THE CHOOSING
BY ADVANTAGES
DECISIONMAKING
SYSTEM

THE CHOOSING
BY ADVANTAGES
DECISIONMAKING
SYSTEM

JIM SUHR

Foreword by Mark Johnson

QUORUM BOOKS
Westport, Connecticut • London

Library of Congress Cataloging-in-Publication Data

Suhr, Jim, 1933–
    The choosing by advantages decisionmaking system / Jim Suhr ;
foreword by Mark Johnson.
      p. cm.
    Includes bibliographical references and index.
    ISBN 1–56720–217–9 (alk. paper)
    1. Decision-making. I. Title.
HD30.23.S86   1999
658.4'03—dc21   98–18499

British Library Cataloguing in Publication Data is available.

Library of Congress Catalog Card Number: 98–18499
ISBN: 1–56720–217–9

First published in 1999

Quorum Books, 88 Post Road West, Westport, CT 06881
An imprint of Greenwood Publishing Group, Inc.

Printed in the United States of America

The paper used in this book complies with the
Permanent Paper Standard issued by the National
Information Standards Organization (Z39.48–1984).

10 9 8 7 6 5 4 3 2 1

JK

Contents

Foreword

Have you ever received a gift at just the time you needed it most? Have you ever received a gift that solved your most pressing need and changed your life? I have. It is the information you are about to read in this book.

The reason this gift came to me is because the most important thing we do in the Forest Service is make quality decisions—with your participation in the decisionmaking process. We make decisions about your National Forests because you have given us that charge through the laws your representatives have passed for you.

We decide if people can use the National Forests for things they want to use them for. We decide if it is in your best interest to use the land and its resources, to make changes to them, or to leave them as nature placed them. This is the job you have given us. This is the most important job we do. But because you are so diverse in what you think should happen on your National Forests, nearly every decision we make is going to disappoint someone. For every person who wants something from or for their National Forests there is someone else who wants something entirely different.

I was in the center of one of these situations. I was faced on one side by a rancher who wanted his livestock to be allowed to continue grazing on National Forest land, as they had done for forty years and his father's had done for at least forty before that. On the other side stood a state fish and game agency that had filed a lawsuit to force us to stop permitting grazing livestock in an area where the rancher's livestock grazed because of the damage it was doing to the habitat of an endangered species of fish. The two parties were frightened by the power of the other, disputing at every turn the other's position. In short, they were focusing on each other and I was in the middle.

How could I get the people in this polarized situation to start helping create a solution instead of focusing on the negative aspects of the other's position? At stake was a good and caring person's ability to keep earning a living at a business he loved. At stake was the potential extinction of a beautiful fish. At stake was the reputation of the Forest Service as an agency of quality management and caring managers. At stake was a costly lawsuit. At stake was this whole set of things, to say nothing about my young career. How could we ever pull this off? This was the state of my mind when I received the gift.

The gift was the basic part of a decisionmaking system that provides an opportunity to focus on the problem and not each other's positions. It offers a way of creating solution alternatives, soundly deciding on the best alternative to implement, and completing this chosen solution in a collaborative and effective way. I was able to share this gift with the people who knew and cared about this part of your National Forest. As a result of all our efforts, a plan of action was formulated which satisfied all parties involved and allowed us to better manage your National Forest.

You are about to learn about this gift. I use it every day. After fifteen years, I am still thankful for having a way to soundly decide both easy and tough decisions in my life at work and away from it. I hope it comes to you at just the time you need it. The likelihood of it being "just at the right time" is fairly good, for if there is one thing you and I do nearly all the time, it's deciding. As Jim Suhr has often reminded me, "If you are going to make a decision, it might as well be a good one." The book you are about to read will give you the ability to make a good decision and be sure about it.

You have in your hand the potential to change your life forever. I look back on when this knowledge changed my life as the most exciting part of my life up to that point. Now, you are about to take the same steps. What a wonderful growing experience you are about to have.

Mark Johnson
U.S. Forest Service

Acknowledgments

Typically, in each organizational unit (and in each family) where Choosing By Advantages is being successfully used there is at least one CBA advocate—one CBA champion. An effective CBA champion initiates the implementation process, energizes it, and keeps it going. For example, it was through the efforts of Richard Cripe, Billy Garrett, Roger Brown, Richard Turk, and others in the National Park Service, and Kurt Gernerd in the Department of the Interior that CBA was adopted as the process the Park Service is now using to set priorities in its line item construction program. Probably, without the efforts of these individuals, the Park Service would have selected a different process.

Several CBA champions have been long-term participants in the development of the CBA system. Without the ideas from Richard Harris, Lee Collett, Mark Johnson, Larry Gorringe, and Geri Rivers—and others in the Forest Service who have been CBA champions for many years—the development of CBA would not have been successful.

Others who made significant contributions during the development of the CBA system include Jeff Sirmon (retired Forest Service deputy chief for international forestry) and Stan Tixier (retired president of The Society for Range Management). The following also contributed: Bill Schnelle, Terry Harwood, Keith Schnare, Russ Rogler, Dayton Nelson, Bob Harmon, Don Rivers, Jim Nelson, Bob Larkin, John Phipps, Clyde Thompson, Melissa Blackwell, Paul Nordwall, Randy Tate, Paul Oakes, Rick Brazell, Clyde Lay, Don Nebeker, Ted Wood, Doug Barber, Alan Pinkerton, Lars Lind, Dave Iverson, Bill Brooks, Cindy Chojnacky, Jon

Leonard, Fleet Stanton, and Sterling Wilcox in the Forest Service, as well as Bruce Bishop at Utah State University and Lynn Cameron of the Cameron Insurance Agency in Moscow, Idaho.

Don Tomisak, Gary Calgrove, Ron Hamann, and others in the 3M Company; Dave Gradick and others in the Animal and Plant Health Inspection Service; and Dave Blackner, Melissa Blackwell, Lee Collett, Mark Johnson, Roberta Beverly, and others in the Forest Service provided many excellent suggestions about how to implement CBA in organizations. Also, thanks to Pat Gardiner, Susan McDaniel, Dick Bryner, and others who helped in the production of materials for early versions of the CBA training process.

Special contributions from Harry Siebert, Bob Terrill, Andrew McConkie, Bonner Ritchie, Stewart Marquis, Ross Carder, Mac McKee, Ned Herrmann, Rusty Broughton, and Ginger Brown are acknowledged in the introduction and in the chapters that follow.

I thank, most of all, my wife and best friend Margaret, our son Steve, and our daughters Lisa and Julie. They provided many years of continuous encouragement and support. Although developing and simplifying the CBA system required thousands of family hours—in addition to thousands of official hours in the Forest Service—they never complained. And their reviews, insights, comments, and suggestions were immeasurably valuable.

Special thanks go to Margaret, who is a teacher—she taught piano lessons to private students for many years and now teaches CBA skills—and to Julie, who is an economist. Especially since 1990, when I retired from the Forest Service, they have actively participated in the development of the CBA system, and with designing and presenting CBA workshops. Many improvements in the CBA system and in the contents and structure of this book came from participants in the workshops.

In 1990, Margaret, Julie, and I co-founded the Institute for Decision Innovations, Inc. Following is our mission statement: "Helping people make better choices by advancing the art of decisionmaking, through research, education, and consultation." Our goal—and the reason for this book—is to help people improve the quality of their lives by helping them learn and skillfully use sound methods of decisionmaking. For this purpose, Decision Innovations granted permission to include in this book all of the illustrations and descriptions that were developed by Decision Innovations—as needed, without restrictions.

Those listed above, and the many others I have failed to name, are not just CBA champions. They are people who want to make the world a better place in which to live.

Introduction

The greatest of all human abilities, I believe, is the ability of everyone to make mental, emotional, and physical choices. Limited only by the availability of alternatives, which is typically a flexible limit, you can choose what foods to eat, what beverages to drink, and how to exercise. You can choose such things as medical procedures, a career, and a home to live in. And you can choose the quality of your relationships with others. To a large extent, you can choose between success or failure in your personal life, your family life, and your work life. In most situations, you can choose to be happy or sad in response to your environment.

Organizations, like individuals, are continuously shaping their futures by their day-to-day and minute-to-minute choices. They are able to choose—in fact, they must choose—their executives, leaders, front-line employees, consultants, and contractors. As additional examples, they choose their strategic plans; their products and services; their activities, projects, and programs; and their equipment and supplies. Similarly, nations choose their relationships with other nations. They choose between war and peace. The world's people are continuously choosing the quality and future of life on earth.

Of course, there are many things people cannot choose. But they can choose how to make choices. And, as will be shown in part I, this could be the most important of all the choices they will ever make—because it will affect so many of the other choices they will make. The available methods range from sound and simple to unsound and very complex. This book will help you make an informed decision about whether or not to choose an exciting new way to make choices, one that is exceptionally sound and surprisingly simple: Choosing By Advantages.

To help you make an informed decision, part II shows that the CBA methods use correct data. Parts III and IV show that they use data correctly. Parts II, III, and IV show, also, that the typical methods in common use today—including the so-called Rational Methods—do not use correct data and do not use data correctly. Therefore, they do not qualify as sound methods. But first, part I briefly reviews why it is important for everyone to learn and skillfully use sound methods.

Every day we see undesirable outcomes that are caused by unsound decisions. Unfortunately, people usually blame themselves or other people for faulty decisions. But far too often, faulty decisions that seem to be people-caused are actually methods-caused. It is time to stop blaming people for methods-caused faulty decisions.

As demonstrated by the evolution of decisionmaking methodology, especially during the past two centuries, the need for methods that are sound, clear, simple, and effective became obvious (at least to those who produced the evolution of decisionmaking methodology) many years ago. And, as shown in the chapters that follow, CBA satisfies this need. Now that the CBA concepts and methods have been developed and validated, the next challenge is to make them available to as many decisionmakers as possible, including those in business and government organizations, as soon as possible.

Executives, leaders, architects, engineers, training and development specialists, counselors, consultants, and other professional decisionmakers need to be sure they are using the very best sound methods of decisionmaking. Their time is precious, and the cost of just one unsound decision can be very significant. Therefore, professional decisionmakers can ill-afford to use primitive methods of decisionmaking—methods that are severely inadequate in a complex, rapidly changing, modern society. And they can ill-afford to use modern methods that are too slow, too complex, or unsound—such as Choosing By Advantages and Disadvantages, Choosing By Pros and Cons, and the so-called Rational Methods, to name a few. They also cannot afford to have the other members of their organizations using inadequate or unsound methods.

The challenge to training and development professionals is two-fold. First, they need to be continuously making sound decisions, themselves, about what and how to teach (teaching is a decisionmaking process). Second, they need to be teaching sound methods. (Chapter 7, and parts of other chapters, present some of the things we have learned about how to teach the CBA concepts and methods.)

Of course, everyone is a decisionmaker. Therefore, even if you are not a professional decisionmaker, you are a decisionmaker; and your decisions do matter. Furthermore, your methods do matter. Because methods do matter, the main purpose of this book is to "sell" CBA to you. I will try to persuade you to thoroughly learn and skillfully use CBA in your personal life, your family life, and your work life. I am confident that CBA will have a very positive impact on your life, and on the lives of those who are affected by your decisions. But only if you learn it and use it.

AN OVERVIEW OF CBA CONCEPTS AND METHODS

CBA is a decisionmaking system, not an individual method. (The methods in the CBA system are unified by one set of definitions, principles, and models.) CBA is also a decisionmaking process, not just a step in the process. (The CBA process begins at the moment when a decision is needed—before alternatives are formulated—and it doesn't end until the decision has been implemented and evaluated.)

The CBA *system* is in sharp contrast with the ***disjointed collection of methods*** in common use today—each with its own vocabulary, its own philosophy, and its own models of the decisionmaking process. By simplifying, clarifying, and unifying the art of decisionmaking, Choosing By Advantages helps good decisionmakers become excellent, and excellent ones even better.

CBA Definitions

Four words in the CBA vocabulary represent four of the concepts that very often make the difference between sound and unsound decisionmaking. The CBA definitions of these words are repeated several times in this book so that by the time you finish it you will be comfortably using them in your active vocabulary.

A <u>factor</u> is
- an element, or a component, of a decision.
- a container for criteria, attributes, advantages, and other types of data.

A <u>criterion</u> is
- a decision-rule, or a guideline.
- any standard on which a judgment is based.
- any decision that guides further decisionmaking.

An <u>attribute</u> is

- a characteristic or consequence of *ONE* alternative.

An <u>advantage</u> is

- a difference between the attributes of *TWO* alternatives.

As you know, these are not new words. They all are commonly used, and they are included in modern dictionaries. Furthermore, their CBA definitions are consistent with their dictionary definitions—and with their on-the-street definitions. However, there are a few additional commonly used words that are included in the CBA vocabulary but not in modern dictionaries.

Although most dictionaries do include matchmakers, shoemakers, and troublemakers, they do not include decisionmakers. I believe that decisionmakers are very important people, and they should be included. Therefore, the word *decisionmaker,* and related words such as *decisionmaking,* are included in the CBA vocabulary. I hope they will soon be included in dictionaries.

CBA Principles

In the CBA system, the principles of sound decisionmaking are central. The definitions and models explain the principles, and the methods apply the principles. In conjunction with many other sound-decisionmaking maxims, this book presents four vital foundation principles, called *the cornerstone principles of sound decisionmaking:*

- The Pivotal Cornerstone Principle: To consistently make sound decisions, decisionmakers must learn and skillfully use sound methods of decisionmaking (part I).

- The Fundamental Rule of Sound Decisionmaking: Decisions must be based on the importance of advantages (part II).

- The Principle of Anchoring: Decisions must be anchored to the relevant facts (part III).

- The Methods Principle: Different types of decisions call for different sound methods of decisionmaking (part IV).

CBA Models

In addition to the need for clearly, accurately, and consistently using the CBA definitions, sound decisionmaking also requires using the CBA patterns of thought and speech, and the CBA models of the decisionmaking process. Therefore, although individual words and their definitions are important, the CBA vocabulary isn't just a set of words. It also includes patterns of speech, and models of the decisionmaking process.

In combination, three of the models that are featured in this book demonstrate that CBA is a breakthrough in the improvement of human performance. The cause-effect model (chapter 1) and the generalizing-specifying model (chapter 13) show that human performance is a decisionmaking process. Therefore, individuals and organizations can substantially raise their levels of performance by improving the way they make decisions. The sound-decisionmaking model (chapter 20) shows how they can improve the way they make decisions.

CBA Methods

Obviously, the future success of both individuals and organizations will depend on their mental, emotional, and physical choices. What might not be so obvious is that their choices will depend on their methods of decisionmaking. To consistently make sound decisions, they must learn and skillfully use sound methods—in particular, CBA methods. This book presents the following CBA methods:

Special methods for complex and very complex decisions
- Special methods for money decisions
- Other special methods for complex and very complex decisions

Simple methods for simple decisions
- The Tabular Method
- The Two-List Method
- The Simplified Tabular Method
- The Simplified Two-List Method
- Instant CBA

Very simple methods for very simple decisions
- The Recognition–Response Process
- Other very simple methods for very simple decisions

To facilitate the discussion of using correct data, part II presents the Simplified Two-List Method, Instant CBA, and the Recognition–Response Process. To facilitate the discussion of using data correctly, chapter 8 presents the Tabular Method for choosing between only two alternatives, and chapter 9 presents the Two-List Method. The other methods that are listed are presented in part IV.

A BRIEF HISTORY OF CHOOSING BY ADVANTAGES

Each of the cornerstone principles of sound decisionmaking has a long, evolutionary history. For example, as is detailed in chapter 18, it took more than a century for the fundamental rule of sound decisionmaking to evolve from its initial form to its present form. And, as shown in chapter 23, it took more than two centuries for decisionmaking methodology to evolve from primitive decisionmaking methods to Choosing By Advantages. This section presents, briefly, only the recent history of CBA.

The basic concepts that initially stimulated the development of the CBA system came from the book, *Science and Sanity: An Introduction to Non-Aristotelian Systems and General Semantics*, by Alfred A. Korzybski (1958 [1933]). In 1959, while working as an engineer in the California Department of Water Resources, I began experimenting with ways to make better decisions in the project development process by applying principles of general semantics. That was my first effort in the development of the CBA system.

From 1965 until 1969, in connection with one of my first assignments as an engineer in the U.S. Forest Service, on the Manti-LaSal National Forest, Forest Engineer Harry Siebert, Forest Supervisor Bob Terrill, and other members of the Forest leadership team gave my efforts a major boost. In a four-year pilot test, they successfully applied several of the concepts that later produced the CBA system, in managing the National Forest.

Applying Korzybski's concepts and other related management concepts (which are still included in the CBA system, although many of them are beyond the scope of this book) improved our ability to effectively organize our work and accomplish our highest priority activities on schedule. One of the benefits from applying these concepts was that they steered us away from a crisis-to-crisis management process toward a smooth-running, well-oiled management process. But the major benefit, in relation to the history of CBA, was that it raised many questions about how to make decisions.

For example, although we were more often accomplishing our highest priority activities on schedule, were we selecting the right activities as our highest priority? We asked ourselves the following questions:

How can we consistently make *sound* decisions?

How can we *clearly* show that our decisions are sound?

How can we *simplify* sound decisionmaking?

These questions were the driving force in the further development of the CBA system. Today, CBA answers all three. As this book will demonstrate, the CBA definitions, principles, models, and methods are *sound, clear,* and surprisingly *simple.*

A second pilot test, beginning in 1969, on the Ashley National Forest, was also successful. But we still faced the same set of questions. To look for answers and to further the development of CBA, Forest Supervisor Andrew McConkie made arrangements for obtaining help from the University of Michigan, where I spent the next year doing graduate studies.

Professors at the University of Michigan, especially in the fields of economics, ecology, and organizational behavior, provided many insights about a wide variety of decisionmaking tools and methods. Several professors—particularly Bonner Ritchie, who taught organizational behavior classes, and Stewart Marquis, who had studied general semantics and who taught urban and regional planning classes—provided many ideas about how to create and implement an effective system of decisionmaking.

During the next twenty years, the further development of the CBA system was sponsored by the headquarters of the Intermountain Region of the Forest Service, with assistance from the Rocky Mountain Research Station and Utah State University. Several national forests and Forest Service regions pilot-tested various components of the system. Because the regional office level is an intermediate level in the Forest Service, this location made it practical for me to interact with and obtain suggestions from individuals and groups in all levels of the Forest Service. It also provided a variety of opportunities to obtain help from outside the Forest Service.

Two who participated extensively in the design of CBA, at its most critical time, were Ross Carder, who was in the research arm of the Forest Service, and Mac McKee, who was a graduate student at Utah State University. Carder and McKee helped keep the CBA development process going when there were many who thought it should be discontinued.

In 1981, after many years of searching for sound methods, I had the good fortune of discovering, or realizing, the fundamental rule of sound decisionmaking: Decisions must be based on the importance of advantages. This rule is so very simple, I am still amazed that it hadn't already been recognized and adopted as the standard of how to make decisions. But when I first thought of it, I had serious doubts. It seemed too good to be true. Nevertheless, within a few months this rule had been validated. And that is when CBA came to life. But there were still many questions. One seemed to be particularly important: What is the correct way to include money in the decisionmaking process?

Resolving this question required lengthy discussions with economists, educators, and others. However, the answer turned out to be quite simple: Decisions must be based on the importance of advantages, not on the importance of dollars. (This is detailed in chapter 24, which transforms the methods for nonmoney decisions, presented in the first twenty-three chapters, into methods for money decisions.)

In the next step, selecting a name for the system, we asked the following question: What do sound methods have in common? And the answer: Sound methods base decisions on the importance of advantages. Therefore, in 1986, the name Choosing By Advantages was selected.

It soon became obvious that learning how to choose by advantages and learning how to teach how to choose by advantages had to go hand-in-hand. Ned Herrmann, the author of *The Creative Brain* (1988) and the developer of ACTAL (Applied Creative Teaching and Learning), and Rusty Broughton, the president of Interpersonal Dynamics, Inc., provided many valuable ideas about how to teach CBA—and therefore, what parts of the CBA system to include in this book, and how to include them. Ginger Brown, a teacher at Bates Elementary School in North Ogden, Utah, developed *A Series of Lessons for CBA Decision-Making Skills* (1993) for her master's degree. As a result, we are now able to successfully teach CBA even to elementary school students. Numerous others, especially CBA workshop participants, also provided many helpful suggestions.

In connection with various projects and programs in the Forest Service, the CBA definitions, principles, models, and methods were pilot-tested and validated (and improved) in a wide variety of decisionmaking situations. And they continue to be improved: In 1990, I retired from the Forest Service to write this book and to establish the Institute for Decision Innovations, Inc. The purpose of Decision Innovations is to further develop the CBA system—building on what was completed in the Forest Service— and to make CBA available to individuals, families, organizations, and communities.

As stated in the acknowledgments, Decision Innovations contributed many of the illustrations and descriptions in this book. The following models and displays—also included in this book—were developed in the Forest Service:

- The Generalizing–Specifying Model
- The Sound-Decisionmaking Model
- A model of how to simplify learning how to choose by advantages, showing that CBA organizes the art of decisionmaking into three overlapping areas: sound, congruent, and effective decisionmaking

- A display of sound methods
- Two formats for organizing and displaying the data required for sound decisionmaking: the Two-List Format and the Tabular Format

Nationally, the Forest Service is using CBA for only certain types of decisions, such as setting priorities among capital investment proposals. But locally, in field offices, some work units have adopted CBA as the standard of how to make all types of decisions—from the simplest to the most complex.

In response to discussions with the Forest Service, evaluation teams in the National Park Service are using CBA to set priorities in their line item construction program. And some in the Park Service are using CBA for other decisions, as well. (Virtually all types of decisions call for CBA methods.) A tri-agency team from the Federal Highway Administration, the Idaho Transportation Department, and the Forest Service is using CBA to set priorities among Idaho Forest Highway construction proposals. Many improvements in the CBA system have resulted from these and other applications by individuals, families, and organizations.

AN EXAMPLE OF CHOOSING BY ADVANTAGES

A quality steering team I was observing had been struggling with a decision that was simple, but important, when the team leader said to me, "Jim, take us through the CBA Process; we're spending too much time on this decision."

With very little guidance, the team members quickly used the Simplified Two-List Method (one of several CBA methods for simple decisions). First, they listed the advantages of each alternative. Second, without numerically displaying the importance of each individual advantage, they selected the alternative that obviously had the greatest total importance of advantages. (It was not the one with the greatest number of advantages.) Satisfied with their selection, they moved on to other items of business.

Obviously, this example raises a lot of questions. Different people ask different questions, but many ask: "Why didn't the team members list both the advantages and the disadvantages of each alternative? Why did they list only the advantages?" This book will answer these and other questions, in detail. For now, here is a brief answer: Decades ago, researchers found that sound methods of decisionmaking base decisions on the *differences* among alternatives. In 1981, after many years of searching for sound methods, I realized that a difference between two alternatives is, simultaneously, an advantage of the one and a disadvantage of the other.

Because a disadvantage is exactly the same thing as an advantage, except for its perspective, Choosing By Advantages *and* Disadvantages causes double-counting and other mistakes. Because it causes critical mistakes, it doesn't qualify as a sound method. However, as part II demonstrates, it can easily be transformed from unsound to sound. And when it is transformed—when it is simplified, clarified, and corrected—it becomes Choosing By Advantages. Similarly, when other unsound methods, such as the so-called Rational Methods, are simplified, clarified, and corrected, they become CBA methods. So, the next question becomes: Do the CBA methods qualify as sound methods?

Sound Versus Unsound

Sound methods are defined, briefly, as those that use correct data and use data correctly. Therefore, they do not cause or encourage critical mistakes. The CBA methods have been thoroughly tested, for several years. They have also been carefully examined, many times by many people, without finding any critical mistakes.

To make sure the CBA system would be sound, simple, understandable, and practical, each component was field-tested in a wide variety of decisionmaking situations—including personal and family situations, as well as work situations. Those who field-tested CBA and contributed to its design include scientists, engineers, ecologists, foresters, equipment operators, landscape architects, psychologists, economists, and educators—to name a few. Contributors included executives, leaders, and front-line employees, mostly in the Forest Service. But some were in other government agencies, and some were in universities and business organizations. Because CBA has been so thoroughly studied, we can say, with a reasonably high degree of certainty, that the CBA methods are sound methods.

In contrast, careful examinations have clearly demonstrated that the typical methods in common use today do not qualify as sound methods. They either cause or encourage critical mistakes—such as omissions of key relevant facts, multiple-counting, distortions of facts, or distortions of viewpoints. And when objective studies demonstrate that a method causes critical mistakes, we can say, objectively, that it doesn't qualify as a sound method.

Fortunately, we don't need to throw away the unsound methods. They can easily be transformed from unsound to sound. Also, a method isn't disqualified by minor mistakes, only by critical mistakes. Furthermore, decisions about how to make decisions are like all other decisions: They are, at least in part, subjective. That is, they depend on personal preferences. Therefore, sound methods for choosing how to make choices do not just take the relevant facts into account, such as whether or not a method is sound. They also take personal preferences into account. They take both facts and preferences into account, in the right way, at the right time.

Of course, methods do not make decisions. People make decisions. Also, obtaining and using correct data isn't always a possibility; and sometimes, when it is a possibility, it's too expensive. Therefore, those who use sound methods don't always make sound decisions. At the same time, those who use unsound methods don't always make unsound decisions.

Although there are CBA methods for practically all types of decisions, CBA is certainly not a panacea. And it doesn't produce perfection. Instead, it produces improvement. As stated earlier, it helps good decisionmakers become excellent ones, and excellent ones even better. Those who learn and use the CBA concepts and methods are able to make excellent decisions more often than ever before. Very soon, therefore, I hope you will choose CBA as your way to make choices.

Simple Versus Complex

I realize that learning the CBA concepts and methods can be a challenging task. And I am assuming—perhaps incorrectly—that you are unfamiliar with CBA. Therefore, to minimize the need for you to go back and reread as you move from chapter to chapter in this book, some of the concepts are repeated. One thing that I will repeat is that if the CBA concepts and methods are unfamiliar to you, they are likely to seem complex—for a while. But in reality, as you will discover, they are surprisingly simple. For example, it is much simpler to list only the advantages of each alternative, rather than listing the advantages and disadvantages. Be careful: ***Do not confuse unfamiliarity with complexity.***

The number of repetitions of key points (some are repeated several times) and their levels of detail are based on the results from trying various options in CBA workshops. The questions answered in this book are those that have been asked repeatedly in the workshops and during CBA decision meetings. A few of the illustrations are hand lettered, and some are hand drawn sketches—to demonstrate how they are typically prepared and used in real-world situations.

Now that you have been introduced to the CBA concepts and methods, you are ready to examine them in detail, starting with the pivotal cornerstone principle. Of course, I hope that you won't just examine them. I hope that you will practice them, and use them, even when it isn't obvious that you need to use them. Then, you will be able to skillfully use them in situations where it becomes obvious that you definitely need them. And finally, I hope—most of all—that you will enjoy your journey of learning and using CBA.

Part I

The Pivotal
Cornerstone Principle

A few philosophers, educators, and others recognized the following initial version of the pivotal cornerstone principle of sound decisionmaking, many years ago: To consistently make sound decisions, decisionmakers must use sound methods of decisionmaking. The recognition of this principle stimulated the evolution of decisionmaking methodology—from primitive decisionmaking to Choosing By Advantages. Nevertheless, many educators and others have apparently still not recognized this principle. They say, "Just use whatever works for you."

While we were testing different ways to teach the CBA concepts and methods, we found that the initial version of this principle was inadequate. Therefore, it was expanded. It still includes using sound methods, as described in chapter 1. But it now also includes learning how to use sound methods, as described in chapter 2. The pivotal cornerstone principle, in its present form, is that *to consistently make sound decisions, decision-makers must learn and skillfully use sound methods of decisionmaking*.

Most people are able to make reasonably good decisions, with or without using sound methods of decisionmaking. But we all need to make better decisions. Our future depends on it. And to make better decisions, we need to learn and skillfully use the very best methods of decisionmaking. For example, elected officials in governments need to become highly skilled in using the CBA methods. Of course, CBA cannot replace the political process; and it shouldn't. Instead, CBA needs to be integrated into the political process. Similarly, it needs to be integrated into the lives and behaviors of individuals, families, organizations, and communities.

For those who have fully accepted the pivotal cornerstone principle, skillfully using sound methods is one of their basic values. (For the same reasons that people with high integrity would never cheat or lie or steal, they would never knowingly use unsound methods of decisionmaking—methods that cause multiple-counting, omissions, distortions, or other critical mistakes.) Those who accept this principle will be the most successful in learning and using the CBA concepts and methods. This is why this cornerstone principle is called the pivotal cornerstone principle.

The sketch that follows shows that the fundamental rule of sound decisionmaking, the methods principle, and the principle of anchoring were discovered in response to the pivotal cornerstone principle. It shows, also, that when the cornerstone principles converged, Choosing By Advantages came into existence. And finally, it shows that after CBA was developed, the pivotal cornerstone principle was expanded, to include learning how to use sound methods.

A Sketch of the History of CBA

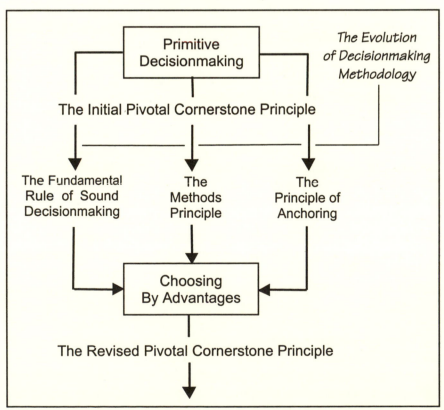

1

Decisionmakers Must
Use Sound Methods

THE IMPORTANCE OF MAKING SOUND DECISIONS

I have asked hundreds of participants in CBA workshops why it is important to make sound decisions, and the responses have always been outstanding. Here are a few examples:

- Sound decisions save time. You don't have to keep doing things over again.

- They produce better outcomes at home, not just at work.

- Better use of resources.

- Higher levels of job satisfaction. Less conflict and less stress.

- Sound decisions are more likely to be accepted and implemented.

- Happier people. More fun.

- Because my decisions affect other people.

- Because our future depends on it.

In the workshops, no one has ever responded by arguing that it isn't important to make sound decisions. It appears, therefore, that those who decide to attend CBA workshops agree that it is important to make sound decisions. The cause-effect model on the following page depicts this basic principle. It shows that our decisions do matter.

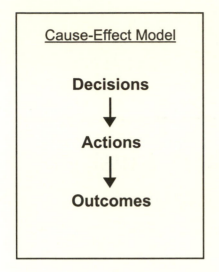

This model shows that our outcomes—good and bad—are caused, in large measure, by our actions. And our actions are caused, in large measure, by our decisions. Therefore, by improving our decisions, we will be able to achieve higher levels of success and happiness.

As everyone knows, there is plenty of room for improvement. Undesirable outcomes, caused at least in part by unsound decisions, are all around us.

Among those who have not attended CBA workshops, a few have told us that decisions do not matter. Some have said that decisionmaking is an illusion. They argue that human performance is entirely the product of only two factors: nature (heredity) and nurture (environment).

In contrast, CBA recognizes that human performance is the product of at least three factors: *nature, nurture,* and *choice.* We are not like puppets on strings. Instead, we are continuously making the following types of choices:

- Mental choices

- Emotional choices

- Physical choices

THE IMPORTANCE OF USING SOUND METHODS

Although few people say that decisions do not matter, many say that decisionmaking methods do not matter. In a CBA workshop, for example, one of the participants—who seemed to think that I would agree with what he was saying—explained to the other participants, "Of course we need to remember that there are many methods of decisionmaking, and that, on average, they will all produce the same results."

Although he was confident, he was wrong. In reality, methods do matter. Unsound methods, far more often than sound methods, produce unsound decisions. So remember: To consistently make sound decisions, decisionmakers must use sound methods.

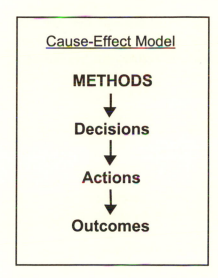

Cause-Effect Model

METHODS
↓
Decisions
↓
Actions
↓
Outcomes

This version of the cause-effect model shows that our outcomes are caused, in large measure, by our decision methods. Our *methods* produce our decisions. Our *decisions* guide our actions. And our *actions* cause our *outcomes*.

Every link in this chain must carry the full load. And for many, the first link is their weakest link. Therefore, they can substantially increase their levels of success and happiness by improving their methods of decisionmaking.

I often use this version of the cause-effect model to show why the CBA system is needed. But some remain unconvinced, at least for a while. To explain why—in their view—CBA isn't needed, people often make "just" statements, such as the following:

"My advice is to *just* use your intuition."

"I wish people would *just* use good judgment."

"If people would *just* use common sense, most of our problems would disappear."

My response is that these three statements—without the word *just*—actually support the need for CBA. The first two prescribe a very important CBA method, presented at the end of chapter 26: Using Good Intuition, Coupled with Good Judgment.

In CBA, "good intuition" means intuitively using correct data. "Good judgment" means intuitively using data correctly. Therefore, the key to using good intuition is to practice using correct data, as described in part II, until you intuitively use correct data. And the key to using good judgment is to practice using data correctly, as described in part III, until you do it intuitively. This means that the key to good intuition and good judgment is to practice Choosing By Advantages, until it becomes intuitive. Unfortunately, many people intuitively use unsound methods—such as Choosing By Advantages and Disadvantages—because they have practiced using unsound methods, many times.

The third statement gets to the heart of the matter. It wouldn't make sense for someone to knowingly use unsound methods of decisionmaking.

Unsound methods do not use correct data, and they do not use data correctly. That is why the CBA methods are so essential. Again, as shown in parts II and III, the CBA methods use correct data, and they use data correctly.

Some of the differences between sound and unsound methods of decisionmaking are like the differences between edible and poisonous mushrooms: Although they are not easy to see, they do matter.

2

Decisionmakers Must Learn How to Use Sound Methods

This chapter is about a serious problem that CBA facilitators have faced, over and over again: Typically, when someone asks them to facilitate the CBA process in a decision meeting, the participants expect to be able to use sound methods—specifically, CBA methods—without learning how to use them. And that can be a very expensive mistake. The cost of not learning how to use sound methods can be enormous.

It is easy to see why it takes several years of formal education to qualify as an engineer or a doctor, and why it takes special training to become an expert electrician or violinist. But apparently, it isn't easy to see why it takes special training to become an expert decisionmaker.

THE PURPOSE OF DISCOVERY

As we all know, Columbus and other explorers didn't invent, create, or construct the American continents. They discovered the continents. Then, they constructed maps and wrote descriptions so that it would be much easier for others to find the same continents. To help others—that is one of the purposes of discovery.

Similarly, I didn't invent the distinctions between factors, criteria, attributes, and advantages. And I didn't invent the cornerstone principles of sound decisionmaking. I discovered them, and described them. And I constructed the CBA methods—so that others can easily apply the things that I discovered—without having to spend decades to discover them on their own. And that brings us to the purpose of education.

THE PURPOSE OF EDUCATION

In the CBA system, the purpose of education is to help people make better choices. And the purpose of making better choices is to improve the quality of life. For organizations, making better choices will improve the quality and profitability of their products and services.

Typically, under today's concept of education (the old concept) children in families, students in schools, and adults in organizations are told what to decide. Under the CBA concept, they are taught how to decide. When following the CBA concept, parents, educators, and leaders will continue telling what to decide, when doing so is appropriate—but only when appropriate. A major improvement is that they will be able to use CBA to explain why the right choice is the right choice.

Of course, educators will continue providing information that is needed in the decisionmaking process. And they will continue providing basic skills; including reading, writing, history, art, music, science, mathematics, computer skills, social skills, and so forth. (In CBA, these skills are viewed as decisionmaking skills.) The major difference is that in the CBA concept of education, basic sound-decisionmaking skills will no longer be neglected.

If we naturally acquired all of the skills we need to consistently make wise choices—mental, emotional, and physical—there would be no need for the educational system. Of course, we do acquire many skills naturally while we are small children. But, as indicated by the three comparisons that follow, many skills are not naturally acquired. They must be taught. Therefore the educational system is essential.

Examples of Skills That Are and Are Not Naturally Acquired

NATURALLY ACQUIRED	NOT NATURALLY ACQUIRED
• Crawling and Walking	• Piloting a Jet Airplane
• Talking	• Reading and Writing
• Instinctive Decisionmaking Skills	• Sound Decisionmaking Skills

Under the old concept, sound decisionmaking is viewed as a natural process, and methods do not matter. ("Just use whatever works for you.") In the CBA concept, sound decisionmaking is recognized as a set of skills that must be taught, and methods do matter. ("Decisionmakers must *learn* and *skillfully use* sound methods.") I believe that changing from the old to the new will require changes in culture and values, because so many members of today's society have not yet accepted using sound methods as one of their basic values.

Unfortunately, as stated above, many people expect to acquire sound-decisionmaking skills naturally, or simply from experience. But that is an unreasonable expectation. Because sound-decisionmaking skills are not naturally acquired, they need to be progressively taught in all levels of the educational system—from the pre-school level to continuing education for adults. To help people more often make successful choices (and more often feel very good about their choices) sound-decisionmaking definitions, principles, models, and methods must be included in the curriculum, and emphasized.

Teachers and students need to learn the definitions of the four sound-decisionmaking terms—factors, criteria, attributes, and advantages. They also need to learn the cornerstone principles of sound decisionmaking. And they need to know how to apply these definitions and principles. Especially, they need to understand the fundamental rule of sound decisionmaking and the principle of anchoring. (As shown in part II, the fundamental rule pertains to using correct data; and as shown in part III, the principle of anchoring pertains to using data correctly.)

How much time will this take away from other subjects? Probably, none. In fact, it could substantially increase the time for other subjects. I expect that it will take less time to teach CBA than it now takes to deal with the problems that will be prevented by CBA.

THE CANOE DECISION

Part II will use a hypothetical canoe purchase decision—the choice between Canoe C and Canoe K for downriver canoeing (not white-water canoeing)—to illustrate the four definitions and the fundamental rule. Then, using this same example, part III will tie together the fundamental rule and the principle of anchoring.

Why is a hypothetical decision used? Why wouldn't it be a good idea to use a real-world example? Because, while learning CBA, it is essential for students to focus on the *process,* not the *content,* of each example. Therefore, starry-brown and kelly-blue—the colors of the canoes in the example—are colors that probably do not exist in the real world. And much of the other data might be just as unrealistic as the two colors.

There are a few things about the choice between Canoes C and K that are realistic. For example, the stakeholders—those who will be using the canoe—decided that, for them, the maximum acceptable canoe weight is 80 pounds. They decided, also, that if the two canoes were exactly alike in every factor except in their weights, they would prefer the lighter-weight canoe. However, because there were significant differences between the two canoes in five factors, not only in weight, it was impossible for the stakeholders to know, in advance, whether to select the lighter canoe or the heavier one.

Therefore, instead of just weighing the two canoes, they "weighed" the advantages of the one against the advantages of the other. In response to the fundamental rule of sound decisionmaking, they selected the alternative with the greatest total importance of advantages.

Part II

The Fundamental Rule
of Sound Decisionmaking

There is no such thing as a totally objective decision, and there never will be. Furthermore, there is no such thing as a totally objective method of decisionmaking, and there never will be. An objective method of decision-making is an impossibility. All decisions and all methods of decision-making are value-laden. Methods that qualify as sound methods are both objectively sound and subjectively sound. Therefore, we need to emphasize that the CBA methods are sound, not merely objective.

For all types of decisions, from the simplest to the most complex, all methods of decisionmaking require deciding preferences. For complex decisions, all methods also require deciding, or weighing—either explicitly or implicitly—intensities of preferences. The most critical difference between unsound and sound methods is that unsound methods weigh the wrong things. Parts II and III will demonstrate that the following are examples of unsound methods:

- Methods that weigh advantages and disadvantages

- Methods that weigh pros and cons

- Methods that weigh factors, goals, roles, or categories

- Methods that weigh criteria or objectives

- Methods that weigh attributes, characteristics, or consequences

As will be restated several times in this book, virtually everyone is a decisionmaker. We all make countless decisions, every day. Individually, most of our decisions are not very important. Some, however, are very important. And all our decisions, collectively, are very important. Therefore, everyone needs to memorize, understand, and consistently apply—all day, every day—the fundamental rule of sound decisionmaking: *Decisions must be based on the importance of advantages.*

Now would be a good time for you to memorize this rule. It would take only a few minutes. And later—for example, while you are going for a walk or riding a bus to work—check to see if you can still remember it. During CBA workshops, we encourage the participants to write the fundamental rule on a 3" x 5" card and to carry it with them until they have it memorized. I hope you will do the same.

An outline of the CBA process for complex decisions is shown below. Phase III is the topic of this book. By the time you finish reading this book, I hope you will have memorized the key words for remembering the four central activities—the activities of the decisionmaking phase—in addition to memorizing the fundamental rule of sound decisionmaking. The words to memorize are attributes, advantages, importance, and total importance.

The CBA Process

Phase I. The Stage-Setting Phase

Phase II. The Innovation Phase

Phase III. The Decisionmaking Phase

1. Summarize the *attributes* of each alternative.

2. Decide the *advantages* of each alternative.

3. Decide the *importance* of each advantage.

4. Choose the alternative with the greatest *total importance* of advantages.

Phase IV. The Reconsideration Phase

Phase V. The Implementation Phase

The outlines for simple, day-to-day and minute-to-minute decisions are much simpler than the one above. For example, as shown in chapter 9, the Two-List Method requires only three of the four central activities. The Simplified Two-List Method requires only two. And the Instant CBA Process requires only one.

3

What, Exactly, Is an Advantage?

One of the most significant of all the features in the CBA system is its vocabulary. Sound decisionmaking calls for the accurate and consistent use of an effective, carefully designed, sound-decisionmaking vocabulary. Remember, anyone who is not using the CBA vocabulary is not using CBA.

CBA assigns a precise meaning to the term *advantages,* and this gives a precise meaning to the fundamental rule of sound decisionmaking. Similarly, CBA gives precise meanings to several other sound-decisionmaking words, especially, *factors, criteria,* and *attributes.* This chapter reviews the distinctions between attributes and advantages, and demonstrates that a disadvantage is exactly the same thing as an advantage, except for its perspective.

Attributes and advantages are both contained in factors. Factors also contain criteria, preference charts and preference curves—presented in chapter 10—and other types of data. So, let's briefly define the term *factor.* In the CBA vocabulary, this term has two definitions, as follows:

- A *factor* is an element, or a component, of a decision.

- A *factor* is a container for criteria, attributes, advantages, and other types of data.

As stated at the end of chapter 2, the canoe decision is divided into five factors. They are: weight, finish smoothness, color, stability, and keel depth.

ADVANTAGES ARE NOT ATTRIBUTES

Although motor oil looks like pancake syrup, it wouldn't make sense to use their labels interchangeably. Similarly, it wouldn't make sense, in a decisionmaking system, to use the terms "attributes" and "advantages" interchangeably. Nevertheless, some of their dictionary definitions are practically the same. In the CBA vocabulary, although not in dictionaries, there is a sharp distinction between attributes and advantages.

In CBA, as in one of the dictionary definitions, an *attribute* is defined as a quality or characteristic belonging to a person or thing. It is a distinctive feature. Synonyms include quality, quantity, characteristic, consequence, distinction, feature, and trait. In the canoe example, the attributes of the two canoes in the first factor, weight, are:

- Attribute of Canoe C: 65 pounds.
- Attribute of Canoe K: 75 pounds.

Attributes, as well as advantages and disadvantages, are often mis-labeled as pros and cons. Although the idea of pros and cons is emotionally attractive, it usually isn't very logical. Therefore, in most situations, the pros-and-cons methods should be avoided. An exception is when we are faced with a take-it-or-leave-it proposal, in which case Ben Franklin's method (Reasons-Pro Versus Reasons-Con) is applicable.

So, why should we usually avoid these methods? Because they cause conflicts. And why do they cause conflicts? Because usually, if not always, an attribute can be viewed as either a pro or a con, depending on what it is being compared with. For example, some would view a 70 pound weight as a reason-pro, because 70 pounds is lighter than 75 pounds. Others would view this same weight as a reason-con, because it is heavier than 65 pounds. Similarly, a 65 pound weight could be viewed as either a pro or a con. And so, too, a 75 pound weight.

When the pros-and-cons methods are used, what typically happens is that the proponents of a particular proposal describe most of the attributes of their proposal as reasons-pro, while the opponents describe most of these same attributes as reasons-con. Both sides argue about whether a particular attribute should be labeled as a pro or a con. And that is a pointless argument.

An attribute is neither good nor bad (pro nor con), except in comparison with another attribute. Therefore, in the CBA vocabulary, attributes are never labeled as pros and cons. Instead, they are labeled as *attributes,* in accordance with the following definition:

- An *attribute* is a characteristic or consequence of *ONE* alternative.

ADVANTAGES ARE DIFFERENCES BETWEEN ATTRIBUTES

In dictionaries, the term *advantage* has a wide range of meanings. Some are in agreement with the CBA definition, and some are not. The definition, "A factor favorable or conducive to success" is definitely not in agreement with CBA. On the other hand, "benefit or improvement" and "gain" are definitions in agreement with CBA.

The CBA definition is an on-the-street definition—one that is commonly used. For example, when participants in CBA workshops are asked, "Which canoe has the advantage in weight?" they select Canoe C, because it is easier to carry than Canoe K. And when asked, "How large is the weight advantage of Canoe C, compared with Canoe K?" they say that Canoe C has an advantage of 10 pounds. This illustrates the CBA definition of an advantage:

- An *advantage* is a favorable dissimilarity in quality or difference in quantity between the attributes of *TWO* alternatives.

The distinction between an attribute and an advantage should be as sharp and clear to you as the distinction between a house and a horse. Therefore, the chapters that follow will review this distinction, several times. Briefly:

- An *attribute* is a characteristic of *ONE* alternative.

- An *advantage* is a difference between *TWO* alternatives.

A disadvantage is exactly the same thing as an advantage, except for its perspective. For example, when the participants in CBA workshops are asked, "Which canoe has the disadvantage in weight?" they select Canoe K. And when asked, "How large is the disadvantage of Canoe K, compared with C?" they say that K has a disadvantage of 10 pounds. Again, the *advantage* of Canoe C is the 10 pound difference between 65 pounds and 75 pounds. And surprisingly, the *disadvantage* of Canoe K is exactly the same 10 pound difference between 65 pounds and 75 pounds.

As demonstrated by this example, the following sound-decisionmaking principle is remarkably simple: If we list a difference between two alternatives as an advantage of the one, and then if we list that same difference as a disadvantage of the other, we have double-counted the difference. And double-counting is a critical mistake. To remind us of this principle, CBA defines a disadvantage as follows: Without exception, a disadvantage of one alternative is an advantage of another.

When there are three or more alternatives, Choosing By Advantages *and* Disadvantages doesn't just cause double-counting. It causes multiple-counting. It also causes omissions, distortions, and confusion. Therefore, too often, it causes faulty decisions. To simplify and clarify the decisionmaking process, and to more often make sound decisions, list all differences among alternatives as advantages. If some of the differences are initially listed as disadvantages, they can easily be transformed into advantages, as in the following examples:

How to Transform Disadvantages into Advantages

DISADVANTAGES OF C	ADVANTAGES OF K
Rougher finish	Smoother finish
Worse color	Nicer color
Taller keel	Shorter keel

The term *disadvantage,* as it is defined in CBA, is used occasionally in the CBA process. But the phrase "the advantages and disadvantages of each alternative" is never used—except in the training process, to explain why it isn't used. Furthermore, the term *disadvantage,* as it is typically defined in dictionaries, is never used in the CBA process. So, while you are learning the CBA process, practice not using the term *disadvantage* at all. Then, after you are skilled in using CBA, be careful how you use this term. At first, this probably seems like a trivial concern. But it certainly isn't trivial. To consistently make sound decisions, clear, accurate, and effective thinking and communicating are essential.

Whenever practicable, non-comparison terms are used when describing attributes, and comparison terms are used when describing advantages. Following are examples:

Attributes Versus Advantages

ATTRIBUTES OF K	ADVANTAGES OF K
Smooth finish	Smoother finish
Kelly-blue color	Nicer color
5/8 inch keel	Shorter keel

In some cases, there isn't an easy way to use comparison terms when describing advantages. But in the canoe decision, we can easily use comparison terms in all of the descriptions of the advantages.

Another distinction that must be sharp and clear is the distinction between a criterion and a factor. A criterion is a decision rule or a guideline. It is a decision that guides further decisionmaking. A factor contains criteria. An example of a factor is weight. In the canoe decision, this factor contains two criteria:

- *A Must Criterion:* According to the stakeholders, the maximum acceptable attribute in the canoe weight factor is 80 pounds. Therefore, all canoes weighing more than 80 pounds were simply ruled out during the innovation phase of the CBA process.

- *A Want Criterion:* When comparing two canoes with different weights, the stakeholders in this example prefer the lighter weight— but not necessarily the lighter canoe, because other factors must also be taken into account. This criterion tells us that Canoe C has the advantage in weight.

In addition to distinguishing between factors, criteria, attributes, and advantages, it is essential to distinguish between objective data and subjective data. This distinction is reviewed in the following chapter.

4

Two Central Questions
and Four Central Activities

Two basic types of data are required in sound methods of decisionmaking: objective and subjective. Objective data pertain to the attributes or the advantages of the alternatives. The following objective question and its answer pertain to the color attribute of Canoe C. (Even if the answer is untrue, it is an objective answer. Why? Because it pertains to a characteristic of the canoe; it doesn't pertain to a preference of a person.)

Objective Data

Q. What is the color of Canoe C?

A. Starry-brown.

Subjective data pertain to someone's preferences, or the intensities of their preferences, as shown in the following example. (Again, even if the answer is untrue—even if the person who answered the question actually prefers the starry-brown color—the answer is subjective.)

Subjective Data

Q. Which do you prefer, the color of Canoe C (starry-brown), or the color of Canoe K (kelly-blue)?

A. Starry-brown is acceptable, but I strongly prefer the kelly-blue color.

Most items of data are neither purely objective nor purely subjective. And this brings us to a third type of data that must often be used in the decisionmaking process. It is often necessary to use subjectively colored words or phrases—such as fair, good, very good, and excellent—when describing the attributes of the alternatives. Items of data that include subjectively colored words or phrases are called subjectively colored data. Following is an example:

Subjectively Colored Data

Q. How stable is Canoe C? (This is an objective question.)

A. Canoe C has excellent stability. (This is a subjectively colored response.)

We cannot avoid using subjective data and subjectively colored data in the decisionmaking process. What is important, therefore, is to be aware that we are using such data. We must never argue, or believe, that we are using totally objective data. We must be aware, also, that some of our objective data—not only subjective and subjectively colored—come from inside our minds. Items of data that come from inside our minds, whether valid or not, are likely to *feel* better to us than valid data that come from outside. This might explain why people so often feel more comfortable with bad decisions than with good decisions. And I suspect that this is one of the major causes of faulty decisionmaking. Remember, sometimes our feelings are correct. But sometimes, they are totally incorrect.

THE TWO CENTRAL QUESTIONS

As demonstrated in the chapters that follow, two questions are central in the CBA process. Both pertain to the advantages of the alternatives. And both must be answered correctly, accurately. The first is objective, and the second is subjective:

How large are the advantages of each alternative?

How important are the advantages of each alternative?

THE FOUR CENTRAL ACTIVITIES

In Phase I of the CBA process, we define the purpose of the decision, and begin identifying the factors—the containers for the data. We also identify the criteria, including the musts and wants. In Phase II, we formulate alternatives and determine their attributes. For difficult, complex, or controversial decisions, we describe each attribute, in each factor, in detail.

The focus of this book is Phase III, the decisionmaking phase. The four central activities of the CBA process—the activities in Phase III—answer three questions, including the two central questions, as follows:

What are the advantages? And how large are the advantages?

1. Summarize the Attributes of each alternative.

2. Decide the Advantages of each alternative.

How important are the advantages?

3. Decide the Importance of each advantage.

4. If the costs of the alternatives are equal, choose the one with the greatest Total importance of advantages.

The first two questions pertain to using correct data, and the remaining chapters in part II respond to this question. The third question pertains to correctly using correct data, and all the chapters in parts III and IV respond to this question. To simplify learning how to choose by advantages, first learn and practice using correct data. Then, learn and practice using data correctly.

Again, the key words for remembering the four central activities: Attributes, Advantages, Importance, and Total importance. If you haven't done so already, take a few minutes to memorize them. Julie Nelson has invented an easy way to remember them. Using the letters highlighted, she tells decisionmakers: To make a sound decision, double-a it.

THE DECISIONMAKING PHASE
OF THE CBA PROCESS

The following outline of Phase III shows that the second central activity—deciding advantages—requires two tasks.

1. Summarize the Attributes of each alternative.

2. Decide the Advantages of each alternative.

    a. Decide the least-preferred attribute in each factor.

    b. Determine the differences from the least-preferred attributes. These differences are the advantages of the alternatives.

3. Decide the Importance of each advantage.

4. If the costs of the alternatives are equal, choose the one with the greatest Total importance of advantages.

Three of the items in the following chart (two of the activities and one of the tasks) are objective; the others are subjective. As stated before, those that are objective reveal the characteristics of the alternatives, and those that are subjective reveal the preferences of people. Mark the three that are objective and the two that are subjective.

Objective Versus Subjective, Revisited

Objective	Subjective		Activities and Tasks
☐	☐	1.	Determine the attributes of each alternative, in each factor.
☐	☐	2a.	Decide the least-preferred attributes—one in each factor.
☐	☐	2b.	Determine the differences from the least-preferred attributes.
☐	☐	3.	Decide the importance of each difference— each advantage.
☐	☐	4.	For each alternative, calculate total importance.

As this demonstrates, the decisionmaking phase of the CBA process moves back and forth between objective and subjective: First, determining the attributes of the alternatives is objective. Second, deciding the least-preferred attributes, is subjective. Then, once the least-preferred attributes have been decided, determining the advantages—the differences from the least-preferred attributes—is objective. Next, deciding the importance of each advantage is subjective. (To make a sound decision, one must decide the importance of each advantage with care and precision.) Finally, once the importance of each advantage has been decided, calculating the total importance for each alternative is objective.

This chapter has shown that the CBA methods are—in part—subjective. However, as the chapters that follow will demonstrate, no other methods are as objective as the CBA methods. And no methods—not even the CBA methods—will ever be totally objective. That would be impossible.

5

Sound Methods Do Not Weigh
Advantages and Disadvantages

This chapter shows how easy it is to transform a popular unsound method—Choosing By Advantages *and* Disadvantages—from unsound to sound. (When it is transformed, it becomes Choosing By Advantages.) The example we will use in this transformation is the choice between Canoe C and Canoe K.

To demonstrate the transformation, we first construct a typical display of so-called advantages and disadvantages and convert it into a display of attributes. Then, using the data shown in the display of attributes, we construct two effective formats for displaying the data for the decision: the Tabular Format, which most often is used for choosing from three or more alternatives, and the Two-List Format, which is used for choosing from only two alternatives. The data in these formats answer the first central question: How large are the advantages of each alternative? Part III will answer the second question: How important are the advantages?

Perhaps what is most significant in the transformation from unsound to sound is the vocabulary change. To make the transformation, the CBA definitions that were presented in chapter 3 are essential. By walking through the first two central activities of the CBA process, this chapter shows the CBA definitions in action—especially, the following:

- An *attribute* is a characteristic, or consequence,
  of *ONE* alternative.

- An *advantage* is a difference between the attributes
  of *TWO* alternatives.

ACTIVITY NO. 1: SUMMARIZE THE ATTRIBUTES

Although decisions must not be based on the importance of advantages *and* disadvantages, listing the "advantages" and "disadvantages" of each alternative can be used in a brainstorming process, as an aid in determining the attributes of the alternatives. You can find out a lot about each alternative by asking some, or all, of the following questions:

1. What do you *like* about each alternative?

2. What do you *dislike* about each alternative?

3. What are the *advantages* of each alternative?

4. What are the *disadvantages* of each alternative?

5. What is *interesting* about each alternative?

6. What is *different* about each alternative?

In the canoe-purchase example, we asked only two of these questions: What are the advantages and what are the disadvantages of each alternative? Unfortunately, those who provided the answers to these questions were unskilled in using the CBA vocabulary. Therefore, while some items in the display truly were advantages and disadvantages, others were attributes that were mislabeled. This is the typical result from asking for the advantages and disadvantages of each alternative.

In Choosing By Advantages *and* Disadvantages, the decisionmaker is expected to study the four lists—the advantages of C, the disadvantages of C, the advantages of K, and the disadvantages of K—and to make a sound decision by using good judgment. But this method doesn't organize the data properly, and it doesn't construct a bridge from the data to the decision. Therefore, this method is actually a primitive method, called the Instinctive Method. Following is an outline of this method:

The Instinctive Method

In response to beliefs, thoughts, feelings, observations, displays of data, or whatever triggers the need for a decision, those who use this method:

1. Make assumptions to fill in data gaps.

2. Jump to a conclusion.

When asked, "Why did you select Alternative C?" or, "Why did you select K?" the decisionmaker displays the same four lists, as if they disclose the rationale for the decision.   But the four lists provide little help in choosing the preferred alternative, and even less help in disclosing the rationale for the decision. Following is the result, in the canoe decision, from asking for the advantages and disadvantages of each alternative:

Display of So-Called Advantages and Disadvantages

Advantages of Canoe C	Advantages of Canoe K
1. Weighs Only 65 Pounds	5. Smoother Finish than C
2. Very Good Flotation	6. Nice Color (Much Nicer than C)
	7. Weighs Only 75 Pounds
Disadvantages of Canoe C	Disadvantages of Canoe K
3. Rougher Finish than K	8. Not Quite as Stable as C
4. Unattractive Color	9. Has a Keel that is a Little Too Deep

Note: Do not use Choosing By Advantages and Disadvantages. It is an unsound method.

This display shows that asking for the advantages and disadvantages of each alternative is likely to produce duplications of data. Surprisingly, it is also likely to produce omissions.   Before deciding, therefore, it is essential to reorganize the data—to eliminate the duplications and other mistakes. When actually choosing from only two alternatives, we usually transform the display of "advantages" and "disadvantages" directly into a display of advantages, using the Two-List Format. But in the CBA training process, first, we construct a display of attributes.   Then, based on the display of attributes, we construct a display of attributes and advantages, using the Tabular Format. Then, we construct the display of advantages.

In the canoe decision, we examined the items of data in the initial display, one-by-one, and asked ourselves, "Does this item describe a characteristic of one alternative (an attribute), or does it describe a difference between two alternatives (an advantage)?" If it described an attribute, we included it in the display of attributes.   Whenever it was necessary to fill in data gaps, we physically examined the two canoes. We didn't simply make assumptions. Following is the result:

Display of Attributes

Attributes of Canoe C	Attributes of Canoe K
Weighs 65 Pounds	Weighs 75 Pounds
Moderately Smooth Finish	Very Smooth Finish
Starry-Brown Color	Kelly-Blue Color
Excellent Stability	Very Good Stability
7/8-Inch Keel	5/8-Inch Keel
Note: Both Alternatives Have the Same Total Cost.	

In the original display, the first item (Weighs Only 65 Pounds) is listed as an advantage of Canoe C. Now, here are the questions we asked ourselves: Is this actually an advantage (a difference between two alternatives)? Or, is it an attribute (a characteristic of one alternative)? Of course, what the first item actually describes is a characteristic of only one alternative. Therefore, it is an attribute—not an advantage. In the display of attributes, this attribute of C and the corresponding attribute of K are shown side-by-side for easy comparison. (Notice, in each case, that the word "only" has been dropped. This removed unnecessary subjectivity.)

The second item in the original display tells us that Canoe C has "Very Good Flotation." But the original display doesn't include the flotation attribute of Canoe K. To determine the flotation of Canoe K, we examined Canoe K. What we found is that both canoes have "Very Good Flotation." Because there is no difference in this factor, the flotation attributes will not affect the decision. Therefore, they are not included in the display of attributes.

Similarly, both canoes have the same cost. Therefore, this is not a money decision. However, the statement that the costs are the same does need to be included (at the bottom of the attributes display). Why? To choose the proper CBA method, as is explained in chapter 24, we need to know whether the costs are equal or unequal. As shown in chapter 24, money decisions call for special methods. (The first twenty-three chapters present sound methods for nonmoney decisions. To use these methods for money decisions, they must be modified. However, the modifications are not very large and not very difficult to make.)

The third item (Rougher Finish than K) truly is a disadvantage, as shown in the original display. But this same difference between the two canoes is shown, again, as the fifth item (Smoother Finish than C). This is an example of double-counting. Neither of the attributes in smoothness is shown in the original display. Therefore, to complete the display of attributes in this factor, we had to examine both canoes. And what we found is that Canoe C has a moderately smooth finish, while K has a very smooth finish. In the remaining factors—color, stability, and keel depth—there were more omissions; we had to collect additional data.

Item 9, which pertains to keel depth, illustrates a very common mistake. This item states that Canoe K "Has a Keel that is a Little Too Deep." This statement is misleading. What we discovered, by talking to those who provided the data, is that this statement is based on a comparison between Canoe K and a third canoe—an imaginary one with an ideal keel for downriver canoeing. By examining Canoes C and K, we found that while K has a 5/8-inch keel—which is a little too deep—Canoe C has a 7/8-inch keel, which is even deeper. Therefore, *compared with C,* Canoe K actually has an advantage in keel depth.

People often make the mistake of comparing a real alternative with an ideal, imaginary one. And in many cases, the imaginary alternative is very unrealistic. This mistake is too often what happens when people make judgments about their children, their spouses, their employers, their employees, and their political leaders. What then happens, of course, is that no one can measure up to the ideal.

ACTIVITY NO. 2: DECIDE THE ADVANTAGES

To simplify complex decisions, CBA divides its major activities, as needed, into bite-size tasks. For example, the second central activity—deciding advantages—requires two simple tasks.

2. Decide the advantages of each alternative.

   a. Decide the least-preferred attribute in each factor.

   b. Determine the differences from the least-preferred attributes. These differences are the advantages of the alternatives.

Task No. 2a: Decide the Least-Preferred Attributes

People have asked, many times, "When deciding the advantage, or advantages, in a factor, why do we start by deciding the least-preferred attribute? Why not the most-preferred?" The following chart shows that identifying the most-preferred attribute would establish a base for deciding disadvantages, not advantages.

Disadvantages Are Differences from Most-Preferred Attributes

	Canoe C	Canoe K
Attributes:	65 Pounds (Most Preferred)	75 Pounds
Disadvantage:		10 Pounds Heavier

As shown, Canoe K has a 10 pound *disadvantage*, compared with C. But this same 10 pound difference in weight is an *advantage* of Canoe C. When we choose between the two canoes, we must count, but not double-count, this 10 pound difference. To avoid double-counting, we must count it either as a disadvantage of K or as an advantage of C, but not both. To simplify and clarify the decisionmaking process, CBA counts this 10 pound difference as an advantage of C.

Advantages Are Differences from Least-Preferred Attributes

	Canoe C	Canoe K
Attributes:	65 Pounds	75 Pounds (Least Preferred)
Advantage:	10 Pounds Lighter	

This chart shows why we start by identifying the least-preferred attributes, rather than the most-preferred. It shows that deciding the least-preferred attribute in a factor establishes a base for deciding advantages. It also shows that an advantage can be defined as *a difference from the least-preferred attribute.*

As stated before, deciding the least-preferred attributes is a subjective task. To demonstrate that it is subjective, consider the colors in the canoe purchase example:

- Some persons would select the starry-brown color of C as the least-preferred attribute in this factor. To them, Canoe K would have the advantage in color.

- Some would select the kelly-blue color of K as the least preferred. To them, Canoe C would have the advantage in color.

- Some would be indifferent between these same two colors. To them, neither canoe would have an advantage in this factor. Remember: *If there is no difference or no preference, there is no advantage.*

All of these viewpoints are valid. So the question is, "Which one is the appropriate viewpoint for the decision?" In this case, the stake-holders—those who will be affected by the decision—strongly prefer the kelly-blue color. Therefore, according to the stakeholders, the starry-brown color is the least preferred. And, for this particular decision, the stakeholders' viewpoint was selected as the appropriate viewpoint. However, what should be remembered is that different decisions call for different viewpoints. And the appropriate viewpoint must be selected for each decision, according to the purpose and circumstances of the decision.

In the Two-List Format, which is demonstrated at the end of this chapter, the attributes of the alternatives are usually not displayed in writing. Therefore, the decisionmaker must perceive the attributes in his or her mind, one pair at a time, and must decide the least-preferred attribute in each pair. This task usually happens in an instant. (In the Two-List Format, the advantages are always displayed in writing—even though the attributes are usually not displayed in writing.)

Task No. 2b: Determine the Differences

After deciding the least-preferred attributes—one in each factor—the decisionmaker determines the differences from the least-preferred attributes. *These differences are the advantages of the alternatives.* Determining the differences should be a scientific, objective task.

As you can see, an advantage is very different from an attribute. Nevertheless, these terms—*attributes* and *advantages*—are often used interchangeably, and that is a mistake. Here is why they must not be used interchangeably—especially, during the decisionmaking process: If numerical weights, ratings, or importance scores must be assigned (explicitly or implicitly) they must always be assigned to advantages—never, to attributes.

As stated before, comparison terms—such as *larger, smaller,* and *smoother*—are used, whenever practicable, when describing advantages. For example, Canoe C has a "slightly *greater* stability" than Canoe K. But comparison terms cannot always be used. An example is when one canoe has a shoulder bar and the other doesn't. Obviously, it would be awkward to use a comparison term when describing this type of advantage. In this type of situation, the advantage would be described as "With versus without _____ ." Following is a description of the shoulder-bar advantage, preceded by the descriptions of its associated attributes:

Attribute of Canoe N: Does not have a shoulder bar.

Attribute of Canoe W: Does have a shoulder bar.

Advantage of Canoe W: With versus without a shoulder bar.

When listing this type of advantage, we sometimes abbreviate by simply listing the attribute, or by not including "versus without" in the description. For example, we could list "A shoulder bar" or "With a shoulder bar" as the advantage of W. But when judging importance, it is the importance of the actual advantage (with versus without a shoulder bar) that must be judged—not the importance of the attribute. (Incidently, pertaining to Canoes C and K: Each has a shoulder bar. Therefore, neither C nor K has an advantage in this factor.)

THE TABULAR FORMAT FOR TWO ALTERNATIVES

The standard Tabular Format—the one for choosing from several alternatives—is presented in chapter 22. This section presents the one for choosing from only two alternatives.

The Tabular Format and the first two central activities of the Tabular Method are presented at this time for three reasons: First, this format is an excellent vehicle for practicing the CBA vocabulary. Second, by walking through the first two central activities of the Tabular Method, we are responding to the first central question: How large are the advantages of each alternative? Third, we are setting the stage for presenting three CBA methods that you will be able to use immediately: the Simplified Two-List Method, the Instant CBA Process, and the Recognition–Response Process. Following are the first two activities of the Tabular Method:

1. Summarize the attributes of each alternative.

2. Decide the advantages of each alternative.

     a. *Underline* the least-preferred attribute in each factor.

     b. *Summarize* the advantages of the alternatives—the differences from the least-preferred attributes. (On the following page, to highlight the advantages, they have been circled.)

The Tabular Format for Two Alternatives

FACTORS	ALTERNATIVES	
	CANOE C	CANOE K

CANOE WEIGHT
  Attributes:
 	
  Advantages:
	65 Pounds
	
	(10 Pounds Lighter)
		<u>75 Pounds</u>

FINISH (Smoothness)
  Attributes:
 	
  Advantages:
	<u>Mod. Smooth</u>	Very Smooth
		
		(Moderately Smoother)

COLOR
  Attributes:
 	
  Advantages:
	<u>Starry-Brown</u>	Kelly-Blue
		
		(Much Nicer Color)

STABILITY
  Attributes:
 	
  Advantages:
	Excellent
	
	(Slightly Greater)
		<u>Very Good</u>

KEEL DEPTH
  Attributes:
 	
  Advantages:
	<u>7/8 Inch</u>	5/8 Inch
		
		(Slightly Better Keel)

TOTAL IMPORTANCE OF ADVANTAGES:		
TOTAL COST:	Both Alternatives Have the Same Total Cost.	

Notice the distinctions between factors, attributes, least-preferred attributes (which are underlined), and advantages. Notice, also, that non-comparison words are used when describing the attributes, while comparison words (lighter, smoother, nicer, greater, and better) are used when describing the advantages. Because the advantages are circled, it is instantly obvious that Canoe C has two advantages, while K has three. And that takes us to the second central question: Do the two advantages outweigh the three, or do the three outweigh the two? This question will be answered in part III. For now, simply notice that in the Tabular Format spaces are provided for showing both the importance of each individual advantage and the total importance of advantages for each alternative.

(If you were attending a sound-decisionmaking workshop, the discussion leader would now be pointing to different items in the display and asking you to name them. For example, you would be responding by saying that canoe weight, finish, color, stability, and keel depth are the factors. As another example, 65 pounds is an attribute, while 75 pounds is a least-preferred attribute. And the 10 pound difference in weight is an advantage of Canoe C. So, take a few minutes to practice pointing to the various items in the Tabular Display and naming them.)

THE TWO-LIST FORMAT

As detailed in chapter 22, the Tabular Format is primarily for choosing from several alternatives—three or more, but not a large number. However, it is also used for difficult two-option decisions. For simple two-option decisions, the Two-List Format is usually preferred. Therefore, before you practice the Tabular Format, practice the Two-List Format—at least for a few simple decisions.

The Two-List Format

Advantages of Canoe C	Advantages of Canoe K
• 10 Pounds Lighter • Slightly Greater Stability	• Moderately Smoother Finish • Much Nicer Color • Slightly Better Keel Depth
Total Importance:	Total Importance:
Both Alternatives Have the Same Total Cost	

Often, at this point in CBA workshops, at least one of the participants will say, "I don't understand why we should ignore the disadvantages." Of course, the answer is that we must not ignore the disadvantages. They must be included in the evaluation; and in all CBA methods, they are included (as advantages). They must be counted, but they must not be double-counted.

THE SIMPLIFIED TWO-LIST METHOD

As in the Tabular Format, space is provided in the Two-List Format for displaying importance scores. However, for most of your simple, two-option decisions, you won't need to display importance; and precise judgments about importance won't be necessary.

For two-option decisions where the advantages need to be displayed but where precise judgments about importance are unnecessary, the Simplified Two-List Method is often used. In this method, we list the advantages. Then, we simply ask ourselves, "Do the advantages of the one alternative outweigh the advantages of other? Or do the advantages of the other outweigh the advantages of the one?"

The Simplified Two-List Method, for Nonmoney Decisions

---

1. In the Two-List format, list the advantages of each alternative.

2. Without deciding the importance of each individual advantage, choose the alternative that obviously has the greatest total importance of advantages.

You can begin using the Simplified Two-List Method immediately for many of your nonmoney decisions. Later, after studying chapters 24 and 25, you will be able to use it for money decisions as well. But this method isn't adequate in some cases. The canoe decision is an example. After listing the advantages of Canoes C and K, the decision wasn't obvious, to the stakeholders. Therefore, as shown in chapter 9, they used the Two-List Method, instead of the Simplified Two-List Method, for the canoe decision.

6

Instant CBA and the Recognition–Response Process

INSTANT CBA

Instant CBA is the same as the Simplified Two-List Method, except for two things: First, the advantages are mentally perceived, instead of being listed on paper. Second, the two activities in the Simplified Two-List Method become one activity with two simultaneous tasks. The following outline is for nonmoney decisions:

Instant CBA, for Nonmoney Decisions

1a. Mentally perceive the advantages of each alternative.
1b. At the same time, without deciding the importance of each individual advantage, simply choose the alternative with the greatest total importance of advantages.

To learn the Instant CBA Process, start by practicing the Simplified Two-List Method—for simple, hypothetical decisions. *List* the advantages of the alternatives. Then ask yourself: "Do the advantages of the one outweigh the advantages of the other? Or do the advantages of the other outweigh the advantages of the one?" Next, practice the Instant CBA Process. *Perceive* the advantages in your mind, instead of listing them on paper; and decide. Keep practicing until you automatically use the Instant CBA Process, whenever it is applicable, without even thinking about it.

THE RECOGNITION–RESPONSE PROCESS

Instant CBA is the appropriate CBA method for many simple, two-option decisions. But very simple decisions call for very simple CBA methods, such as the Recognition–Response Process—which is discussed, in more detail, in chapter 26. Expert decisionmakers, those who most often make excellent decisions, use the Recognition–Response Process for at least 85 to 90 percent of their decisions.

The Recognition–Response Process

1a. **Observe** the situation and **recognize** that you have either considered or experienced similar situations before.

1b. At the same time, correctly **respond** to the present situation.

An expert draws from a mental reservoir containing countless excellent previous decisions. Often, she or he simply reuses a previous decision, adjusted to fit the present situation. Of course, those who seldom make excellent decisions also use the Recognition–Response Process for most of their decisions. Why do they seldom make excellent decisions? One of the differences between those who usually do make excellent decisions and those who usually do not is that excellent decisionmakers are better observers. Another major difference is that excellent decisionmakers are more responsive to feedback. They don't keep making the same mistakes, over and over again. Perhaps the greatest difference is that they have a better supply of excellent previous decisions in their reservoirs. So, how can you fill your reservoir with excellent decisions?

By using the other CBA methods for the 10 to 15 percent of your decisions that do not call for the Recognition–Response Process, you will be continuously filling your reservoir with excellent decisions. Therefore, practically all of your decisions, including your Recognition–Response decisions, will be based on the importance of advantages. And you will be making excellent decisions more often than ever before.

The Simplified Two-List Method, Instant CBA, and the Recognition–Response Process do not require high levels of skill. They are easy to learn and easy to use. But they do require higher levels of skill than other CBA methods. So, let's look at the skill-learning process.

7

The Five-Step
Skill-Learning Process

The five-step process (learn, unlearn, relearn, practice, and teach) was initially designed for learning CBA skills. However, this same process can be used for learning other skills, as well.

1. *Learn* one set of CBA concepts and methods at a time.

2. *Unlearn* (learn to not use) the unsound methods that CBA will replace. For example, if you have been using Choosing By Advantages and Disadvantages, or other methods that you now know are unsound, I hope you will never use them again.

3. *Relearn* the CBA concepts and methods—as many times as necessary. Very soon, for example, I hope you will reread and restudy the first seven chapters of this book.

4. *Practice* the CBA definitions of factors, criteria, attributes, and advantages. Keep on practicing them until they become a natural part of your everyday vocabulary. Also, practice the CBA methods. Start with simple, hypothetical decisions. Then, practice with simple, unimportant, real-world decisions. Eventually, after you have finished reading and studying this book, you will be able to use CBA for nearly all your decisions.

5. *Teach* the parts of CBA that you have learned. At first, teach mostly by example—by using CBA for your own decisions. Teaching CBA to others will not only be a service to them; it will also strengthen your own understanding of the CBA process.

To thoroughly learn the entire CBA system, use Five Steps Plus One. In this process, the five basic steps are repeated several times—at least once for each new set of concepts and methods. After completing the five steps for one set of definitions, principles, models, and methods, repeat these same steps for the next set, then the next, the next, and so forth. Then, teach by formal instruction.

Five Steps Plus One

LEARN

To develop the CBA system, we not only had to learn such things as how to simplify sound decisionmaking, we also had to learn *how to learn* such things as how to simplify sound decisionmaking. The CBA training process is the result of many cycles of designing, testing, and improving. Improvements were made concurrently both in how to choose by advantages and how to learn how to choose by advantages. The two had to go hand-in-hand.

When you teach CBA, you can take advantage of our experience. For example, we needed to find the best sequence for presenting the cornerstone principles. So we asked ourselves, "Should the principle of anchoring precede the fundamental rule, or should the fundamental rule precede the principle of anchoring?" After trying several variations of each option, and after weighing their advantages, we selected the sequence that is used in this book.

Surprisingly often, participants in CBA workshops want to skip the basics. Some want to start using the concepts and methods for complex decisions, before learning the concepts and methods for simple decisions. Participants in basic sound decisionmaking workshops have often asked how to get a group of people to agree on the importance of advantages, which requires multiple-viewpoint decisionmaking skills, before they have learned the basic single-viewpoint decisionmaking skills that are presented in this book. That is like trying to use calculus before learning arithmetic (which, as you know, is impossible).

Ideally, everyone would gradually learn the basic concepts and methods of Choosing By Advantages *while they are learning other basic skills*— before becoming professional economists, engineers, teachers, counselors, consultants, leaders in organizations, or journalists.

An Ideal Skill-Learning Sequence

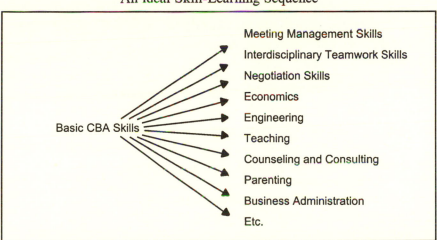

Following are examples of learning the basic CBA skills in a logical sequence:

- Part II presents the definitions of key sound-decisionmaking words, the fundamental rule of sound decisionmaking (which pertains to using correct data), and three CBA methods—in preparation for learning how to use data correctly.

- Part III presents the principle of anchoring (which pertains to using data correctly) and two additional CBA methods—in preparation for learning the methods that are presented in part IV.

- Part IV shows that CBA simplifies the art of decisionmaking and simplifies correctly using correct data by organizing the art of decisionmaking into three overlapping areas: sound decisionmaking, congruent decisionmaking, and effective decisionmaking.

UNLEARN

Obviously, the ideal way to learn the CBA system isn't a possibility for those who have already begun their professional careers, before having an opportunity to learn CBA. They will not only need to learn how to skillfully use sound methods, they will also need to unlearn the use of unsound methods. To unlearn unsound methods, they will need to clearly understand why the unsound methods are unsound. And, of course, they will need to consistently use sound methods. If you haven't done so already, start using CBA, today—for your simple, nonmoney, two-option decisions. And don't worry about perfection. *It is better to use sound methods approximately, rather than using unsound methods precisely.*

The key to unlearning unsound methods, I believe, is to clearly understand that unsound methods, such as Choosing By Advantages and Disadvantages and Choosing By Pros and Cons, do cause or encourage critical mistakes, and that these mistakes too often cause tragic outcomes. Only those who can see that it is essential to learn and use sound methods are likely to make the necessary effort to unlearn unsound methods.

When we first started conducting CBA workshops, we assumed that all we would need to do is to show that the CBA methods are sound and simple. The assumption was that the workshop participants would immediately stop using methods that are unsound and too complex. But that was a false assumption. Until we began strongly emphasizing the need for unlearning commonly used unsound methods, along with emphasizing the first cornerstone principle (decisionmakers must learn and skillfully use sound methods), almost no one stopped using the unsound methods.

Of course, before someone can skillfully use sound methods, they must start using sound methods. For now, therefore, I recommend abbreviating the first cornerstone principle as follows: To consistently make sound decisions, *decisionmakers must learn and use sound methods.*

RELEARN

Relearn the Four Key Definitions

To be able to understand and use the CBA concepts and methods, four words in the CBA vocabulary must be used with exceptional precision:

A factor is

- an element, or a component, of a decision.
- a container for criteria, attributes, advantages, and other types of data.

A <u>criterion</u> is

- a decision-rule, or a guideline. (Some are "musts." Others are "wants.")
- any standard on which a judgment is based.
- any decision that guides further decisionmaking.

An <u>attribute</u> is

- a characteristic or consequence of *ONE* alternative.

An <u>advantage</u> is

- a difference between the attributes of *TWO* alternatives.

Only if necessary, CBA decisionmakers display the data and the rationale for a decision in writing. They establish *criteria* for a decision during the stage-setting phase of the CBA process. During the innovation phase, they formulate alternatives and determine their *attributes*. And if necessary, they describe the attributes, in detail, in each *factor*. During the decisionmaking phase, they summarize the attributes, if necessary, and decide the *advantages*.

Relearn the Fundamental Rule of Sound Decisionmaking

This is such an important principle that decisionmakers need to memorize it; they need to be able to apply it for virtually all of their decisions; and they need to be able to explain it. Here, again, is the rule: *Decisions must be based on the importance of advantages.*

People ask, "What are the exceptions? In what situations should we not base decisions on the importance of advantages?" There are no exceptions. This rule applies to all types of decisions, from the simplest to the most complex. However, as shown in part IV, different types of decisions call for different methods of Choosing By Advantages. For example, while complex decisions require explicitly weighing advantages, very simple decisions require implicitly weighing advantages.

Relearn the Key Words for Remembering the Four Central Activities

The following chart shows, again, that sound methods move back and forth between the objective and subjective sides of the decisionmaking process—and that the key words for remembering the four central activities are *attributes, advantages, importance,* and *total importance.*

The Decisionmaking Phase of CBA for Complex Decisions

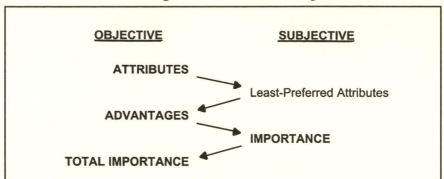

PRACTICE

Think about the old question of which came first, the chicken or the egg. Now, think about this question: Which needs to be first; learning CBA, using CBA, or choosing CBA? The answer: Making sound decisions about how to make decisions requires the skillful use of CBA, and skillfully using CBA requires learning and practicing CBA. A good way to practice is to start with a decision where one alternative is obviously preferred. So, for practice, let's choose between two methods of decisionmaking: Choosing By Advantages *and* Disadvantages, and Choosing By Advantages.

Following is a display of advantages for this decision. In my view, the two large advantages of Choosing By Advantages far outweigh the one small advantage of Choosing By Advantages *and* Disadvantages. Do you agree?

A Two-List Display of Advantages

Advantages of Choosing By Advantages and Disadvantages		Advantages of Choosing By Advantages	
• More Familiar		• Simpler To Use • Produces Better Decisions	
Total Importance:		Total Importance:	

Practice by revising the Two-List Display for this decision. What additional advantages should be included on either side? (For example, CBA produces better interpersonal relationships, with less conflict.) And, which of the advantages in the display should be excluded? (Of course, as someone becomes more and more familiar with CBA, the difference in familiarity becomes less and less important. Therefore, I believe that, for you, CBA has all the advantages—at least, for simple, two-option decisions—because you are now familiar with CBA. Do you agree?)

After listing the advantages of Choosing By Advantages, use your list as a stimulus for action. Use it to encourage yourself to start using CBA today. There are some who protest: "But I'm not ready to use CBA." So I ask, "Why not?" "Because I still don't know how to decide the importance of advantages." My reply: "If you don't know how to decide the importance of advantages, you certainly don't know how to decide the importance of advantages and disadvantages."

Actually, everyone knows how to decide importance (intensities of preferences). They have been doing it all their lives. Long ago, when they selected a new toy, they had to decide—at least implicitly—the intensities of their preferences. Later, when they chose from a menu in a restaurant and when they selected a new car, they based their decisions on the intensities of their preferences.

What most people have not been doing, at least not correctly, is *numerically disclosing* the intensities of their preferences. Furthermore, they haven't been deciding (weighing) the importance of the right things. They haven't been weighing advantages. And this is why, far too often, they have been making unsound decisions.

Obviously, an essential step in learning how to disclose your viewpoint about the importance of advantages will be to just start doing it. But it is important to do it correctly; so very soon, study part III to be sure you clearly understand how to anchor your decisions (about importance) to the relevant facts. Studying and practicing are the keys. Old decisionmaking habits can be replaced by practicing new ones.

Perhaps the most difficult habits to change (in the change to Choosing By Advantages) are vocabulary habits. Changing to sound-decisionmaking patterns of speech can be difficult. Why? Because, when we need to use a phrase or a sentence to express a thought, we seldom have time to carefully select exactly the right combinations of words—particularly during the decisionmaking process. While we are concentrating on the content of a decision, we automatically use our old patterns of thought and speech.

To acquire sound-decisionmaking habits, we must practice the sound-decisionmaking patterns while we are not making decisions. Start with the three patterns that are highlighted below—especially the two that are sound and simple. (Of course, those that are unsound, conflict-causing, or too complex must be avoided.) Practice and practice those that are sound and simple, until you use them automatically. (Notice in the last two examples that the word IN is emphasized as a reminder that a factor is a container and that advantages are contained IN factors.)

Describing What Data to Include in a Set of Data
for a Decision:

- Unsound and Conflict-Causing: Be sure to include all the pros and cons of each alternative.

- Unsound and Too Complex: Be sure to include all the advantages and disadvantages of each alternative.

- Sound and Simple: *Be sure to include all the advantages of each alternative.*

Dividing a Decision into Factors:

- Unsound: What factors will be important in this decision?

- Sound: *IN what factors will there be differences among the alternatives?*

- Sound and Simple: *IN what factors will there be advantages?*

When you are talking with someone who is unfamiliar with CBA, it might be better, at first, to use the phrase, *differences among the alternatives,* instead of the single word, *advantages.* But use the word *advantages* when talking with someone who is familiar with CBA. Practice, many times, using the pattern that is sound and simple: "In what factors will there be advantages?"

Practicing is good, but practicing with feedback—especially feedback from a CBA facilitator—is much better. If you are not a member of an organization that has a CBA facilitator, exchange feedback between yourself and someone else who is also learning CBA. Most of all, help one another to adopt the CBA patterns of thought and speech. Again, start with the three that are highlighted above. Later, adopt the additional patterns that are presented in chapter 14. As indicated, there is no need to finish learning CBA before beginning to use CBA. In this regard, the study of decisionmaking is similar to the study of mathematics. In the same way that a person can use arithmetic before learning algebra and calculus, she or he can use the basic CBA concepts and methods before learning the advanced concepts and methods.

In review: Sound methods for complex decisions require four central activities, represented by the following key words: attributes, advantages, importance, and total importance. In chapter 5, you learned the Tabular Format and the Two-List Format. You also learned that the Simplified Two-List Method requires only two central activities, with the following key words: advantages and total importance. And only the advantages are displayed in writing. Chapter 6 encouraged you to practice the Simplified Two-List Method, until you automatically use the Instant CBA process whenever it is applicable.

A good way to practice is by displaying the choice between Canoe C and Canoe K. Start by drawing a box—manually, not with a computer. Then, divide the box into six areas, as follows:

The First Steps in Creating the Two-List Format

Advantages of C	Advantages of K

Next, use dashed lines to subdivide the two largest areas, as shown on the following page. (Notice that these lines do not extend all the way from the top to the bottom of the display.) In this step, be sure to use dashed lines, rather that solid lines. In CBA workshops, most of the participants do this correctly. But initially, some make the mistake of using solid lines where dashed lines are needed, and that decreases the clarity of their displays.

The Two-List Format

Advantages of c	Advantages of k

You are now ready to list the advantages of the two alternatives. The following display shows what to avoid. It shows an unclear way to list the advantages:

This Is Not an Acceptable Way to List Advantages

Advantages of c	Advantages of k
10 Pounds Lighter Slightly Greater Stability	Moderately Smoother Finish Much Nicer Color slightly Better keel

This Is an Improvement

Advantages of c	Advantages of k
• 10 Pounds Lighter • Slightly Greater Stability	• Moderately Smoother Finish • Much Nicer Color • slightly Better keel

In the Two-List Format, use bullets, as shown above, to clearly distinguish one advantage from another. For the same purpose, use double-spacing between advantages, as follows:

This Is an Effective Way to List Advantages

Advantages of c	Advantages of k
• 10 Pounds Lighter • slightly Greater Stability	• Moderately Smoother Finish • Much NicerColor • slightly Better keel

TEACH

After you have reached a comfortable level of skill in using CBA for simple, two-option decisions, I strongly recommend taking yourself to a higher level by teaching what you have learned, so far, to at least one other person.   Start by using numerical illustrations to define *attributes* and *advantages*.   Also, using these same illustrations, demonstrate that a disadvantage of one alternative is an advantage of another.

Here is an illustration that works very well: We need to choose between two basketball players. The selected player will be the new center for the team.   Therefore, one of the factors we will be considering—along with strength, quickness, and other factors—is height. The following sketch shows the heights of players A and E:

The Height Attributes of Players A and E

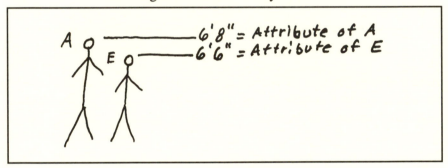

After drawing the sketch, review the definition of an ***attribute*** (a characteristic or consequence of one alternative). Then, show that an advantage is not the same thing as an attribute by asking: "Which one of the basketball players, A or E, has the advantage in height?" Nearly everyone gives the same answer: Player A has the advantage. Then ask: "How large is the advantage of Player A, compared with E?" Again, nearly everyone gives the same answer: Player A has a two-inch advantage—compared with Player E.

Add the two-inch advantage to the sketch, as on the following page. Use this sketch to review the definition of an ***advantage*** (a difference between the attributes of two alternatives). Then ask, "Which one of the players has the disadvantage in height?" Answer: Player E. Then ask, "How large is the disadvantage of Player E—compared with A?" Answer: The same two inches.

The Height Advantage of Player A

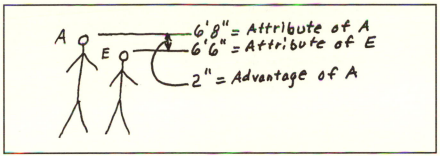

Use both numerical and nonnumerical examples—use as many as necessary—to demonstrate that, without exception, a disadvantage of one alternative is an advantage of another. After defining attributes, advantages, and disadvantages, teach others, mostly by example, to always base their decisions on advantages. Teach them to never base their decisions on advantages and disadvantages.

After you have studied part III, teach others why it would be a mistake to base decisions on the importance of factors, goals, roles, categories, objectives, criteria, or attributes. Also, after you have studied part III, teach them how to anchor their decisions to the relevant facts. Then, learn and teach the methods that are presented in part IV.

You don't need to wait until you have learned the principles that are presented in part III, and the methods that are presented in part IV, before you can begin using and teaching those you have learned in parts I and II. Parents can immediately begin teaching their children the concepts of *alternatives, attributes,* and *advantages.* For example, soon after a child becomes mature enough to understand choosing between two toys, the parents can ask, "How is this alternative better than that one? And, how is that alternative better than this one?"

By using it themselves, parents can immediately begin teaching the CBA vocabulary. When planning a family activity, for example, they can ask, "What are the advantages of going in July, rather than August? And what are the advantages of going in August?" At the same time, they can avoid using such words as *pros, cons,* and *disadvantages.* For family decisions, parents can demonstrate how to use the Simplified Two-List Method, so their children can see the process in writing. Parents can also help the school system find ways to include sound decisionmaking as a basic subject in a crowded curriculum.

Parents, teachers, and others need to become highly skilled in describing attributes and advantages—using non-comparison terms when describing attributes and comparison terms when describing advantages. For example, parents and teachers need to help their children and students form sensory-rich, motivational pictures of the advantages of:

- Becoming educated, contributing, successful members of society

- Learning such skills as reading, writing, music, art, science, history, and mathematics

- Learning how to choose by advantages

- Treating others with kindness and respect

- Living free from addictions

Instead of *telling* your children, or your students, the advantages of—for example—treating others with kindness and respect, *ask* them to list the advantages. Ask them to list the advantages of living free from addictions, the advantages of learning to read and write, and so forth. If they list an attribute, give them feedback. Explain: "That's an attribute, not an advantage."

When you are teaching CBA, you are taking your students on a journey. This book follows one of the routes that successfully leads to the destination of understanding and skillfully using the CBA process. There are other successful routes. But routes that appear to be shortcuts are likely to be dead ends. For example, it might seem sensible to skip some of the definitions or some of the concepts that you have learned so far, or to skip some of the histories that will be presented later. Routes such as those have been explored, and they have seldom led to success.

If everyone could see the need for learning and using sound methods, teaching CBA would be a snap. To find out approximately how many are able to see this need, I surveyed three university classes. I asked the students to list the subjects that, in their opinion, should be taught in the educational system. In response, they listed forty-nine subjects. But none of the students—not even one—listed decisionmaking.

This seems to be typical. Apparently, many people do not view decisionmaking as a skill that needs to be taught. Instead, they perceive that sound decisionmaking is a natural skill, or one that can be acquired simply from experience. To change this perception, CBA workshops now emphasize that sound decisionmaking is not a natural skill. This has increased our success in teaching CBA; it will increase your success, as well.

Another thing that has increased the success of CBA workshops is that they now include histories of the cornerstone principles. These histories review the step-by-step improvements that produced the CBA system. Because CBA workshops with these histories have been more successful than those without, they are presented later in this book so that you can use them when you teach CBA. Presenting these histories has been viewed, by some, as a negative way to teach. In their view, we are being negative about the old methods, those that are being replaced by CBA. They apparently think that we view the differences between the old and new as disadvantages of the old. Also, that we are criticizing people for not using CBA in the past. But that would be an unjust criticism. Obviously, it wasn't possible for anyone to use CBA—at that time—because the CBA principles hadn't been brought together, and the CBA methods hadn't been developed.

In my view, presenting the histories of CBA is a positive way to teach. The differences between the old and the new are advantages. Furthermore, we are complementing those who made the improvements—also, those who will accept and apply the improvements in the future.

There are other advantages of including at least some of the histories of CBA in the training process: Comparing and contrasting two things—in this case, the old and the new—is often a more effective way to teach than not comparing and contrasting. Also, presenting these histories helps the participants to more clearly see that the art of decisionmaking is a broad field of study, and that CBA isn't just a "flavor of the month." They need to know that the CBA principles have always been valid in the past, and they will always be valid in the future.

If more parents, students, leaders in organizations, and educators—including those who conduct training seminars for adults—viewed the art of decisionmaking as a vital subject, that would be a giant step in the right direction. But it needs to be viewed as more than a subject. It needs to be viewed as a vital field of study. For example, as you know:

- Decisionmakers can choose not to be teachers. But teachers cannot choose not to be decisionmakers. They are continuously deciding what and how to teach.

- Decisionmakers can choose not to be doctors. But doctors cannot choose not to be decisionmakers. And we, their patients, certainly want them to use sound methods.

- Decisionmakers can choose not to be engineers. But engineers cannot choose not to be decisionmakers. Engineers are continuously making vital, quality-of-life decisions.

Clearly, we could improve our own lives and the lives of others if we all were continuously studying the art of decisionmaking and improving our decisionmaking skills.

TEACH BY FORMAL INSTRUCTION

To graduate from each level in the educational system, the applicable level of CBA competency could—and I think should—become a graduation requirement. As stated, people can choose not to become doctors, lawyers, truck drivers, engineers, or airline pilots. But they cannot choose not to become decisionmakers. Everyone is a decisionmaker. Furthermore, those in many fields are professional decisionmakers (decisionmaking is their primary job); and each person needs to become fully competent in his or her field, or profession. While practically everyone needs to learn at least the basic concepts and methods of Choosing By Advantages, professional decisionmakers need to learn more than the basics.

Because virtually everyone needs to know how to choose by advantages, many CBA instructors are needed, in all levels of the educational system. Perhaps what is most important, in the long run, is that elementary school teachers need to learn, use, and progressively teach the basic CBA concepts and methods to all of their students.

Unfortunately, many of the decision methods that teachers are being taught, today, are unsound. Therefore, many of the methods that they are teaching are unsound. To make matters worse, they are not teaching the sound-decisionmaking vocabulary. And they are not teaching the basic sound-decisionmaking principles. They are not even teaching the corner-stone principles of sound decisionmaking—because they have never been taught these principles.

When teaching CBA, use the teaching aids that are described in this book. For example, chapter 8 describes using a balance scale to introduce the principle of anchoring—which is the centerpiece of the CBA system. It is very important for you to buy or borrow a balance scale, so that you can physically demonstrate weighing pennies versus dimes. (You can buy an inexpensive scale at a school supply store.) Using the scale as an aid, make sure that those you are teaching clearly understand the difference between anchored versus unanchored objective questions and judgments, before you try to teach them the difference between anchored versus unanchored subjective questions and judgments. As another example, be sure to at least describe the bridge design experiment, presented in chapter 12. (If those in the group you are teaching aren't likely to be offended by participating in the experiment, do it, instead of just describing it.)

Teach Your Students that Unsound Methods Must Not be Used

As extensive studies have demonstrated, several of the decisionmaking methods that came into use before the CBA system was developed are unsound. Nevertheless, they are still being taught today. Unfortunately, unsound methods are being taught in all levels of the education system— from the elementary school level to the continuing–education level.

In particular, the methods that some call THE Rational Methods, and we call Weighting-Rating-and-Calculating, or WRC, are very unsound ("weighting" is the same as "weighing"). As is shown in part III, the WRC methods violate several basic sound decisionmaking principles. Even so, they are viewed by many—apparently, throughout the world—as the standard of how decisions should be made. Therefore, educators will need to teach decisionmakers to stop using the WRC Methods. Similarly, educators will need to teach decisionmakers to stop using Choosing By Advantages and Disadvantages, Choosing By Pros and Cons, and other unsound methods.

Teach Your Students that Sound Methods Must be Used

People make some of the most important decisions of their entire lives before and while they are teenagers. And they continue making important decisions throughout their lives. Therefore, they need to be taught, as soon as possible, how to skillfully use sound methods.

To gain acceptance, when you teach and use CBA, in some situations it might be necessary for you to point out that CBA is not based on a theory, or a philosophy. Instead, it is based on practical realities. Here is an example: In the first factor in the canoe decision, the 10 pound difference between 65 pounds and 75 pounds can be viewed as an advantage of the one alternative or as a disadvantage of the other. As you know, this is a practical reality, not a theory.

Furthermore, if a decisionmaker counts this difference as an advantage of the one alternative and then counts this same difference as a disadvantage of the other, that is an example of double-counting. Again, this is a practical reality. Nevertheless, some have argued that CBA cannot be valid, because they think that it disagrees with a particular economic theory, or human behavior theory. Of course, the question of whether CBA agrees or disagrees with a particular theory is actually irrelevant. What is relevant is the fact that the CBA concepts and methods are sound.

As stated in part I, sound-decisionmaking skills are like reading skills, writing skills, and many other skills that are essential in a modern society. They are not natural skills; and they are not acquired simply from experience. As shown in part II, decisionmakers must be taught how to use correct data. And, as is shown in parts III and IV, they must be taught how to use data correctly. (They must be taught how to choose by advantages.)

Of course, those who have adequate reading skills will be able to learn the sound-decisionmaking concepts and methods that are included in this book through self-teaching—by reading and studying the book. But young children and many adults do not have the level of reading skill that is required for self-teaching these concepts and methods. They will need to be taught by their parents and their school teachers, or by CBA instructors. Therefore, the subject of sound decisionmaking (Choosing By Advantages) needs to be included at the very beginning of the educational process. Then, it needs to be continued throughout the educational process. And it must be taught correctly. This is both a major challenge and a golden opportunity for parents, educators, leaders in organizations, and specialists in the field of training and development.

Part III

The Principle of Anchoring

The principle of anchoring is the centerpiece of the CBA system. It is the key to correctly using correct data. In particular, it is the key to correctly taking viewpoints into account in the decisionmaking process. Therefore, it is the key to sound decisionmaking. As follows, the principle of anchoring and the fundamental rule go hand-in-hand.

Q. How can we consistently make sound decisions?
A. The principle of anchoring:
   Decisions must be anchored to the relevant facts.

Q. How can we anchor our decisions to the relevant facts?
A. The fundamental rule of sound decisionmaking:
   Decisions must be based on the importance of advantages.

On the surface, the principle of anchoring seems simple, and its meaning seems obvious. But surveys, experiments, and observations of meetings have demonstrated that its meaning isn't at all obvious. In fact, very few decisionmakers adequately understand this principle.

Although decision methods that violate the principle of anchoring are unsound, such methods are commonly presented—as if they were sound—in books about problem solving and decisionmaking. To make matters worse, they are taught in school classes, university classes, and seminars for business and government leaders. As a result, methods that violate the principle of anchoring are widely used today. Fortunately, they can be transformed from unsound to sound, as is demonstrated in part III.

I should point out that I am not the only person who recognized this principle.   Others also recognized it, long ago.   For example, when I described the concept of anchoring to a professor at the University of Colorado, many years ago, he said that he fully agreed with the concept I had presented.   Then he said, "We call it anchoring."   And that is when I began calling it anchoring.

In essence, the principle of anchoring is that sound methods require anchored versus unanchored questions and judgments.   This is what sets the CBA methods apart from other methods.   Without using anchored questions and judgments, it would be very difficult, if not impossible, for decisionmakers to consistently base their decisions on the relevant facts.   Therefore, the primary purpose of part III—all twelve chapters—is to bring about a change from the traditional use of unanchored questions and judgments to the skillful use of anchored questions and judgments.

Why does it take twelve chapters to explain just one principle?   Perhaps it is simply because the principle of anchoring has many parts, and for most decisionmakers they are unfamiliar.   But some have said that learning the principle of anchoring *requires* a paradigm shift—changing to a different set of beliefs pertaining to the decisionmaking process.   And a member of the Utah House of Representatives said that choosing CBA *is* a paradigm shift.

CBA facilitators help individuals and organizations anchor their decisions to the relevant facts, and this often requires explaining the concept of anchoring.   One facilitator said that explaining this concept is like explaining the shape of the earth at a time when everyone believed that it was flat.   The idea that the world was spherical probably didn't seem to make sense, at first.   But once people thoroughly understood the world's actual shape, they couldn't continue believing that it was flat.   Now, the belief that the world is spherical is the one that makes sense.   And the belief that the world is flat is nonsense.   (This is an example of a paradigm shift.)

Similarly, for many, the anchoring concept doesn't seem to make sense, at first.   But once they understand this concept, they can see that if a method of decisionmaking calls for unanchored judgments, it is unsound.   The CBA methods require anchored questions and judgments.   Therefore, they are the methods that make sense.   The old standard methods—those that require unanchored questions and judgments—are nonsense.

One person who is now a CBA champion has said that learning the concept of anchoring was like seeing an optical illusion—except that it turned out to be a reality.   She said that while she was learning this concept, she could see it for a moment.   And then she couldn't.   Then she could, and then she couldn't. Eventually, however, she couldn't not see it. (This supports the argument that, for many, choosing CBA is a paradigm shift.)

When I first started conducting CBA workshops, I didn't realize how difficult it would be to teach the principle of anchoring. I put together what I thought was a clear, concise explanation of this vital principle, and I expected my explanation to be successful. But it wasn't. The success rate from that first explanation was practically zero. What happened is that most of the workshop participants continued using the old standard (unsound) methods of decisionmaking. Others began using CBA in name only. (They had not made the shift.)

As I continued conducting CBA workshops, I tried several different explanations of the anchoring concept. And in every case, the success rate was very low. Because none of the explanations worked by themselves, I then tried using presentations with two explanations. This improved the success rate, slightly. So I kept adding more explanations, more examples, more details, and more repetitions—and I tried using different combinations of explanations in different sequences. As a result, the success rate from full-length CBA workshops is now reasonably high. And this book is based on the successful workshops.

Recently, what I realized is that none of the individual presentations explains the anchoring concept as a whole. Each individual explanation covers only one essential, or only a few essentials, of the principle of anchoring. Likewise, each chapter in this book explains only one essential, or only a few essentials, of this principle. Anchoring is what the entire CBA system is about. Anchoring is what CBA does. Therefore, the more you learn about CBA, the greater will be your understanding of the principle of anchoring.

Here are a few things about CBA that seem important to me. Which of these seem important to you?

- What might be most important is that you don't need to discard the **sound** methods you are already using. (To consistently make sound decisions, sound methods must be used.)

- Perhaps what might be most surprising is that if you are using **unsound** methods you don't need to throw them away, either. Just make improvements. (In most cases, unsound methods can easily be transformed from unsound to sound.)

- The CBA system has a coordinated-separates structure. Therefore, you don't need to make an all-or-nothing decision about whether to adopt the CBA system. Just choose the components that you will need for your decisions. After you select a set of components, you don't need to learn them all at the same time, but you do need to learn them in the right sequence.

- To learn how to skillfully use sound methods for very simple decisions, one must first learn how to use sound methods for simple decisions.

- Although learning CBA is easier than learning mathematics, the two have the following similarity:

  In the field of mathematics, one must learn arithmetic before learning advanced mathematics.

  In the field of decisionmaking, one must learn the basic CBA concepts and methods before learning the advanced CBA concepts and methods.

- For both simple and complex decisions, the CBA methods have major advantages, when used by expert decisionmakers, compared with the methods in common use today:

  The CBA methods are faster—especially for simple decisions—because they quickly clarify the situation.

  The CBA methods produce better decisions because they are sound methods.

8

Anchored Versus Unanchored Questions and Judgments

This chapter and the other eleven chapters in part III respond, collectively, to the most often asked question about the CBA process: How should we decide the importance of advantages? The answer is the principle of anchoring: Decisions about importance must be anchored to the relevant facts. Sound methods of decisionmaking require anchored questions and judgments. In sharp contrast, methods that require unanchored questions and judgments are unsound. This chapter starts the lengthy process of illustrating this critical difference between sound and unsound methods.

The first section of this chapter describes how to use a balance scale to compare the weight of a fixed number of pennies versus the weights of different numbers of dimes. A chart of these comparisons, coupled with questions and answers based on the chart, will demonstrate the difference between anchored and unanchored *objective* questions and judgments.

The second section demonstrates the Tabular Method by completing the decisionmaking phase of the CBA process, for the canoe decision. Then, using the canoe decision, the third section compares the "weight" (importance) of the one advantage in the color factor—the difference between the starry-brown color and the kelly-blue color—versus the "weights" of different advantages in the stability factor. A chart of these comparisons, coupled with questions and answers based on it, will demonstrate the difference between anchored and unanchored *subjective* questions and judgments. The fourth section outlines the reconsideration phase. For some decisions, this fourth phase—which is too often neglected—is the most important of the five phases of the CBA process.

ANCHORED VERSUS UNANCHORED OBJECTIVE QUESTIONS AND JUDGMENTS

You, yourself, can weigh pennies versus dimes. All you need is a balance scale, 25 pennies, and about 35 or 40 dimes. Because this is an objective demonstration, the outcome should not be influenced by someone's viewpoint or preferences. Here is the demonstration:

1. Establish a unique numerical scale of weight—just for this experiment—as follows: 25 pennies weigh 100 lunar grams.

2. Place the 25 pennies on the left-hand side of the balance scale.

3. Add dimes to the right-hand side until you find the crossover point—the point where the pennies and the dimes weigh the same. You will find, before the crossover point, that 28 dimes weigh less than 25 pennies. On the other side of the crossover point, 30 dimes weigh more than 25 pennies. The scale is very nearly balanced when you weigh 25 pennies versus 29 dimes. Therefore, 29 dimes weigh approximately 100 lunar grams. Now, construct a chart to display the lunar-gram weights of 25 pennies and various numbers of dimes.

The Weight of Twenty-Five Pennies Versus the Weights of Dimes

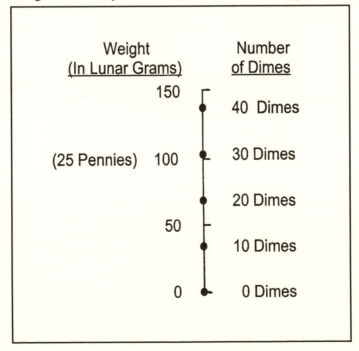

The following questions and answers, which are based on the chart, illustrate the difference between anchored versus unanchored *objective* questions and judgments.

Anchored Question:	Which weighs more, 25 pennies or 20 dimes?
Anchored Judgment:	25 pennies.
Anchored Question:	Which weighs more, 25 pennies or 40 dimes?
Anchored Judgment:	40 dimes.
Anchored Question:	Which weighs more, one penny or one dime?
Unanchored Question:	Which weighs more, pennies or dimes?
Unanchored Judgment:	Pennies.
Unanchored Judgment:	Dimes.
Unanchored Judgment:	They both weigh the same.

Notice that the three anchored questions are specific. Therefore, they are answerable questions. But the unanchored question can be interpreted in an infinite number of ways, from one extreme to another. Its meaning isn't tied down; it isn't anchored. Therefore, it isn't an answerable question. Here are additional examples of unanchored questions:

Q. How long is a piece of string?

Q. What color is a Plymouth car?

Q. What is the temperature of a rock?

You probably remember the following third-grade riddle: Which weighs more, a pound of feathers or a pound of gold? Was that an anchored question, or was it unanchored? Of course, it was anchored. However, as expected, some third graders gave the wrong answer. They said that a pound of gold weighs more than a pound of feathers. But they were thinking of density, not weight. Now, how could we change the riddle from anchored to unanchored? Here is the unanchored version: Which weighs more, feathers or gold?

PHASE III OF THE CANOE DECISION, CONTINUED

Following is an outline of Phase III (the decisionmaking phase) of the Tabular Method for Choosing from Two Alternatives. This section completes the third and fourth activities in this phase, for the canoe decision. Then, using this decision, the next section illustrates the difference between anchored and unanchored subjective questions and judgments.

The Decisionmaking Phase of the Tabular Method
(This version is for choosing from only two alternatives.)

---

1. Summarize the **attributes** of each alternative.

2. Decide the **advantages** of each alternative.

    a. Underline the least-preferred attribute in each factor.

    b. Summarize the differences from the least-preferred attributes.
        These differences are the advantages of the alternatives.

3. Decide the **importance** of each advantage.

    a. Circle the advantages.

    b. Select the paramount advantage (the most important of all the
        advantages).   Then, establish a scale of importance for the
        decision by assigning the paramount advantage an importance of
        1, 10, or 100—or any convenient number.

    c. Weigh all the other advantages on this same scale of importance.

4. If the costs of the alternatives are equal, choose the one with the
    greatest **total importance** of advantages.

Chapter 5 demonstrated the first two of the four central activities, and
the first task of the third. We are now ready for the task of selecting the
paramount advantage. When you involve others in this task, you will
probably need to explain the difference between weighing advantages and
weighing factors. Otherwise, they are likely to select what they see as the
paramount factor, thinking that they are selecting the paramount advantage.
One way to illustrate the difference is to sketch a bucket, nearly full of
water. The bucket represents a factor—a container for data. The water
represents the advantages and other data contained in the factor.

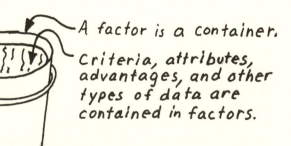

A factor is a container.

Criteria, attributes, advantages, and other types of data are contained in factors.

Task No. 3b: Select the Paramount Advantage and Establish a Scale of Importance

Once the distinction between weighing advantages and weighing factors is clearly understood by the participants in the decisionmaking process, selecting the paramount advantage becomes a very simple, doable task. For a complex, controversial decision, this one task can take several hours, or even several days. But for a simple decision, the paramount advantage can be selected by inspection. In the canoe example, expert CBA decision-makers are able to answer the following question, almost instantly—if they have the correct data for the decision:

Q. Which one of the five advantages is the paramount advantage?

A. The advantage in color. As shown on Page 75, this advantage was assigned an importance score of 100. This established a 0 to 100 scale of importance for the decision. (Note: The scale is *zero* to one hundred, not *one* to one hundred. Also, the scale can be extended beyond one hundred, if necessary.)

An observer is likely to ask: How did they decide that the advantage in color is the paramount advantage? Explaining how the paramount advantage was selected is like explaining how to ride a bicycle. It is easier to show than to explain. Fortunately, with practice, this task eventually becomes almost as automatic as riding a bicycle. For now, therefore, we will simply show, mechanically, how the advantage in color was selected.

To select the paramount advantage, if the decision is a difficult decision, simplify by using the Defender–Challenger Process. This process divides the one task into a series of bite-size steps. The canoe decision requires four defender–challenger comparisons, as follows:

(1) Select one of the advantages—it doesn't matter which one—as the initial defender, and select another as the initial challenger. In this case, let's select the first advantage of Canoe C, *the advantage in weight,* as the initial defender. (This is very important: We are not selecting *weight*, because weight is a factor, not an advantage.) Let's select the second advantage of C, the advantage in stability, as the initial challenger. Here is the first comparison:

Q. In your view, which of the two advantages of Canoe C is the most important one: the 10 pound advantage in weight, or the very small advantage in stability?

A. The very small advantage in stability. However, they both have about the same importance.

(2) The advantage in stability now replaces the advantage in weight as
     the defender. Next, let's select the advantage of Canoe K in finish
     smoothness as the second challenger, as follows:

   Q. Which of the following advantages is the most important
       one: the very small advantage in stability, or the moderately
       small advantage in finish smoothness?

   A. The advantage in stability.   The difference in smoothness
       isn't very important.

(3) This answer retains the stability advantage as the defender. Next,
     let's arbitrarily select the advantage in color, as the third chal-
     lenger. (We could have selected the advantage in keel depth.)
     Here is the third comparison:

   Q. Which of the following advantages is the most important
       one: the very small advantage in stability, or the large
       advantage in color?

   A. The large advantage in color.

(4) The advantage in color now replaces the advantage in stability as
     the defender. And the advantage in keel depth becomes the final
     challenger, as follows:

   Q. Which one of the following is most important: the advantage
       in color, or the advantage in keel depth?

   A. The advantage in color. (This answer selects the advantage
       in color as the paramount advantage.)

At this point in CBA workshops, some of the participants still try to
weigh factors, instead of weighing advantages. Therefore, at least one of
them will now say, "I don't understand why they didn't select stability as
the paramount *factor*. Isn't stability more important than color?"

In response, divide the Defender–Challenger Process into even smaller
steps to show, in more detail, how the paramount ***advantage*** was selected.
To do this, choose between the advantages in stability and color, as follows:
Select the advantage of Canoe C in the stability factor (the very small
difference, in the stability factor, between Canoe C and Canoe K) as the
defender. Select the advantage of Canoe K in color (the large difference
between the kelly-blue and starry-brown colors) as the challenger.

Selecting the Paramount Advantage and
Establishing a Scale of Importance for the Decision

FACTORS	ALTERNATIVES	
	CANOE C	CANOE K
CANOE WEIGHT Attributes: Advantages:	65 Pounds (10 Pounds Lighter)	75 Pounds
FINISH (Smoothness) Attributes: Advantages:	Mod. Smooth	Very Smooth (Moderately Smoother)
COLOR Attributes: Advantages:	Starry-Brown	Kelly-Blue (Much Nicer Color) 100
STABILITY Attributes: Advantages:	Excellent (Slightly Greater)	Very Good
KEEL DEPTH Attributes: Advantages:	7/8 Inch	5/8 Inch (Slightly Better Keel)
TOTAL IMPORTANCE OF ADVANTAGES:		
TOTAL COST:	Both Alternatives Have the Same Total Cost.	

Next, construct a display with a range of stability advantages (stability differences)—listed in order of importance. Include, in the list, a few advantages that are more important and a few that are less important than the defender. (In the following display, the defender is italicized.)

Advantages (Differences), Listed in Order of Importance

- A very large difference in stability
- A large difference in stability
- A small difference in stability
- *The very small difference in stability between Canoes C and K*
- An extremely small difference in stability
- A non-advantage (no difference, at all) in stability

Point out that in the stability factor—as in all other factors—a non-advantage (no difference, at all) does not have any importance, at all. Point out, also, that an advantage of almost zero has an importance of almost zero. Then, find *the decisionmaker's crossover point* by asking a series of questions, as follows:

Q. Let's start at the bottom of the list. Which would be more important, in your view, no difference at all in stability, or the large difference between Canoes C and K in color?

A. Obviously, the difference in color.

Q. Which would be more important, to you, an extremely small difference in stability—a difference so small that only an expert canoeist would be able to detect it—or the large difference in color?

A. The large difference in color.

Q. Which is more important, *the very small difference in stability between Canoes C and K* (the very small advantage of C, in the stability factor), or the large difference in color?

A. The difference in color. In our view, it truly is a large difference. The starry-brown color is acceptable, but the kelly-blue color is much nicer—in our view.

This answer tells us that the crossover point is *above* the very small advantage of C in stability. Therefore, we know that the advantage of K, in color, is the paramount advantage. We don't need to find the crossover point; but we can find it, by asking at least one more question:

Q. Which is more important, a small difference in stability, or the large difference between Canoes C and K, in color?

A. A small difference in stability is more important than a large difference in color. (Now we know that the crossover point—the location of the color advantage—is *below* a small difference in stability, as shown in the following list of advantages.)

Advantages (Differences), Listed in Order of Importance

- A very large difference in stability
- A large difference in stability
- A small difference in stability
- *The large difference in color between Canoes C and K*
- The very small difference in stability between Canoes C and K
- An extremely small difference in stability
- A non-advantage (no difference, at all) in stability

Obviously, the questions and answers that placed the difference in color at the location shown in the chart are subjective. That is, they disclose the preferences of the stakeholders, not the characteristics of the alternatives. And this is crucial: To accurately disclose the preferences of the stakeholders, the questions must be answered with care and precision.

You and I might not agree with the judgments made in the canoe decision. For example, we might not agree that the large difference in color is less important than a small difference in stability. On the other hand, we might not agree that it is more important than a very small difference in stability. But that doesn't matter, because we are not the stakeholders. Therefore, our viewpoints are not the appropriate viewpoints for this decision.

The stakeholders were able to accurately select the paramount advantage because they tried out both canoes. With these and other canoes, they performed several eddy-turns and other maneuvers in a challenging stretch of a beautiful river. Therefore, they know exactly what they mean when they label the attributes of Canoes C and K, in the stability factor, as *excellent* and *very good*. Furthermore, they know exactly what they mean when they describe the stability advantage, as follows: "What we learned is that there is only a very small difference, in stability, between these two canoes. Canoe C has only *slightly greater* stability than K."

The stakeholders also know how and how often they will be using the selected canoe. For example, they know that they will not be using it very often. But they will be seeing it very often, because it will be stored in their garage, next to their nice car. Therefore, a large difference in color is quite important to them.

As will be shown again, later in this chapter and in the chapters that follow, the previous set of questions and answers demonstrates that it would never make sense to say that stability is more important than color—because a very small difference in stability is not more important than a very large difference in color. Stability, in general, is not more important than color, in general. At the same time, it would never make sense to say that color is more important than stability—because a very small difference in color is not more important than a very large difference in stability. Color, in general, is not more important than stability, in general.

What might not be so obvious is that it would never make sense to say that stability and color—the two factors—are equal in importance. Why not? The answer is simple: When comparing an advantage in one factor with all of the possible advantages in another factor, there will be a crossover point. For example, there are some advantages in stability that are less important and some that are more important than the advantage of Canoe C, in color.

At first glance, it might appear that the stakeholders selected color as "the paramount factor." Nothing could be farther from the truth. They absolutely did not select color as the paramount *factor*. Instead, they selected the large difference in color as the paramount *advantage*. Remember: A factor is not the same thing as an advantage. Factors are containers. They contain criteria, attributes, advantages, and other types of data. This is why the sound-decisionmaking vocabulary is key to sound decisionmaking. For example, we must never say "color," when we mean "the advantage in color."

Task No. 3c: Weigh All the Other Advantages

After selecting the paramount advantage, weigh all the other advantages on the same scale of importance. (They can be weighed in any order.) The participants in the canoe decision were able to accurately judge the importance of each of the other advantages, compared with the paramount advantage—and compared with each other—because they had formed a clear, accurate, sensory-rich perception of each advantage before deciding. They did this when they tried out each of the canoes. (The results from this task and from Activity No. 4 are shown in the following Tabular Display.)

Weighing the Importance and Total Importance of Advantages

FACTORS	ALTERNATIVES	
	CANOE C	CANOE K
CANOE WEIGHT Attributes: Advantages:	65 Pounds 10 Pounds Lighter | 70	75 Pounds
FINISH (Smoothness) Attributes: Advantages:	Mod. Smooth	Very Smooth Moderately Smoother | 5
COLOR Attributes: Advantages:	Starry-Brown	Kelly-Blue Much Nicer Color | 100
STABILITY Attributes: Advantages:	Excellent Slightly Greater | 75	Very Good
KEEL DEPTH Attributes: Advantages:	7/8 Inch	5/8 Inch Slightly Better Keel | 10
TOTAL IMPORTANCE OF ADVANTAGES:	145	115
TOTAL COST:	Both Alternatives Have the Same Total Cost.	

The importance scores reveal the intensities of the stakeholders' preferences. For example, in their view, the advantage in stability is 75 percent as important as the advantage in color. The advantage in finish smoothness is 5 percent as important as the advantage in color.

To make a sound decision, we must accurately weigh each of the advantages, compared with the other advantages. (Weigh only the advantages—not the criteria, attributes, or other types of data.) As I will say many times, the importance, or weight, of each advantage must be judged with care and precision. Although judgments about importance are subjective, they must never be arbitrary. They must be anchored to the relevant facts. What does this mean? One of the essentials of the principle of anchoring is that in order to accurately decide the importance of one advantage, compared with another, the magnitude of each must be taken into account. (This is why we must ask the following central question, as stated in chapter 4: How large are the advantages?)

We must also know, for each advantage, the magnitudes of its associated attributes. Selecting the paramount advantage, to establish a scale of importance for the decision, illustrates this essential. When we select the paramount advantage—also, when we decide the importance of each of the other advantages—we must make anchored judgments. To do this, we must know three things in relation to each advantage—even if we don't display them:

1. The magnitude of the attribute of the one alternative (65 pounds, for example)

2. The magnitude of the attribute of the other alternative (75 pounds)

3. The magnitude of the difference between the two attributes

In the Tabular Display, notice where the importance scores are located— next to the advantages, not the factors or the attributes. Remember that each importance score pertains to a difference between two attributes. We must get rid of the traditional concept—that we should be deciding the importance of the attributes, themselves. This change from the traditional way to make decisions is crucial. Also crucial, as stated before, is that decisions must never be based on the importance of factors.

Activity No. 4: Choose the Preferred Alternative

Now, let's go from the third to the fourth central activity of the Tabular Method. As you saw, all four tasks in the third central activity—deciding importance—are subjective. You also saw that judgments about importance must be anchored to the relevant facts. The fourth activity—calculating totals—is objective. The results in the canoe decision (145 and 115) are shown in the preceding Tabular Display.

The completed Tabular Display shows that, in total, the two advantages of Canoe C outweigh the three advantages of K. Therefore, according to the stakeholders, Canoe C is the preferred alternative. To show that C is preferred, the total importance for C has been double-underlined. You or I might not agree with this decision, but that doesn't matter because we are not the stakeholders. Therefore, neither of our viewpoints is the appropriate viewpoint for this decision.

Notice that the Tabular Format guides us through the four central activities of the Tabular Method, as follows:

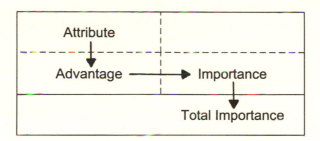

First, summarize the attributes; second, decide the advantages; third, decide importance; and fourth, calculate total importance. Notice, also, that non-advantages are represented by blank spaces, not zeros. Remember: There is no such thing as a zero advantage. Corresponding with non-advantages, wherever there is no importance there is a blank space, not a zero. Zeros would clutter the display.

Although the *criteria* for the decision are not shown in the Tabular Display, they were not left out of the decisionmaking process. Remember that various types of criteria come into play during the process: During Phase II, the criteria guide the formulation of alternatives and the identification of their attributes. In particular, the must-criteria rule out the unacceptable alternatives. Then, during Phase III, the want-criteria identify the least-preferred attributes. Now, as you did in chapter 5, use the Tabular Display (on page 79) to review the distinctions between *alternatives, factors, attributes, least-preferred attributes,* and *advantages*. And notice, again, that because the advantages have been circled, we can instantly see that Canoe C has two advantages, while K has three.

Now, using the canoe decision, the next section shows the difference between anchored and unanchored subjective questions and judgments. When you teach CBA, you will probably find that this is the most difficult of all the CBA concepts to teach. For nearly everyone, apparently, using anchored subjective questions and judgments is very counter-intuitive.

ANCHORED VERSUS UNANCHORED SUBJECTIVE QUESTIONS AND JUDGMENTS

Earlier, to demonstrate the difference between anchored and unanchored *objective* questions and judgments, we weighed various numbers of dimes versus a fixed number of pennies. Now, to demonstrate the difference between anchored and unanchored *subjective* questions and judgments, we will weigh two advantages in the stability factor versus the one advantage in the color factor. Because it will pertain to the viewpoints of the stakeholders, this will be a subjective demonstration.

1. Establish a numerical scale of importance as follows: For this decision, and only for this decision, the advantage in color has an importance of 100.

2. At the bottom of the scale, show that when there is no advantage there is no importance.

3. As we did when we weighed dimes against pennies—also, as we did when we selected the paramount advantage—identify the crossover point. Following is the result:

The Advantage in Color Versus Advantages in Stability

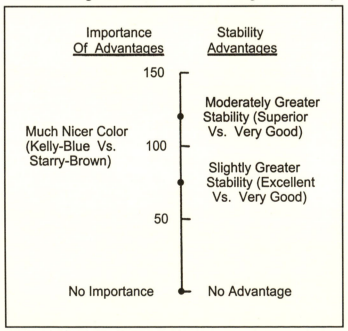

As their chart indicates, the stakeholders decided that the very small difference between Excellent Stability and Very Good Stability has an importance of 75. Then, to take themselves above the crossover point, they considered the possibility of a third canoe—one with Superior Stability. And they decided that the difference between Superior and Very Good has an importance of 120. The following examples, which are based on the chart, illustrate the difference between anchored versus unanchored *subjective ordinal* questions and judgments:

> Anchored Question: Which is more important, Much Nicer Color or Slightly Greater Stability?
> Anchored Judgment: Much Nicer Color.

> Anchored Question: Which is more important, Much Nicer Color or Moderately Greater Stability?
> Anchored Judgment: Moderately Greater Stability.

> Unanchored Question: Which is more important, color or stability?
> Unanchored Judgment: Color is more important than stability.
> Unanchored Judgment: Stability is more important than color.
> Unanchored Judgment: Both factors, stability and color, have the same importance.

The above demonstrates, again, how the stakeholders used anchored questions and judgments when selecting the paramount advantage and establishing a scale of importance for the decision. In the next task, they weighed all the other advantages on the established scale of importance. That is, they directly or indirectly compared all the other advantages with the paramount advantage. Again, they used anchored questions and anchored judgments. Following are examples of anchored versus unanchored *subjective cardinal* questions and judgments:

> Anchored Question: How important is Slightly Greater Stability, compared with Much Nicer Color?
> Anchored Judgment: 75.

> Unanchored Question: How important is stability, compared with color?
> Unanchored Judgment: (Any answer to an unanchored question is an unanchored judgment.)

The preceding questions and answers show why we must no longer use the old standard methods of decisionmaking: In the old standard methods, individual numbers, called factor weights, are assigned to the factors. Supposedly, these weights represent the importance of the factors. But they don't. They can't. Because factor weights are unanchored judgments, it is impossible to assign valid weights, ratings, or scores to factors. Therefore, instead of basing decisions on the importance of factors, sound methods base decisions on the importance of advantages.

How should we respond to an unanchored question? Of course, the best response is to not answer it. But the natural, automatic response is to *assume* a specific meaning of the question, and then to *answer* the assumed question. Assuming and answering is the Instinctive Method, introduced in chapter 5. In many decisionmaking situations, unfortunately, this primitive method produces unsound decisions. To make matters worse, it very often produces unnecessary, dysfunctional conflicts.

Several years ago, for example, members of the Forest Service made a very costly mistake—one that they are still paying for. They asked members of the public a number of unanchored questions, such as the following: "Which is more important, to you, wilderness or development?" Of course, these unanchored questions produced emotionally charged, unanchored judgments; and the result was polarization—instead of effective, interactive decisionmaking.

PHASE IV OF THE CANOE DECISION

At the end of the decisionmaking phase, double-underlining the greatest total importance only tentatively identifies the preferred alternative. If the decision is important, this should not be viewed as a final decision—at least, not yet. Before making the final decision, challenge and reconsider the initial decision. In the canoe decision, the stakeholders asked themselves:

- Are there any additional alternatives that should have been considered? For example, is there a canoe that has the weight and stability of C and the color of K?

- Are there any additional advantages that should have been included?

- Do the importance scores accurately represent the viewpoints of the stakeholders?

- Based on examining each alternative as a whole, are there any adjustments that need to be made? For example, are there any significant interdependencies among the factors? If so, were they taken into account?

- Are any other changes needed?

If you find that the decision should be changed, change it. But once the decision has been finalized, go for it; make it a successful decision. And to make it a successful decision, make adjustments, if necessary—based on the importance of advantages—during the implementation phase.

After the Tabular Method has been introduced in the CBA training process, the participants are encouraged to learn and practice the Two-List Method, presented in the following chapter, before they continue learning and practicing the Tabular Method. I hope you will do the same. Why? Because the Two-List Method is simpler, mechanically, than the Tabular Method. Also, when you do need to use the Tabular Method, it will usually be the version for choosing from several alternatives, presented in chapter 22.

As shown in the following chart, decisions that call for the Two-List Method are near the middle level of complexity, compared with other decisions.

The CBA Methods that Are Included in this Book

Special Methods for Complex and Very Complex Decisions
- Special Methods for Money Decisions
- Other Special Methods for Complex and Very Complex Decisions

Simple Methods for Simple Decisions
- The Tabular Method
- *The Two-List Method*
- The Simplified Tabular Method
- The Simplified Two-List Method
- Instant CBA

Very Simple Methods for Very Simple Decisions
- The Recognition-Response Process
- Other Very Simple Methods for Very Simple Decisions

Moving upward from the Two-List Method, toward the top of the chart, CBA simplifies decisions that are more complex than those that call for the Two-List Method by taking smaller steps. Moving downward in the chart, CBA simplifies decisions that are simpler than those that call for the Two-List Method by taking fewer steps. Of course, when a method is taking fewer steps, it is also taking larger steps. And larger steps require higher levels of skill than smaller steps. Therefore, the methods at the lowest levels on the chart require the highest levels of skill.

The canoe decision is used in chapter 9 to demonstrate the Two-List Method. This same example is used in the remaining chapters of part III to further explain the principle of anchoring. Other examples will be used, in part IV, to present the additional methods that are shown in the chart.

9

The Two-List Method

The Two-List Method is for moderately simple, two-option decisions. In particular, it is for those where we need to display the rationale for the decision, but not in detail. This chapter presents only the mechanics of the Two-List Method—its outline and its format. For now, just learn these mechanics. In particular, don't worry about exactly how to decide the importance scores, because the discussion of how to decide importance will be continued in the chapters that follow.

Although the Two-List Method is simpler (mechanically) than the Tabular Method, it requires a higher level of skill than the Tabular Method. Why? Because the Two-List Format displays fewer key relevant facts. (Except as shown in chapter 26, it doesn't display the attributes.)

Have you ever read a book about how to play golf? Describing how to use CBA for moderately simple, two-option decisions (those that call for the Two-List Method) is like describing how to swing a golf club. In each case, it takes a lot of words to describe the details of what happens in a very brief period of time. Many of the definitions, principles, and models that are presented throughout this book help to explain the Two-List Method. (For example, chapter 24 describes how to correctly include money in the process.) Therefore, one needs to study the entire book to learn how to skillfully use this method.

There are several CBA methods that are mechanically simpler than the Two-List Method; yet the Two-List Method is not complex. It might seem complex, at first, while it is still unfamiliar. Be careful; do not confuse unfamiliarity with complexity.

Outline of the Two-List Method

---

1. List the *advantages* of each alternative.

2. Decide the *importance* of each advantage.

3. If the costs of the alternatives are equal, choose the one
    with the greatest *total importance* of advantages.

The Two-List Format

Advantages of Canoe C		Advantages of Canoe K	
• 10 Pounds Lighter	70	• Moderately Smoother Finish	5
• Slightly Greater Stability	75	• Much Nicer Color	100
		• Slightly Better Keel Depth	10
Total Importance:	145	Total Importance:	115
Both Alternatives Have the Same Total Cost.			

This display doesn't tell us whether we should or shouldn't buy a canoe. That decision is a money decision, as shown in chapter 24. What the display tells us is that if we decide to buy a canoe, and if the choice is between Canoes C and K, we should select C. And, as stated in chapter 8, it tells us that it would be wise to search for a third alternative—one with the weight and stability of C, and with the color of K.

To learn how to use the Two-List Method, use the Five-Step Skill-Learning Process (as you did in learning the Simplified Two-List Method): Learn, unlearn, relearn, practice, and teach. When teaching the Two-List Method, be sure to thoroughly teach all the definitions, principles, models, and methods that were presented in the first eight chapters. Also, teach those that are presented in the following chapters. They help explain the Two-List Method. When teaching, use the canoe purchase example. It was carefully designed; it has been thoroughly tested; and, it works.

As an aid, you might want to prepare a set of wooden blocks, to be used as shown in the next two illustrations. (I sometimes carry a set of blocks made from balsa wood—each with a different color—in my briefcase.) In the illustrations, each block represents a difference between the two canoes. The tallness of each block represents the importance of its difference. As has been stated many times, any difference between two alternatives can be perceived as positive (an advantage) or as negative (a disadvantage). The first illustration demonstrates a mathematically correct version of Choosing By Advantages and Disadvantages. (In this illustration, all the differences are shown as advantages, except the difference in color.)

To demonstrate how easy it is to change from Choosing By Advantages and Disadvantages to Choosing By Advantages, first stack the blocks as follows. As stated, the tallest block represents the disadvantage of C, in the factor of color. Because this difference is included as a disadvantage, it has a negative importance. The other four blocks represent the advantages of the two canoes in weight, stability, smoothness, and keel depth.

Two Advantages and One Disadvantage Versus Two Advantages

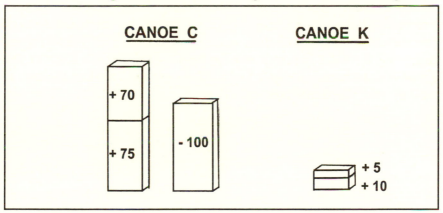

Mathematically, it isn't difficult to see that the total of (70 + 75 - 100) is greater than the total of (5 + 10). Therefore, Canoe C is obviously the preferred alternative. Mathematically and graphically, however, we can make it even more obvious that Canoe C is preferred. So, after explaining that, without exception, a disadvantage of one alternative is an advantage of another, move the block that represents the difference in color to the other alternative. (When it is moved, it becomes an advantage.) After stacking the two advantages of C against the three advantages of K, simply choose the alternative with the tallest stack of advantages.

Two Advantages Versus Three Advantages

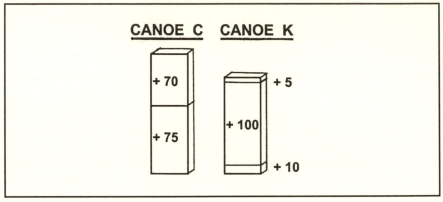

Now that you know the mechanics of the Two-List Method, use it. Keep on using it, even when you don't need it, until you are able to skillfully use it when you do need it. Remember that it is better to use sound methods approximately, rather than using unsound methods precisely. However, it is even better, of course, to use sound methods precisely. And that is something anyone can learn to do, by studying and practicing the CBA concepts and methods. Studying the chapters that follow will increase your ability to skillfully use the Two-List Method, as well as other sound methods.

10

Preference Charts
and Preference Curves

In the CBA training process, preference charts and preference curves help us explain the principle of anchoring. In particular, they help us show why we must base decisions on the importance of advantages. Then, in the decisionmaking process, they help us decide and display the importance of advantages. They do these things by displaying the *relationships* between the attributes, advantages, and importance of advantages in a decision. Although most decisionmakers will seldom, if ever, need to construct them, practically all decisionmakers need to understand them; furthermore, professional decisionmakers need to be able to construct them.

Preference charts are sometimes used in numerical, quantity-valued factors. But they are more often used in nonnumerical, quality-valued factors. Preference curves are used only in numerical factors.

PREFERENCE CHARTS

A preference chart in the factor of stability is shown on the following page. (This chart is similar to the one that was used in chapter 8 to illustrate the difference between anchored and unanchored subjective questions and judgments.) Notice that Canoe L, with superior stability, has been included in this chart.

Notice, also, that in the typical format—which is most often hand drawn and hand lettered, as in this example—the attributes are summarized, instead of the advantages. Nevertheless, the vertical scale shows the importance of the advantages. It does not show the importance of the attributes. As is explained in chapter 17, that would be impossible. For example, Excellent Stability (the attribute of C) does not have an importance of 75; it is the *difference* between Excellent and Very Good (the advantage of C) that has an importance of 75. As another example, Very Good Stability does not have an importance of zero; it is the non-advantage associated with this attribute that has an importance of zero.

Preference Chart Example (Typical Format)

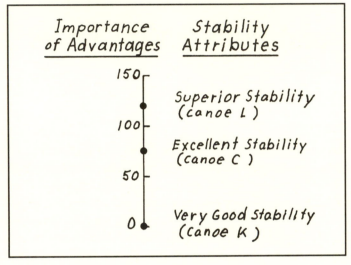

If you want to display *advantages* versus importance of advantages, instead of displaying *attributes* versus importance of advantages, you can use the alternative format, shown in the next illustration. Both formats show that there is nothing wrong with extending the scale above 100. In this example, the difference between Superior Stability and Very Good Stability is more important than the difference in color, which was assigned an importance of 100, as shown in chapter 8. This explains why, in this case, the scale of importance had to be extended above 100.

In response to either of the two formats, people have often questioned this particular preference chart. They say, "There is no such thing as a canoe with superior stability. And besides, words like *superior, excellent,* and *very good* are subjective." Some have said, "Things that cannot be quantified shouldn't be included in the process." But to make a sound decision, it is essential to include all the significant advantages. For example, the stability advantage, which isn't quantified, must be included.

Preference Chart Example (Alternative Format)

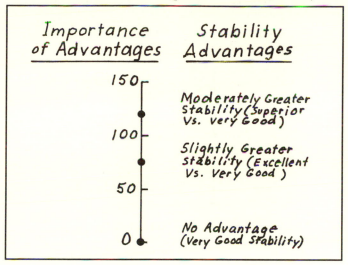

It is true that words like *superior* and *excellent* are subjectively colored. They not only pertain to facts; they also reflect someone's viewpoint. Of course, we cannot avoid using them. Fortunately, we don't need to avoid using them, as follows:

The ideal is to base decisions on actuality (objective reality), not on numbers or words. To come as close as they can to basing their decisions on actuality, the participants must form clear, accurate, sensory-rich perceptions of the actual attributes and advantages of the alternatives. One way to gain these perceptions is through direct personal experience. For example, the participants in the canoe decision tried out the two canoes. Then, they used their own words to remind themselves of what they had experienced. While they were judging the importance of the advantages, their own words—such as *excellent* and *very good*—reminded themselves of the actual characteristics of the alternatives. In many cases, it is better to use detailed, scientific descriptions, instead of personal experience. After studying these descriptions, the decisionmakers can use such words as *excellent* and *very good* to remind themselves of the details.

The next example is typeset, as is occasionally required in real-world situations. In this example, we have added a fourth alternative, Canoe M. Notice that it has Good Stability, which is not quite as good as the stability of Canoe K. To add this fourth alternative, we didn't *extend* the scale downward. We *moved* it downward.

Another Preference Chart Example

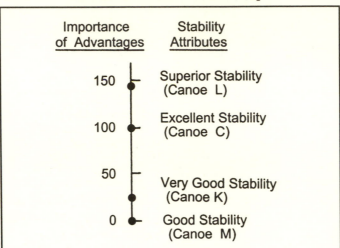

By moving the bottom of the scale downward, from Very Good to Good Stability, we established a new zero point. We could have simply extended the scale downward, but that would have created a negative importance score for the difference between Very Good and Good. And having a negative score, along with positive scores, could have caused confusion.

Notice that when Canoe M was added to the chart, the viewpoint of the stakeholders didn't change. For example, the difference between Excellent and Very Good Stability has an importance of 75—the same as before (it is now the difference between 100 and 25). Also, the importance of the difference between Superior and Very Good is still 120 (it is now the difference between 145 and 25).

The reason the importance of each difference stayed the same is that we are still using the original scale of importance. That is, we are still comparing all the advantages to the original paramount advantage—the difference between the starry-brown and kelly-blue colors, which was assigned an importance of 100. Again, instead of replacing the scale when we added Canoe M, we simply moved it downward.

PREFERENCE CURVES

Decisionmakers need to understand preference curves, as well as preference charts. Preference curves show *relationships*—in numerical factors—between attributes, advantages, and importance of advantages. To show these relationships, each preference curve has three scales; two horizontal and one vertical:

- The first horizontal scale is an attribute scale. It shows attribute quantities.

- The second horizontal scale is an advantage scale. It shows advantage quantities.

- The vertical scale shows the importance of advantages.

To provide an example of each scale, and to show the concept of a preference curve, the following display includes a preference curve and more. In this display, each numbered box represents an advantage, and each is placed, on the advantage scale, at the location of the advantage it represents.

Preference Curve Concept

Each of the following shows the importance of the advantage: the height of the box, the number in the box, and the importance scale. For example, the 5 pound advantage (the difference between 70 and 75 pounds) has an importance of 45. As another example, the 10 pound advantage (the difference between 65 and 75 pounds) has an importance of 70. The curve connecting the tops of the boxes is a preference curve.

Preference-curve shapes vary from one factor to another. Valid shapes include straight lines, S-curves, broken lines, and many others. The preference curve in the canoe weight factor illustrates the typical shape. Economists say that this shape represents the law of diminishing returns. When you are deciding the shape of a preference curve—and when you are constructing the curve—you are deciding the importance of advantages. After you have constructed the curve, it displays your decisions about the importance of advantages.

Following is the preference curve in the canoe weight factor—hand drawn and hand lettered, as in typical, real-world situations:

Preference Curve Example

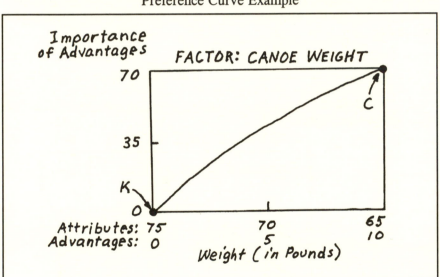

Now, let's look at the three scales. Notice that the least-preferred attribute—75 pounds—is placed at the left-hand end of the attribute scale. The non-advantage of Canoe K, corresponding with the least-preferred attribute, is placed at the same location, at the left-hand end of the advantage scale. It is shown as a zero, even though there is actually no such thing as a zero advantage. Its non-importance is also shown as a zero, at the bottom of the importance scale.

Chapter 11 presents three principles and four considerations to follow when deciding the importance of advantages and constructing a curve. In addition to those four considerations, it helps to think about what would happen if we extended the curve in both directions.

First, think about what would happen if we extended the canoe weight curve toward the left: The curve would become more and more vertical as it approached the maximum weight that could be carried by the person who will most often be using the canoe. The next pound after the very last one that could be carried would be "the straw that broke the camel's back." It would be very important. Therefore, at that point the curve would be very steep. It would be impossible to know exactly which pound would be the last one. And we don't need to know. Instead, we simplify the decision by establishing a practical limit as a must-criterion. In this case, a limit of 80 pounds was established. In response to this criterion, all canoes that weighed more than 80 pounds were simply ruled out before the decision-making phase of the CBA process.

In response to other must-criteria, in other factors, all of the canoes that weighed more than 75 pounds were ruled out. For example, a canoe that weighed 78 pounds was ruled out, due to its unacceptable color. Because none of the remaining canoes weighed more than 75 pounds, that is where the curve begins.

Now, think about what would happen if we extended the curve toward the right. Because it would be moving farther and farther away from "the last straw," the curve would become more and more horizontal. The extended curve would show, for example, that the 5 pound difference between 65 and 60 pounds (to the right of the original curve) is not as important as the 5 pound difference between 75 and 70 pounds. There-fore—because preference curves are usually not straight lines—we must know the magnitudes of the advantages *and their associated attributes,* not just the advantages.

Remember that an advantage of almost zero, in any factor, will have an importance of almost zero. Here are two examples, in the canoe decision: First, as shown earlier, an extremely small difference in stability—one that is almost undetectable—is much less important than a very large difference in stability. Second, as shown by the preference curve in the canoe weight factor, the very small difference between 75.0 pounds and 74.9 pounds has almost no importance.

The only case where an advantage of almost zero would have a significant amount of importance would be in a factor where the part of the curve that is near zero is nearly vertical. And that will seldom happen—if ever—in real-world decisionmaking situations.

Although their concepts apply in many situations, preference charts and curves are actually constructed during the decisionmaking process only in special situations. Some situations require their construction. For example, they are constructed and used in the Prior Anchoring Method, described in

chapter 23 (Prior Anchoring is a CBA method that prevents favoritism
when choosing from contract proposals). They are often used in the CBA
methods for choosing from a large number of alternatives and in those for
choosing from an infinite number of possibilities (these methods are also
presented in chapter 23, along with the Prior Anchoring Method). They are
sometimes used in choosing from several alternatives.

Preference curves might seem complex, at first, while they are
unfamiliar. But they are actually quite simple. And for choosing from a
large number of alternatives, they greatly simplify deciding importance.
When a preference curve is needed, construct it as follows:

1. Place a point at the left-hand end of the advantage scale, at zero on
   the importance scale, to show that a non-advantage has no importance.

2. Place a point at the right-hand end to show the importance of the
   most important advantage in the factor. For example, the 10 pound
   advantage of Canoe C has an importance of 70. (It is 70 percent as
   important as the paramount advantage.)

3. Decide the proper shape of the curve.

4. Draw the curve.

5. Review the curve, and—if necessary—make corrections.

Again, the modern methods that are viewed by many as the standard of
how decisions should be made are called Weighting-Rating-and-Calculating
(WRC). The WRC methods assign numerical *weights* to the factors. Then,
they assign numerical *ratings* to the attributes of the alternatives. And then,
they *calculate* scores—by multiplying the weights times the ratings—as the
basis for the decision. Chapter 12 reveals the underlying pattern of thought
that the WRC methods are based on. It shows that, except for CBA
decisionmakers, nearly everyone uses this same pattern of thought,
automatically. Typically, even those decisionmakers who are totally
unaware of the WRC methods use this same pattern.

In chapter 16, the preference curve that was constructed in this chapter
is used to demonstrate that assigning numerical weights to factors is a
critical mistake: Sound methods do not weigh factors. Chapter 17 uses this
same curve to demonstrate that assigning numerical ratings to attributes is
also a critical mistake: Sound methods do not rate attributes. Therefore,
what the preference curve will prove is that the old standard methods—the
WRC Methods—are unsound. They base decisions on unanchored
judgments.

Before the CBA principles were discovered—and before the CBA definitions, models, and methods were developed—almost no one realized that the typical WRC methods were unsound. With few exceptions, even the leading experts in the field of decisionmaking didn't know that weighing factors and rating attributes were critical mistakes. This is why the WRC methods are still viewed, by many, as the standard of how to make decisions.

It is easy to see why almost no one realized that the WRC methods are unsound: None of their mistakes are easy to see. Therefore, those who learned, taught, and used the WRC methods in the past—also, those who computerized them—should not be criticized. Nevertheless, the typical WRC methods, including those that have been computerized, are definitely unsound and, in the future, should not be used. As I said before and will say again: For the same reasons that people with high integrity would never cheat, lie, or steal, they would never knowingly use unsound methods of decisionmaking.

Although the WRC methods are unsound, we need to thank—not criticize—those who developed them. Compared with some of the older methods, the WRC methods made significant improvements in the decisionmaking process. For example, they emphasize basing decisions on a full range of alternatives. Also, they require determining and displaying the attributes of the alternatives. If the WRC methods had not been developed, the CBA methods might not have been developed—at least, not at this time. The development of the WRC methods set the stage for the development of the CBA methods.

This chapter has shown how to construct preference charts and preference curves as an aid in anchoring decisions about importance to the relevant facts. The following chapter presents three principles and four considerations that aid in deciding importance—and, where applicable, in the construction of preference charts and curves.

Deciding Importance:
Three Principles and Four
Considerations

Except for very simple methods for very simple decisions, all methods of decisionmaking, both sound and unsound, require deciding (weighing) importance (intensities of preferences). The key difference between sound and unsound is that unsound methods require weighing such things as factors, criteria, objectives, goals, roles, categories, consequences, pros and cons, advantages and disadvantages, benefits and costs, attributes, risks, and so forth. (If you can name it, someone has probably tried it.)

In contrast, sound methods require weighing—either explicitly or implicitly—the importance of advantages. And this is why we gave the name Choosing By Advantages to sound methods. This chapter is a further response to the question that is most often asked about Choosing By Advantages: How should we decide the importance of each advantage?

People often ask, "Isn't a decision about the importance of an advantage just an arbitrary decision?" The answer is that decisions about importance must not be arbitrary. Decisionmakers must decide the importance of each advantage with care and precision. The key is to use sound-decisionmaking patterns of thought and speech. Here is a pattern that must not be used: How important is keel depth, compared with color? And here is the one that must be used: How important is the advantage in keel depth, compared with the advantage in color?

For those who are experienced in using CBA, deciding importance is usually not a difficult activity. But for those who are not, this activity can be the most difficult of the entire CBA process. People often imagine that if they were using some other process, deciding importance would either be unnecessary or not difficult. That is wishful thinking. In reality, for those who are using unsound methods, correctly deciding importance isn't just difficult, it's impossible—even for simple decisions. That is why unsound methods so often produce unsound decisions.

- As is shown in chapter 16, it is impossible to correctly decide the importance of factors, goals, roles, or categories.

- As is shown in chapter 17, it is impossible to correctly decide the importance of "pros-and-cons" (good and bad attributes), even if they are properly described. Similarly, it is impossible to correctly decide the importance of objectives or criteria.

- Deciding the importance of advantages and disadvantages is possible, but the Choosing By Advantages and Disadvantages methods are unsound. (Some of these methods *encourage* people to make critical mistakes; others *require* them to make critical mistakes.)

DECIDING IMPORTANCE: THREE PRINCIPLES

For simple decisions, it is never difficult for a skilled CBA decision-maker to correctly weigh advantages. For complex decisions, it is sometimes difficult, but always possible. To simplify and clarify this activity—and to anchor each decision to the relevant facts—decisions about importance must be based on at least three principles:

1. There is no such thing as a zero advantage. Therefore, in a display of rationale, such as a Two-List Display or a Tabular Display, a non-advantage and its non-importance are represented by *blank* spaces. (As shown in chapter 10, exceptions are in preference charts and preference curves, where non-advantages are represented by zeros.)

2. All the advantages of all the alternatives must be weighed on the *same* scale of importance, and that is the only purpose of selecting a paramount advantage. (Selecting the paramount advantage establishes a scale of importance for the decision.)

3. *Decisionmaking is NOT a branch of mathematics.* Therefore, we must *decide,* not calculate, the importance of each advantage—based on the following and other considerations.

(I hope you will mark this page and the following page, and refer to them often. They could be the most valuable pages in the entire book. To anchor decisions to the relevant facts, the preceding three principles and following four considerations are vital—especially, the four considerations.)

DECIDING IMPORTANCE: FOUR CONSIDERATIONS

When we are deciding importance, if we don't know the purpose and circumstances of the decision, the needs and preferences of the stakeholders, the magnitudes of the advantages, and the magnitudes of their associated attributes, we are deciding by accident. Deciding By Accident is a popular method. And it sometimes produces sound decisions—by accident. But it doesn't qualify as a sound method. So, base your decisions about importance on the following considerations:

1. The *purpose* and circumstances of the decision. (CBA is purpose driven. Therefore, the CBA process begins by identifying a purpose to be achieved, not by identifying a problem to be solved. If there is a problem, however, the activity of defining the problem and finding its root cause is included in the stage-setting phase of the CBA process.)

2. The needs and preferences of the customers and other *stakeholders,* including those who will be affected by the decision and others who will be interested in the decision.

3. The magnitudes of the *advantages.* (In the typical situation, as demonstrated by the typical preference curve shape, an advantage of almost zero has an importance of almost zero.)

4. The magnitudes of the *associated attributes.* (Usually, as demonstrated in chapter 10, the relationships between attributes, advantages, and importance of advantages are nonlinear. That is, preference curves are usually not straight lines.)

There are, of course, many other types of information that sometimes should be considered when deciding importance, in addition to these four considerations. For example, because the advantages of the alternatives are prospective future advantages, they are uncertain, at least to some degree, and significant uncertainties must be taken into account. Here is another example of other types of information that sometimes should be considered: Advantages in the distant future do not necessarily have the same importance as if they were in the near future. (The sound methods for weighing distant future advantages and those for dealing with uncertainty are closely related, but they are not the same.)

Advanced CBA concepts and methods—such as those for weighing distant future advantages and those for dealing with uncertainty—are beyond the scope of this book. However, this book provides the essential foundation for the advanced topics.

DECIDING IMPORTANCE: A NATURAL PROCESS

Fortunately, deciding importance is a natural process. People learn how to decide importance, naturally, while they are small children—while they are learning how to crawl, and walk, and talk. However, small children do not learn how to clearly and accurately disclose their decisions about importance, especially how to disclose importance numerically. To make matters worse, both children and adults typically decide the importance of the wrong things. CBA improves the natural process, as follows:

First, CBA requires deciding the importance of the right things. The CBA methods require weighing advantages. In contrast:

- Some of the old methods require weighing the importance of factors, goals, roles, categories, or similar items, and that is a mistake. Others require rating the importance of the attributes of alternatives, and that is another mistake.

- The old standard methods require both mistakes. They require weighing factors and rating attributes.

Second, CBA improves the accuracy of decisions about importance.

To see how to accurately decide the importance of one advantage, compared with another, look at how people decide that they prefer one flavor of ice cream, compared with another. How do they decide? The answer is simple: To make a sound decision, they must clearly and accurately perceive the two flavors. Therefore, they must taste each flavor, before deciding. And that is how to accurately decide the importance of one advantage, compared with another: *Before deciding, form a clear, accurate, sensory-rich perception of each advantage.*

For complex decisions, numerical weights—displayed in writing—are usually essential. They help decisionmakers choose the preferred alternative and disclose the rationale for the decision. They also help decisionmakers when they need to reconsider and improve the decision. But for simple decisions, numerical weights are seldom required. And for very simple decisions, they are never required.

Remember that deciding importance is a subjective activity, and that there will never be an objective way to do a subjective activity. In particular, there will never be an objective way to decide importance. Nevertheless, we must never arbitrarily decide importance. Instead, we must skillfully decide—with care and precision. And skill comes from studying and practicing. Of course, while practicing is good, practicing with feedback is much better. If possible, practice under the guidance of a CBA facilitator or instructor. This is why: In response to a physical mistake—such as touching a hot stove—feedback is usually automatic, and the needed correction is instantly obvious. In contrast, feedback from the mental mistake of using an unsound method of decisionmaking—especially, one that requires deciding the importance of the wrong things—isn't automatic, and it usually isn't immediate. Furthermore, the needed correction (changing from using an unsound method to using a sound method) is almost never obvious—even if the unsound method causes a terrible outcome.

If it isn't possible for you to practice under the guidance of a CBA facilitator, try to practice with someone else who is also learning the CBA process, and give feedback to one another. At the very least, carefully review your own work and give feedback to yourself. What feedback needs to do for you, most of all, is to help you form the habit of using anchored questions and anchored judgments. Keep in mind the principle of anchoring: Decisions about importance must be anchored to the relevant facts. Chapter 12 demonstrates that very few decisionmakers adequately understand this principle, and chapter 15 shows that this lack of understanding is a major cause of human conflicts and miseries.

12

The Bridge Design
Experiment

A very enlightening experiment, called "The Bridge Design Experiment," reveals how we naturally make decisions. It shows that we must be *taught* how to make sound decisions, and that expecting people to acquire sound-decisionmaking skills from experience, without being taught, is an unreasonable expectation. This experiment has demonstrated, over and over, that most people do not adequately understand the principle of anchoring, because they haven't been taught this principle.

For several years, we did this experiment in nearly all of our CBA workshops. But now, we seldom do it during the workshops, because we know what the results would be, and because it sometimes offended some of the participants. However, until we find a good substitute for the experiment, it is essential in the training process to at least describe it. It is a powerful tool in explaining the principle of anchoring.

WHAT HAPPENED IN THE
BRIDGE DESIGN EXPERIMENT

In the experiment, first we described a hypothetical situation where a decision was needed. Second, we asked a question pertaining to this decision. Third, we challenged the participants to give the best possible response to the question. We were careful not to request an answer to the question, because answering is not the best response. The bridge design question is not a good question. It is an unanchored question. Remember: Any answer to an unanchored question is an unanchored judgment.

The Situation

We need to choose between two bridge design alternatives for crossing a deep canyon.

Before we asked the bridge design question, we usually told the participants that it is not a good question. *It's a trap.* However, it didn't seem to make any difference whether or not they were told this. Those who hadn't had CBA training fell into the trap, regardless. Almost without exception, only those who had previously attended CBA workshops were able to avoid the trap. To set the trap, we usually told the participants, correctly, that the bridge design question is a subjective question. It pertains to viewpoints, not facts.

The Question

In your opinion, which of the following is the most important factor in choosing from the two alternatives? Is it economics, safety, or esthetics?

Now, before you read the next section, which describes the typical response of those who are unfamiliar with CBA, think about what the common sense response would be. In other words, what do you think was the most common response to the bridge design question? Here, again, is the question: "In your opinion, which of the following is the most important factor in choosing between two bridge designs for crossing a deep canyon?"

- Economics

- Safety

- Esthetics

The Typical Response

In group after group (every time the experiment was performed), nearly everyone selected safety as the most important factor. This response is apparently the "common sense" response to the question. But selecting safety is not a good response. In fact, it could be the very worst response. In this case, as in many cases, common sense turns out to be nonsense.

Approximately 3 percent of the participants selected economics. Less often, someone selected esthetics, and even less often someone said that the factors are equal in importance or that other factors should be considered. Virtually no one—in most groups, not even one person (except for those with previous CBA training)—responded correctly.

Sometimes, we gave the participants a second chance. But first we reminded them that engineers who design bridges are guided by very rigid safety requirements, or criteria. If they do their jobs correctly, both bridges will meet all the requirements in the factor of safety. As a result, the *differences* in safety will be small, or very small, and not very important. If the concern about safety is properly taken care of during the design phase (the innovation phase), safety should be only a minor concern during the decisionmaking phase.

In their second response, approximately 60 percent of the participants selected economics as the most important factor, and about 40 percent selected esthetics. Almost no one selected safety. Of course, their second response wasn't much better than their first—because answering is not a good response to an unanchored question. But to some extent, we let them off the hook. We told them, again, that *the question* was wrong; it really was a trap. The trouble is, people catch themselves in this trap just as certainly in real-world decisionmaking as in the bridge design experiment. Tragically, it is happening every minute of every day, throughout the world. This trap is causing an enormous amount of avoidable human conflicts and miseries.

WHAT HAPPENS IN REAL-WORLD DECISIONMAKING

In the following discussion, an "important factor" is one that someone is very concerned about. Here is what happens in real-world situations when the CBA process is not being used and when there is a so-called important factor involved in the decision:

1. When everyone is very concerned about one of the factors, this concern strongly influences the formulation and screening of alternatives. In many cases, all the alternatives that are not exceptionally strong in relation to what is viewed as an important factor are simply screened out—prior to the decisionmaking phase of the process.

2. Among the alternatives that are not screened out, the differences that remain within the "important factor" are usually small, or very small, and not very important.

3. Now, here is where many people make the same mistake: Due to their high intensity of feelings, or high level of concern, pertaining to the so-called important factor, the small remaining differences in that factor are assigned far too much weight.

One reason this happens, apparently, is that decisionmakers forget that the unacceptable alternatives were already screened out—prior to the decisionmaking phase of the process. For example, they give safety a large numerical weight—even when the differences in safety are extremely small. And the factor of safety is just one example of where this happens. This violation of the principle of anchoring often causes the best alternative to not be selected. Sometimes, the very worst of those that were not screened out is selected. To make matters worse, methods that weigh factors very often cause interpersonal conflicts among the decisionmaking participants.

In contrast, the principle of anchoring takes us to the very best alternative. It tells us that in all factors the magnitudes of the advantages must be taken into account. For example, if an advantage within "an important factor" is actually large, that advantage (not the factor) should be assigned an appropriately large amount of importance.

The principle of anchoring tells us that before answering the second central question (how important is each advantage) we must answer the first (how large is each advantage). Therefore, when methods of decision-making ask unanchored questions, the best response is to avoid answering them. Unfortunately, however, answering is the instinctive response. Those who answer instinctively make assumptions to fill in data gaps. Then, they jump to conclusions. Because different people make different assumptions, which are likely to be false, unsound methods (especially, those that weigh factors) produce conflicts and unsound decisions, in situations where sound methods (those that weigh advantages) would have produced agreements and sound decisions.

In the unsound methods, the mistake is not that *incorrect* weights are assigned to factors; it is that weights—at all—are assigned to factors. Sound methods do not weigh factors. Here is what needs to be remembered: It is impossible to assign correct weights to factors. In fact, as chapter 16 demonstrates, it is impossible to actually weigh factors, correctly or incorrectly. Nevertheless, whether or not they are asked to weigh factors, that is what many people try to do, and think they have done, in real-world situations. The bridge design experiment shows that, except for CBA decisionmakers, almost no one is aware that what people call weighing factors (which they should call *trying* to weigh factors) is a mistake.

Chapter 13 presents four thinking skills that help people understand why weighing factors is a mistake and how to avoid this mistake. In a complex, rapidly changing, modern society, these four thinking skills are vital thinking skills.

13

Vital Thinking Skills for Sound Decisionmaking

This chapter continues responding to the question of how to decide importance. It shows that, in most cases, the main difference between sound and unsound methods of decisionmaking is that sound methods do and unsound methods do not anchor decisions about importance to the relevant facts. This chapter also shows that anchoring requires the following vital thinking skills: (1) specifying versus generalizing, (2) using low-order versus high-order abstractions, (3) using relevant facts versus low-order assumptions, and (4) using anchored versus unanchored questions and judgments.

We all acquired at least the first two of these vital skills, long ago. Specifying versus generalizing and using low-order abstractions are basic communication skills that we use in our daily conversations. But without CBA training, very few decisionmakers correctly use relevant facts in the decisionmaking process, because very few consistently use anchored questions and judgments.

SKILL NO. 1: SPECIFYING VERSUS GENERALIZING

To begin a detailed explanation of why the bridge design question *is not* a good question, the participants are asked the following, which *is* a good question: "Think about tables, chairs, lamps, bookshelves, and similar items. What are these items called? In other words, what is their classification?" (This is not a trap. It truly is a good question.) Write your answer in the top oval in the following diagram.

The Process of Generalizing

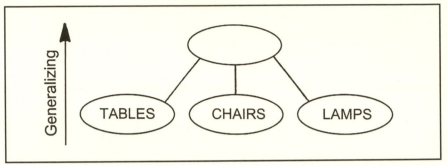

Source: U.S. Forest Service.

- Almost everyone correctly gives the same answer: Tables, chairs, lamps, and similar items are called *furniture*. (There are, of course, other correct answers—but not many.)

- This exercise demonstrates the process of **generalizing**, which is a very useful communication process.

In *Science and Sanity: An Introduction to Non-Aristotelian Systems and General Semantics,* Alfred A. Korzybski, a mathematician/engineer, described in detail the process of generalizing, although that isn't what he called it (1958 [1933]: 371). (Generalizing is an aspect of what he called "the abstraction process.") The publication of *Science and Sanity* was a very important milestone in the development of the CBA system. Korzybski's work, and the work of his students, laid the groundwork for the discovery of the principle of anchoring.

What is general semantics about? It isn't simply about the meanings of words. Instead, it has been defined as a discipline, as a doctrine, and as a field of study. In 1969, *The American Heritage Dictionary* defined general semantics as "A doctrine proposed by Alfred Korzybski (1879–1950) that presents a method of improving human behavior through a more critical use of words and symbols." CBA improves human behavior by improving the way individuals and organizations make choices, which requires a more critical use of words and symbols. Therefore, CBA and general semantics go hand in hand.

CBA recognizes that the abstraction process is a very important part of the decisionmaking process. In *Science and Sanity,* Korzybski presented an excellent model of the entire abstraction process (Korzybski: 398). The model that follows is based on Korzybski's model.

A Model of the Abstraction Process

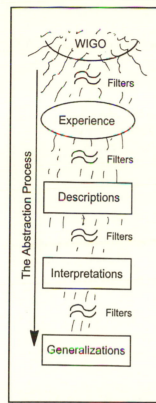

All the world is a process, represented by the initials WIGO, for What-Is-Going-On. (WIGO includes what is happening in neurons, molecules, atoms, etc.)

The first level of abstraction is the experience, or object level. This level pertains to what we see, hear, touch, etc. (No words or labels are involved at this level.)

At the second level, we are able to describe, or name, only a fraction of what we experience. In CBA (not everyone agrees with this), descriptions are called *low-order abstractions*.

At the third level, we interpret our descriptions. In CBA, interpretations of our descriptions—and of our interpretations—are called *middle-order abstractions*.

At the fourth level, we form generalizations or conclusions, based on our interpretations. In CBA, generalizations are called *high-order abstractions*.

According to this model, nothing is static. Even this book isn't static; its molecular activity never stops. This book, and everything else in the universe, is a process. Therefore, it is labeled as What-Is-Going-On (WIGO). Notice the following important distinction: "WIGO" doesn't represent someone's perception of What-Is-Going-On; instead, it represents What-Is-Going-On. WIGO is represented in the model by a parabola—open at the top and never-ending—to show that the total of WIGO is infinite. The few lines that go from WIGO to experience show that we are able to abstract, or experience, only a tiny fraction of WIGO.

The model shows that there are levels, or orders, of abstraction. It also shows that as we move from one level to another we filter our perceptions of WIGO through our personal concepts of the world. Due to these filters, it is impossible for two people to perceive the same thing in exactly the same way. (Notice that when we are moving lower on this version of the model, we are moving to *higher-order abstractions*.)

There are several types of abstracting. Classification, a very common type, is simple. Following is an example:

Low-Order Abstraction: Ten, very sweet, medium-size, grade AAA, navel oranges.

Middle-Order Abstraction: Oranges.

THE ABSTRACTION PROCESS

Middle-Order Abstraction: Fruit.

High-Order Abstraction: Food.

In 1939, S. I. Hayakawa, one of the most famous of Korzybski's students, turned the model over (1939: 126). His revision placed low-order abstractions at the bottom and high-order abstractions at the top. Following is the revised classification example:

High-Order Abstraction: Food.

Middle-Order Abstraction: Fruit.

THE ABSTRACTION PROCESS

Middle-Order Abstraction: Oranges.

Low-Order Abstraction: Ten, very sweet, medium-size, grade AAA, navel oranges.

In his version of the abstraction model, Hayakawa placed WIGO at the bottom, represented by a parabola that is open at the bottom. He described the levels of abstraction as *the abstraction ladder*.

I first became interested in the work of Korzybski and his students in 1958, while I was an engineering student at Utah State University. Their work is what stimulated the development of the CBA system. However, I was more interested in the engineering process, where we move in the opposite direction, compared with abstracting. I was interested in moving from high-order abstractions to descriptions and specifications, and to actions and outcomes.

In 1959, while working as an engineer in the California Department of Water Resources, I began experimenting with ways to apply Hayakawa's abstraction model and other concepts of general semantics to make better decisions in the project-development process. In 1965, on the Manti-LaSal National Forest, the forest engineer, the forest supervisor, and other members of the Forest Leadership Team decided to pilot test, in managing their projects and programs, the concepts that had been pioneered in California. This pilot test produced many improvements.

In 1966, Samuel Bois published *The Art of Awareness: A Textbook on General Semantics*. His book, coupled with Korzybski's book and other books about general semantics, contributed significantly to the further development of the CBA system. Bois called Korzybski's book "an epoch-making classic" (1966: xi). Bois said that in 1964, based on a reader survey, *Saturday Review* listed *Science and Sanity* as one of the most influential books that had been written in the previous four decades. Of the 163 titles mentioned, only 24 were rated higher than *Science and Sanity*. Nevertheless, if you decide to study general semantics to strengthen your understanding of CBA, I recommend starting with *The Art of Awareness*, before studying *Science and Sanity*.

The improvements we made on the Manti-LaSal Forest included breaking away from many concepts that were inconsistent with general semantics—including several pertaining to master planning, multi-year planning, and long-range planning. For example, multi-phase planning and scheduling replaced multi-year planning and scheduling. This was a significant change. Multi-phase planning is flexible and dynamic. It emphasizes using the right levels of abstraction in the planning process. In 1965, for example, we didn't ask ourselves, "Specifically, what should we do *in 1969?"* Instead, we asked ourselves, "In general, what options do we need to have available in 1969? And specifically, what phases of our projects do we need to complete *in 1965,* so the best options will be available in 1969?"

Within three years, the Forest Leadership Team had moved well away from a crisis-to-crisis management process, which is common in many organizations, toward an effective, smooth-running process. But the process wasn't self-sustaining. Therefore, it was soon abandoned, after those of us who were involved in its development moved away from the Manti-LaSal to new assignments. The new assignments that came to me provided numerous opportunities for further developing the CBA system.

In 1968, it became clear to me that four changes would make Hayakawa's abstraction model more effective in revealing how to improve human performance. These four changes produced the following model:

The Generalizing–Specifying Model

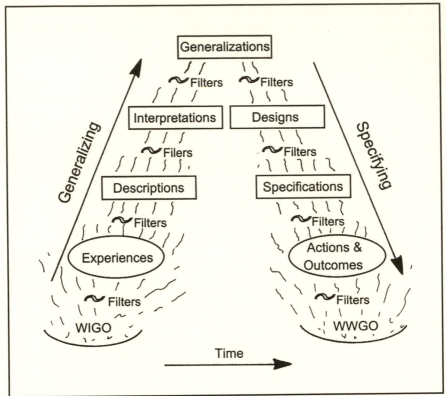

Source: U.S. Forest Service

First, the name for moving upward on the ladder is changed to *generalizing*. (The abstraction process includes more than simply moving upward on the ladder.) The second change shows that generalizing is not outside of WIGO. Instead, it is a very important part of WIGO. Therefore, the parabola is turned over, so that it is open at the top, and generalizing is placed within the parabola. The third change shows that the process takes time.

The fourth change is the one that is the most significant. In this change, the process of *specifying* What-Will-Go-On (WWGO) in the future—moving downward on the abstraction ladder—was added to the model. Compared with generalizing, specifying is not only opposite in direction, it is also very different. Generalizing is simple, straight forward, and predictable. In contrast, specifying is a turbulent, muddy, unpredictable, dynamic, searching–discovering, negotiating–bargaining, *decisionmaking* process.

From the process of specifying there are, nearly always, many correct outcomes. For example, suppose we asked several people to specify the word *chairs*. Each could correctly specify a different type of chair. As shown in the next chart, one person could specify lawn chairs while another could select recliners. Another could choose antique chairs. Someone else could choose barber chairs. And so on.

The Process of Specifying

Source: U.S. Forest Service

Moving even lower on the ladder of abstraction, one person could specify a particular lawn chair, worth about $7. Another could specify a particular recliner chair, worth $700. Yet another could choose an antique chair, worth $70,000. Someone else could specify a large collection of antique chairs, worth millions of dollars. For the word *chairs,* the range of possibilities from one valid meaning to another is enormous.

The number of valid meanings of the word *furniture* is endless. One person could specify a roomful of furniture. Another could specify enough furniture to fill a warehouse. Yet another could specify all the furniture on earth. Similarly, the number of meanings of the words used in the bridge design experiment *(safety, economics,* and *esthetics)* is endless. Therefore, the number of meanings of the bridge design question is also endless. And because the bridge design question does not have a specific meaning, it does not have a specific answer.

Much of the motivation to develop the CBA system was in response to the generalizing–specifying model—particularly the concept of specifying WWGO. The model confirms that steering the course of events and shaping the future is a decisionmaking process. It shows that the things we say and do are not caused only by nature and nurture, or heredity and environment; they are caused by **nature, nurture,** and **choice.** Therefore, human performance, including organizational performance, is a decisionmaking process. The model clearly shows that improving the way people make decisions will improve the performance of both individuals and organizations.

The generalizing–specifying model is just one of several models of the CBA process. The CBA models tell us that by our mental, emotional, and physical choices—by our decisions, motivations, and actions—we are steering the course of events and shaping the future. They also ow that, to a great extent, the future is undecided and unpredictable. We are continuously choosing the future. I believe that skillfully steering the course of events and choosing the future is the most critical challenge facing humankind today. Nothing is more important. And that is why the CBA system was developed.

Choosing By Advantages is not just a step, or a phase, in the decisionmaking process. For a particular decision, the CBA process begins at the moment when the decision is needed, before alternatives are formulated, and it doesn't end until the decision has been implemented and evaluated. Mentally, emotionally, and physically choosing the very best possibilities is the purpose of the CBA system. And it works. It is a major breakthrough. This is why it will be very worthwhile for you to continue learning, using, and teaching the CBA concepts and methods.

SKILL NO. 2: USING LOW-ORDER VERSUS HIGH-ORDER ABSTRACTIONS

In the CBA vocabulary, as shown by the next diagram, words such as food, furniture, and clothing are called *high-order abstractions*. Each has a wide range of valid meanings. (When they are being compared with such words as tables, chairs, and lamps, they are called *higher-order abstractions*.) High-order abstractions are very useful because they point us in a particular direction. For example, when people want to buy a sack of oranges, they go to a food store. If they want a new chair, they go to a furniture store. "And," someone quipped in a CBA workshop, "if they want both food and furniture, they go to a drug store."

In contrast with a high-order abstraction, a detailed description of a particular item, such as a description of a particular bag of oranges or a particular chair, is a *low-order abstraction*. (When being compared with words such as tables, chairs, and lamps, a detailed description is called a *lower-order abstraction*). Between the two extremes are *middle-order abstractions*. Now, here is the key to sound decisionmaking: It doesn't make sense to judge the importance of an abstraction—not even a low-order abstraction. Instead, each judgment about importance must pertain to the particular objective reality that the abstraction represents, and we must use a low-order abstraction to represent it.

An Illustration of Levels of Abstraction

(Food) (Furniture) (Clothing)	High-Order Abstractions
(Tables) (Chairs) (Lamps)	Middle-Order Abstractions
(Lawn Chairs) (Recliner Chairs) (Antique Chairs)	Middle-Order Abstractions
Description of a Particular $7 Lawn Chair Description of a Particular $700 Recliner Chair Description of a $70,000 Antique Chair	Low-Order Abstractions

In particular, what does make sense is to judge the importance of the actual differences among the alternatives. To accurately judge the importance of these differences, we must use clear, accurate, low-order abstractions to describe them. Furthermore, we must include them as advantages—not as advantages and disadvantages. At the same time, high-order-abstraction guidelines, or criteria, can play a very important role in our personal and organizational lives. We can use them to remind ourselves of directions we have selected for ourselves. The following are examples of guidelines that have served very well:

- Safety first. Be prepared.

- Quality is job-one.

- I will be caringly honest in the things I say and in the things I do.

- No other success can compensate for failure in the home.

Here is an example of the need for differing orders of abstraction: More and more business organizations are recognizing that "good ethics" means "good business." Therefore, they are establishing corporate codes of ethics. An effective code of ethics includes high-order, middle-order, and low-order abstractions. It is general enough to cover a wide range of situations, and it includes enough specifics to provide guidance in particular situations.

The following diagram explains why people are correct when they say that we cannot consistently make wise choices if we choose between "apples" and "oranges." It is because the words "apples" and "oranges" are not low-order abstractions.

Another Illustration of Levels of Abstraction

Furniture	Food	Clothing	High-Order Abstractions
Vegetables	Fruit	Cereal	Middle-Order Abstractions
Apples	Oranges	Grapes	Middle-Order Abstractions
Two Very Rotten Apples	Three Very Nice Very Sweet Grade AAA Navel Oranges		Low-Order Abstractions

What if someone asked, "Which would you prefer, apples or oranges?" In that case, because the quantity, quality, and purpose are not specified in the question, the person who is asked to make the choice must either assume a specific meaning of the question—which too often produces false assumptions, conflicts, and unsound decisions—or they must avoid answering it. Of course, the best response is to avoid answering it.

In contrast, if a question is specific we can answer it without making dangerous assumptions. Consider the following question, for example: "Which would you prefer—for eating, not for composting—two very rotten apples or three very nice, very sweet, grade AAA, navel oranges?" Obviously, anyone could easily make this choice.

In the same way that the words *furniture, food,* and *clothing* are high-order abstractions, the words used in the bridge design experiment—*economics, safety,* and *esthetics*—are also high-order abstractions. In many situations, these are excellent words to use. But, as shown in the bridge design experiment, they can easily be misused. Expert decisionmakers know how and when to move higher or lower on the ladder of abstraction (this is Skill No. 1). They also know how to correctly use low-order abstractions (this is Skill No. 2). CBA workshop participants practice these two skills, before moving on to the third skill, and I hope you will do the same.

Before you practice, however, look again at the difference between these two skills: In the first (specifying versus generalizing), we move from one level of abstraction to another. In the second (using low-order abstractions), we don't. Now, here is an example of practicing the first vital sound-decisionmaking skill:

- Discussion Leader (while showing something to the participants): What is this? Workshop Participant: Pliers.

- Discussion Leader (with outstretched arms): What similar items are at the same level? Workshop Participants: Hammer, saw, punch, screwdriver, wrench.

- Discussion Leader (with arms pointing upward): What are those items called? Workshop Participant: Tools. (This is an example of generalizing.)

- Discussion Leader (pointing downward): This time, be specific. What is this? Workshop Participant: That tool is a Stanley, Number 84-100, 6-1/2 inch, red-handled pliers.

In Skill No. 1, we move to low-order abstractions. In Skill No. 2, we use low-order abstractions. For example, we order, from a catalogue, a Stanley, Number 84-100, 6-1/2 inch, red-handled pliers.

SKILL NO. 3: USING RELEVANT FACTS VERSUS LOW-ORDER ASSUMPTIONS

In the third vital skill, we use the right type of low-order abstractions in the decisionmaking process. Specifically, we base decisions on relevant facts, rather than low-order assumptions. Decisionmakers need to clearly understand the difference between basing decisions on relevant facts versus basing them on low-order assumptions. Therefore, after the participants in sound-decisionmaking workshops have practiced the first two skills, they are given two assignments to draw pictures. These assignments help explain the following fundamental difference between sound methods and unsound methods: Sound methods base decisions on relevant facts. Unsound methods base decisions on low-order assumptions.

To set the stage, the participants are informed that while the first is a very doable assignment, the second is impossible. First, the discussion leader asks them to draw an example of food. The following space is provided for you to do this first assignment:

Draw an Example of Food

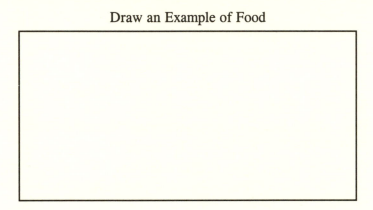

In most workshop groups, several participants draw apples. (In Alamogordo, New Mexico, several drew T-bone steaks.) Others draw bananas. Others draw additional examples of food—such as grapes, pizzas, and shelves full of food. Each person selects a unique example to draw. Even the individual apples that are drawn by different persons are not quite the same.

Next, the participants are instructed to draw a picture of food-in-general—not an example, and not an abstract symbol representing food. You might want to try this assignment. But remember: Do not draw an example. Also, do not draw an abstract symbol—one that, supposedly, would represent the general concept of food. For instance, do not draw a picture of a food store; a picture of a food store is not a picture of food, it is a picture of a store. Furthermore, it isn't even a good symbol for depicting food-in-general. As a symbol, it would represent only certain types of food. You can think of many types of food that are not sold in food stores. For example, food-in-general includes food for wild plants and animals. It even includes food for microorganisms in a meadow.

Draw a Picture of Food-in-General

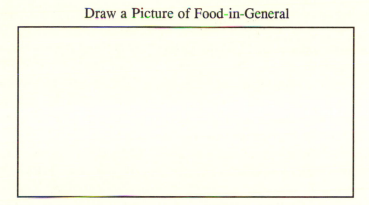

Two or three participants in most groups draw either examples or abstract symbols. But most agree, immediately, that it truly is impossible to draw a picture of a high-order abstraction, such as food-in-general. As everyone knows: "A picture is worth a thousand words." CBA reminds us that a high-order abstraction word, such as *food,* represents thousands and thousands of pictures.

It is impossible to draw a picture of a high-order abstraction because a picture is a low-order abstraction. For example, think of the difference between the word *food* versus a picture of an example of food. The word *food* is a high-order abstraction. It represents food-in-general. In contrast, each drawing of an example of food is a low-order abstraction.

It is important to understand what happened in the first assignment: In order to do it, each person had to assume a picture of food. That is, each assumed a specific meaning of the word *food*. Because pictures are low-order abstractions, assumed pictures are called *low-order assumptions*. And where do assumptions come from? They come from:

- Past experience and present imagination

- Friends and authorities

- Traditions and superstitions

- Many other sources

Basing decisions on low-order assumptions is what we do, automatically, when we do not have the data we need for a decision. As stated before, this is the Instinctive Method of decisionmaking. And when the Instinctive Method is used, our decisions are based, far too often, on false assumptions.

Psychologists tell us that we commonly assume data for a decision, as follows: We combine a small amount of new information from the outside with a large amount of old information, or old perceptions, from the inside—from our filters. Then, we treat the combination as if it all came from the outside. Unfortunately, our assumed data usually feel better to us than those that come from outside. And that is why we are usually comfortable with basing decisions on our assumptions—even when they disagree with the true relevant facts.

Once we are aware of the Instinctive Method, it becomes easy to understand what happened, again-and-again, in the bridge design experiment. In response to the bridge design question, each person assumed a set of specific meanings of the words *economics, safety,* and *esthetics.* For example, in response to the word *safety,* nearly everyone assumed—usually, without becoming aware of this assumption—that one of the bridges would be unsafe. Some assumed pictures of cars or trucks falling into a river, and people getting killed. In this way, each person assumed a specific meaning of the question. Then, each answered his or her assumed question.

Answering—making assumptions and jumping to a conclusion—is the instinctive response to the bridge design question. With the exception of CBA decisionmakers, nearly everyone responds by answering. But answering is not a valid response to an unanchored question.

SKILL NO. 4: USING ANCHORED QUESTIONS AND JUDGMENTS

Here, once more, is the bridge design question: "Which is the most important *factor* in choosing between two bridge designs? Is it economics, safety, or esthetics?" This high-order abstraction question doesn't have a specific meaning. Its meaning can drift from one extreme to another. That is why it is called *an unanchored question.* It is like an unanchored ship in a windy cove: It is likely to crash into nearby rocks. Of course, the best response to an unanchored question is to tactfully avoid answering it. Another good response is to ask questions of your own that will anchor it. For example, you could ask, "How large are the *differences* in each factor?" Then, provide an anchored answer, such as the following: "In my view, *the very large difference in esthetics* is more important than *the extremely small difference in safety.*"

Be sure to explain your answer. If you don't, most people will think you said, "In my view, *esthetics* is more important than *safety.*" And, as you know, that would be an unanchored judgment.

Occasionally, someone responded to the bridge design question by saying, "Your question can't be answered." When I first heard that response, I thought, "Finally, here is someone who already understands the principle of anchoring, before attending a CBA workshop." But I was wrong. When I asked, "Why not?" he said, accusingly, "Because *you* didn't give us enough data." That was a big disappointment. If he had understood the principle of anchoring, he would have known that having data or not having data makes no difference. With or without data, it is a mistake to ask or answer unanchored questions—except for the purpose of stimulating a discussion, or simply making conversation.

Chapter 14 shows how to make better decisions by replacing traditional unanchored questions and judgments with untraditional anchored questions and judgments. After its introduction, it identifies the levels of abstraction of the four sound-decisionmaking terms: *factors, criteria, attributes,* and *advantages.* Then, it shows how to use sound-decisionmaking patterns of thought and speech to anchor decisions to the relevant facts.

14

The Sound Decisionmaking Vocabulary

How do people naturally make decisions? No one knows, exactly, because decisionmaking is a thought process, and thoughts happen in our minds, not out where we can see or hear them. During CBA workshops, several participants have said that they naturally base decisions on advantages. I think that basing decisions on advantages, but not necessarily doing it correctly, might be a natural way to make decisions.

Of course, decisionmaking requires nonverbal thinking, in addition to verbal. Nevertheless, because words and symbols represent thoughts, a vocabulary is a window to the mind. Furthermore, combinations of words and symbols (patterns of speech) represent patterns of thought. Therefore, we can learn a lot about someone's patterns of thought by observing his or her patterns of speech. We have been able to learn a lot about how people make decisions by paying attention to what they say during the decision-making process. One of the things we have observed is that without CBA training they don't use the sound-decisionmaking vocabulary.

To anchor decisions to the relevant facts, the CBA methods require the clear, accurate, and consistent use of the CBA vocabulary. *Anyone who is not using the CBA vocabulary is not using CBA.* The CBA vocabulary isn't just a set of words, although words are important. It includes:

- Models, formats, charts, and diagrams

- Individual words

- Patterns of thought and speech

SOUND-DECISIONMAKING MODELS, FORMATS, CHARTS, AND DIAGRAMS

One of the barriers you are likely to face when you are ready to implement the CBA system, if others must be involved, is that some will resist using both the models for teaching CBA and the formats, charts, and diagrams for using CBA. For example, they are likely to resist using the Two-List Format. It is obvious to nearly everyone that sound decisionmaking requires using correct data. What is apparently not so obvious is that sound decisionmaking also requires correctly organizing and correctly using correct data. In particular, the Two-List Method requires the precise use of the Two-List Format, and the Tabular Method requires the precise use of the Tabular Format.

The CBA formats for displaying data have been carefully designed and thoroughly tested. They are the result of many cycles of field-testing, making improvements, and retesting. So, as stated previously, use each format with accuracy and consistency. For example, use solid lines where solid lines are needed, and use dashed-lines where dashed-lines are needed. Mistakes in formats of displays are like mistakes in spellings of words: A minor mistake will cause a loss of credibility. Major mistakes will cause communication failures and faulty decisions.

Usually, those with high levels of skill in using maps, drawings, charts, diagrams, photographs, and other nonverbal communication tools are able to quickly learn how to use the CBA displays. Those who are unskilled in using nonverbal communication tools can also learn how to use the CBA displays, but for them it usually takes more study and practice.

SOUND-DECISIONMAKING WORDS

For the same reasons that the models, formats, charts, and diagrams in the CBA vocabulary were carefully selected, the words were also carefully selected. Of course, while we were designing the vocabulary, we didn't start with the words and select the definitions. Instead, we started with the CBA concepts and then we selected the words.

As stated many times in this book: To make sound decisions, decision-makers must skillfully use the CBA definitions of the following words: *factors, criteria, attributes,* and *advantages.* The failure to clearly distinguish between the concepts represented by these four words has caused too many faulty decisions. This section repeats their definitions, with some variations from those previously presented. It also presents their levels of abstraction:

- A *factor* is an element, or a component, of a decision.

- A *factor* is a container for criteria, attributes, advantages, and other types of data.

(Names of factors are high-order abstractions.)

There are several synonyms of the term *factor,* as listed in the Rodale *Synonym Finder:* element, part, component, constituent, ingredient; item, detail, point, facet, aspect, thing, and consideration. The CBA definitions and this list of synonyms are in agreement. Notice that the terms *criterion, attribute,* and *advantage* are not synonyms of the term *factor.* Because each of these terms has a distinctly different meaning, CBA doesn't use them interchangeably.

As an illustration of the first CBA definition of the term *factor*—an element or a component of a decision—the canoe decision was divided into five factors. This definition is depicted in the following diagram:

The First Definition of the Term *Factor*

The second definition of the term *factor*—a container for data—reminds us that when we are dividing a decision into factors we do not ask, "What factors will be important in this decision?" Instead, we ask: "*In* what factors will there be advantages?" Remember: Sound methods assign importance scores to the advantages themselves, not to their containers. Be careful, do not confuse the container with its contents.

Remember, also, that sound methods base decisions on the relationships, *in* the factors, between attributes, advantages, and importance of advantages. They do not base decisions on the importance of the factors.

The Second Definition of the Term *Factor*

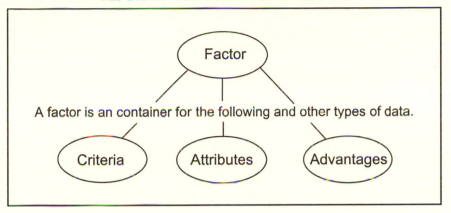

Sound methods also do not base decisions on the importance of criteria. Like attributes and advantages, criteria are contained in factors. In the CBA vocabulary, the term *criterion* has three definitions, as follows:

- A *criterion* is a decision-rule, or a guideline. Some are musts. Others are wants.

- A *criterion* is any standard on which a judgment is based.

- A *criterion* is any decision that guides further decisionmaking.

  (Criteria can be high-order, middle-order, or low-order abstractions.)

Following are several synonyms of the term *criterion,* again as listed in the Rodale *Synonym Finder,* and as used in CBA: measure, gauge, scale, barometer, yardstick, guide, guideline, test; standard, norm, benchmark, point of comparison; model, example, exemplar, precedent, lead; original, prototype, archetype, type, classic example; pattern, paradigm; rule, law, canon, maxim, and code. Notice, again, that the term *factor* is not a synonym of the term *criterion.*

Typically, there are musts and wants in all the factors in a decision, but if they are obvious they are usually not written down. In the canoe decision, for example, based on recommendations from the Twin-Rivers Association of Canoeists, a minimum of flotation was established (but not in writing, because it was easily remembered). This must-criterion, coupled with other must-criteria, narrowed the choice to only two readily available canoes: C and K.

Must-criteria establish attribute limits. Be careful not to set limits that are too restrictive. When establishing your must-criteria, keep the following play-on-words in mind: A must-criterion is a decision-rule. Be careful not to rule out the best alternative.

- An *attribute* is a characteristic, or consequence, of one alternative.

- An *attribute* is neither good nor bad (pro nor con), except in comparison with another attribute.

  (Proper descriptions of attributes are specific. They are low-order abstractions.)

Want-criteria identify the least-preferred attributes, one in each factor, and the differences from the least-preferred attributes are the advantages of the alternatives.

- An *advantage* is either a favorable dissimilarity (in quality), or a favorable difference (in quantity) between the attributes of two alternatives.

- An *advantage* is a difference from a least-preferred attribute.

  (Proper descriptions of advantages are low-order abstractions.)

In review: The CBA definitions of the term *advantage* simply formalize the on-the-street definition. To illustrate this definition, suppose you said to someone, "Please taste these two ice cream cones and tell me, in your opinion, which one has the advantage in flavor." What would be the response if both cones had the same flavor, or if they were equally preferred? In either case, the on-the-street response would be the same: "To me, neither has an advantage in flavor." What the on-the-street vocabulary tells us is that if there is no difference—or if there is a difference but no preference—there is no advantage. It's the same in the CBA vocabulary.

Some of the dictionary definitions of the term *advantage* agree with the CBA definitions. Examples include: benefit, betterment, and gain (an increase, or improvement). Like the CBA definitions, these dictionary definitions pertain to differences. On the other hand, some of the dictionary definitions disagree with CBA by not pertaining to differences. Following is an example: a superior position. (In the CBA vocabulary, an individual position—even if it is a superior position—is an attribute. A favorable difference between two positions is an advantage.) The following dictionary definition strongly disagrees with CBA: a favorable factor.

A Family of Sound-Decisionmaking Terms

The following diagram reviews, in a single display, the relationships—in the canoe a decision—between *factors, criteria, attributes,* and *advantages.* The **key relevant facts** are the advantages and their associated attributes (in the weight factor, they are shown in bold type). In addition, any facts that aid in making judgments about importance are relevant facts.

Relationships Among Key Sound-Decisionmaking Words

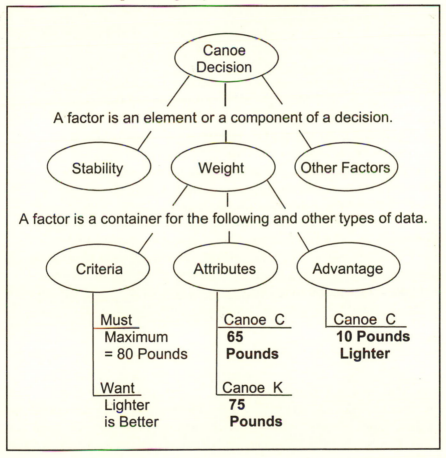

In the CBA vocabulary, as in common usage, a *decision* is a mental choice, or a symbolized choice—also, an emotional choice, or a motivation. In contrast, an *action* is a physical choice. The CBA process includes both mentally and emotionally *deciding,* and physically *doing.*

Some have said, "The CBA vocabulary is too complex." In response, I sometimes ask, "How many words are there in a typical adult's vocabulary?" And they always say that a typical vocabulary contains thousands of words. Then I point out that we are just sharpening the existing definitions—not creating new definitions—of only four sound-decisionmaking terms. The difference is that before the CBA definitions were established, people commonly used these terms interchangeably.

Factors Versus Criteria

In many government agencies, as well as private organizations, the term *criterion* is often used as a synonym of the term *factor*. Members of those organizations confuse the decisionmaking process by saying, "Color and weight are two of the criteria in this decision." Dictionary definitions and CBA definitions both show that color and weight are factors, not criteria. Factors and criteria are not at all the same; they are not even similar. They are closely related to one another, but they are distinctly different from one another. A factor *contains* criteria.

In the canoe example, the first factor, weight, contains two criteria: First, the maximum weight is 80 pounds (this is a must-criterion; it ruled out all canoes weighing more than 80 pounds). Second, lighter is better (this is a want-criterion; it pointed to 75 pounds as the least-preferred attribute in this factor). This same factor (weight) contains two attributes: The 65 pound weight of Canoe C and the 75 pound weight of Canoe K. It also contains one advantage: The 10 pound advantage of Canoe C. In addition, it contains information that helps us decide the relative importance of the 10 pound advantage; and it contains a preference curve.

Factors Versus Advantages

Another distinction that was not sharp and clear before CBA was developed is the distinction between a *factor* and an *advantage*. This distinction needs to be completely internalized so that the CBA definitions of these terms are used without any conscious thought. The reason this distinction is critical is that sound methods never assign numerical weights to factors. When it is necessary to assign numerical weights, they must be assigned to advantages. Again, the relationship between a factor and an advantage is a container–contents relationship. It is similar to the relationship between a horse barn and a horse:

- Names of factors are high-order abstractions. Factors *contain* advantages.

- Descriptions of advantages are low-order abstractions. Advantages are *contained in* factors. As stated before, do not confuse the container with its contents.

Attributes Versus Advantages

Before CBA, there wasn't a sharp distinction, even in dictionaries, between *attributes* and *advantages*. But in a sound-decisionmaking process, the things that are represented by these two words are distinctly different. The distinction between an attribute and an advantage must be as sharp and clear as the distinction between an individual location and a distance between two locations.

- An *attribute* is a characteristic or consequence of *ONE* alternative.

- An *advantage* is a difference between the attributes of *TWO* alternatives.

Advantages Versus Disadvantages

In CBA workshops, we often ask, "What is the difference between an advantage and a disadvantage?" And the answer is, "They are exactly the same—except for perspective." Following, again, is the CBA definition of a disadvantage: Without exception, a disadvantage of one alternative is an advantage of another.

Choosing By Advantages and Disadvantages causes multiple-counting, confusion, omissions, distortions, and faulty decisions—especially when there are three or more alternatives. Therefore, to simplify and clarify the decisionmaking process, and to make sound decisions, all the differences among the alternatives must be listed as advantages, and only as advantages. Obviously, in the choice between Choosing By Advantages and Disadvantages versus Choosing By Advantages, CBA is preferred.

How should you respond when someone suggests listing the advantages and disadvantages of each alternative? As shown in chapter 5, when people are asked to list advantages and disadvantages, they usually list advantages, disadvantages, and attributes. As in dictionaries, most do not clearly distinguish between a characteristic of one alternative and a difference between two. Also, they usually double-count some of the advantages. Nevertheless, a display of so-called advantages and disadvantages can be used as a starting point in the decisionmaking phase of the CBA process. But it is much simpler to start by listing either the attributes, in the Tabular Format, or the advantages, in the Two-List Format. (If someone asks you to list the pros and cons of the alternatives, list their attributes.)

SOUND-DECISIONMAKING PATTERNS
OF THOUGHT AND SPEECH

To make sound decisions, it is essential to use sound-decisionmaking charts, diagrams, and words. But what is absolutely essential is to use sound-decisionmaking patterns of thought and speech. Following are comparisons between the old (unsound) patterns and the new (CBA) patterns (the first two sets are from chapter 7). Do not use the patterns that are unsound, conflict-causing, too complex, or unanchored. Practice the CBA patterns—especially those that are in bold italic type—until you automatically use them without thinking about them.

Describing What Data to Include in a Set of Data
for a Decision:

- Unsound and Conflict-Causing: Be sure to include all the pros and cons of each alternative.

- Unsound and Too Complex: Be sure to include all the advantages and disadvantages of each alternative.

- Sound and Simple: ***Be sure to include all the advantages of each alternative.***

Dividing a Decision
into Factors:

- Unsound: What factors will be important in this decision?

- Sound: In what factors will there be differences among the alternatives?

- Sound and Simple: ***In what factors will there be advantages?***

For most decisions, we don't need to identify the factors. Instead, we simply ask ourselves the following (see ch. 4): What and how large are the advantages of each alternative? When we are able to use the Instant CBA process, we don't even list the advantages on paper. We simply perceive them in our minds. In the canoe decision, for example, we would recognize that Canoe C has two advantages (ten pounds lighter and slightly greater stability), while K has three (moderately smoother finish, much nicer color, and slightly better keel depth). Then we would ask ourselves, "Do the two outweigh the three, or do the three outweigh the two?"

In this case, the stakeholders were unable to choose the preferred alternative without deciding the importance of each individual advantage. Therefore, they listed the five advantages, in the Two-List Format. Then, to establish a scale of importance for the decision, they selected the paramount advantage and assigned it an importance of 100. This was an ordinal decision: Which advantage is first in importance? (There is no need to know which is second, third, and so on. To establish a scale of importance, we just need to know which one is first.)

Asking Ordinal Questions:

- Unanchored: Which factor is more important in this decision, weight or color?

- Anchored: Which advantage is more important in this decision, the difference in weight or the difference in color?

- Anchored: *Which advantage is more important in this decision, the advantage in weight or the advantage in color?*

The level of detail in the two examples of anchored ordinal questions is adequate in nearly all situations. So practice saying *the difference in* and *the advantage in* until you are using these two patterns automatically, naturally, without even thinking about them. (Use *the difference in* when talking with someone who is unfamiliar with CBA.)

There are a few situations where the anchors need to be stronger than those in the two preceding examples. In such situations, use one of the following patterns:

- Strongly Anchored: Which advantage is more important in this decision, the 10 pound advantage in weight or the large advantage in color?

- Very Strongly Anchored: Which advantage is more important in this decision, the 10 (= 75 - 65) pound advantage in weight or the large (= kelly-blue versus starry-brown) advantage in color?

Answering Ordinal Questions:

- Unanchored: Color.

- Anchored: The difference in color.

- Anchored: *The advantage in color.*

After assigning the paramount advantage an importance of 100, the stakeholders decided the importance of each of the other advantages by asking a series of cardinal questions. First, they weighed the advantage in canoe weight against the advantage in color:

Asking Cardinal Questions:

- Unanchored: How important is weight, compared with color?

- Anchored: How important is the difference in weight, compared with the difference in color?

- Anchored: *How important is the advantage in weight, compared with the advantage in color?*

Notice that an anchored question has two anchors, in the same way that a ship has two anchors—one to anchor the bow, and one to anchor the stern. Examples of the two anchors are: *"the advantage in weight"* and *"the advantage in color."* Again, there are a few situations requiring anchors that are stronger or much stronger. In such situations, choose one of the following patterns:

- Strongly Anchored: How important is the 10 pound advantage in weight, compared with the large advantage in color?

- Very Strongly Anchored: How important is the 10 (= 75 - 65) pound advantage in weight, compared with the large (= kelly-blue versus starry-brown) advantage in color?

Because our patterns of thought and speech are mostly patterns of habit, and because they are usually deeply embedded, changing from the typical decisionmaking vocabulary to the sound-decisionmaking vocabulary (the CBA vocabulary) takes time and practice. Some say that changing a pattern of speech requires a conscious effort for at least three to six months. And it doesn't work to practice the CBA patterns only while making major decisions. As everyone knows, success requires practicing "before the game, during the game, and after the game." Be sure to practice the sound-decisionmaking patterns when you are not making decisions. Also, practice them while you are making decisions that are not very important.

One of the obstacles decisionmakers face when making the change from the traditional vocabulary to using anchored questions and judgments is that it is difficult for people to hear themselves and to recognize when they have used questions and judgments that are unanchored. It is much easier for them to change if they have help from a skilled CBA facilitator. (The facilitator will pay attention to what they say and tactfully let them know when they have slipped back into old habits.)

What if a CBA facilitator isn't available to you? As I mentioned before, one option is to practice with someone else who is also learning CBA, so that you can give feedback to one another. A second option is to carefully listen to yourself and to give feedback to yourself. Keep in mind that when you are acquiring and improving a skill, such as Choosing By Advantages: Practicing is good, but practicing with feedback is much better.

Unanchored Question:
Which has the greatest value, food
or food?

Anchored Question:
Which has the greatest value, two small grade-B potatoes
or twelve large grade-A potatoes?

15

It Isn't "Just" a
Matter of Semantics

Usually, if not always, to change from unsound to sound decisionmaking, decisionmakers must change from basing decisions on low-order assumptions to basing them on relevant facts. This requires changes in semantics—in patterns of thought and speech. As stated in chapter 14, patterns of thought and speech are, to a great extent, patterns of habit; and some of the grooves in the patterns are very deep. That is why most people need to practice the CBA vocabulary, with feedback. Because patterns of speech are so automatic, those who practice with feedback usually find themselves being corrected over and over for a while. This can be discouraging. And it has caused some to question whether the required change in vocabulary is worth the effort. They ask, "Does it really make any difference? Isn't it just a matter of semantics?"

Of course it *is* a matter of semantics; but it isn't *just* a matter of semantics. It is a very important matter of semantics. And it isn't just one of the differences between sound and unsound decisionmaking. It is a critical difference.

The following page compares the typical response to an unanchored question with the typical response to an anchored question. Notice that the responses are not just phrased differently. They are opposites in terms of content. Usually, in response to the unanchored question, those participants who answer select *stability*. This is not only an unanchored judgment; it is untrue, as well. It doesn't truly disclose the participants' viewpoint. The same participants, responding to the anchored question, usually select the difference in *color,* and this truly does disclose their viewpoint.

Unanchored Question:	Which is the most important *factor* in the canoe decision: Stability or color?
Unanchored Judgment:	***Stability.***

Anchored Question:	Which is the most important *advantage:* The very small difference in stability or the large difference in color?
Anchored Judgment:	The large difference in ***color.***

These two patterns of speech are opposites, and in many situations they produce opposite decisions. As shown by this example, if you change the phrasing of the question, you are likely to change the answer. If you want correct answers, you must ask correct questions. As an illustration, the following principle is very significant: According to the stakeholders in this decision, if the advantage in stability had been large, and if the advantage in color had been small, the stability advantage would have been far more important than the color advantage. But if we assumed that the advantage in stability is large, and if we assumed that the advantage in color is small, we would be making false, low-order assumptions.

In the old standard methods (those that weight the factors, rate the attributes, and multiply the weights times the ratings to calculate scores), when people think they are assigning weights to factors, they are actually assigning weights to low-order assumptions. Sometimes these assumptions are true and relevant. But too often they are either untrue or irrelevant. In either case (whether the assumptions are true and relevant, or not) people are usually unaware of their assumptions. This is a very significant difference between the old standard methods and the CBA methods:

- The old standard methods base decisions on ***low-order assumptions***.

- The CBA methods base decisions on ***relevant facts.***

In CBA, anchored questions produce relevant facts, which produce anchored judgments (sound decisions). In the old standard methods, unanchored questions produce low-order assumptions, which produce unanchored judgments (unsound decisions). The bridge design experiment demonstrated what happens: The participants unconsciously assumed, apparently, that one of the bridges would be unsafe. Then, based on this assumption, they judged that the difference in safety would be very important.

It should be noted that all questions and judgments are unanchored to some extent. It is a matter of degree. Even when we describe each advantage precisely, there is still some amount of room for interpretation, or misinterpretation, of the description. Nevertheless, descriptions of advantages are far more anchored than names of factors.

THE OLD STANDARD: BASING DECISIONS ON LOW-ORDER ASSUMPTIONS

There are numerous examples, everywhere, that show why the world's people urgently need to change from the old standard patterns of thought and speech to the CBA patterns. Unanchored questions, which produce low-order assumptions and unanchored judgments, are causing countless avoidable human conflicts and miseries, including wars. Following are examples:

Examples of Unanchored Questions: Which is more important:

- Owls or jobs?
- Wilderness or development?
- Health care or education?
- Your family or your work?

More Examples of Unanchored Questions: Who is more trustworthy:

- A Jew or an Arab?
- A Serbian, a Muslim, or a Croatian?
- A person with tan-colored skin or a person with white skin?
- A Catholic or a Protestant?
- An engineer or a lawyer?
- A man or a woman?
- A liberal or a conservative?

Far too often, in response to the need for a decision, people make false, low-order assumptions. Then, tragically, they base their decisions on their assumptions. False assumptions (and unanchored judgments) have produced horrible outcomes. In human history, genocide—the deliberate and systematic extermination of a national, ethnic, or racial group—has been repeated again and again. The mass killing of people, simply because they share a particular high-order abstraction label, is a despicable example of a terrible outcome caused by the old standard methods. Although some of the methods that existed before CBA are sound methods, the old standard methods truly are unsound.

Of course, atrocities are not caused only by unsound methods. They are also caused by the values of those who commit the atrocities. Typically, those who commit atrocities use false assumptions to rationalize their values. In response to false assumptions, many do not value the lives of people who are different from themselves. Some do not value the lives of people who live in distant lands. And some do not value the lives and needs of those in future generations.

In the workplace, as another example, there are men who make false assumptions about women, and there are women who make false assumptions about men. The result is unnecessary conflict, and in many cases, discrimination.

As another example, industrialists too often make false assumptions about environmentalists. Likewise, environmentalists make false assumptions about industrialists. These assumptions produce hatred and conflict, not effective, interactive decisionmaking. In reality, many environmentalists are involved in excellent industrial activities, and industrialists are involved in excellent environmental activities. A number of industrialists have worked hard to protect the environment—some, because it is profitable, and others simply because it is the right thing to do.

Similarly, in some ways, many of those who could be called liberals are conservative, and many of those who could be called conservatives are liberal. It is criminal that we are being bombarded, daily, with venomous anti-liberal and anti-conservative rhetoric.

- Here are ten of the synonyms of the term *liberal:* forward-looking, enlightened, modern, up-to-date; unbigoted, unprejudiced, generous, charitable, unselfish, and kind. I certainly would not wish to be labeled as anti-liberal, would you?

- Here are ten of the synonyms of the term *conservative:* cautious, scrupulous, prudent, careful, punctual, stable; preserving, conserving, protecting, and saving. I certainly would not wish to be labeled as anti-conservative, would you?

As yet another example, some people with one color of skin make false, low-order assumptions about people with another color, and some with another color make false, low-order assumptions about those with the one. Then, based on their false assumptions, they *decide* to murder one or more of those who look different from themselves; and they do it. In response to false assumptions, some members of some religions *decide* to commit horrible crimes against members of other religions; and they do it. Nations *decide* to go to war; and they do it.

As you know, there are countless examples of bad outcomes that are caused by unsound decisions: Some people *decide* to drink and drive; and they do it. Some *decide* to commit numerous other types of crimes; and they do it. Too many young students *decide* to drop out of school; and they do it. In each case, the cause-effect chain is the same:

Methods ——▶ Decisions ——▶ Actions ——▶ Outcomes

This model shows that human performance is a decisionmaking process—a cause-effect chain. Unfortunately, this chain is producing far too many undesirable outcomes because, typically, the first link in the chain is unsound. The standard, today, is a disjointed collection of unsound methods. For example, *methods* that ask unanchored questions produce unanchored judgments *(decisions)*. Unanchored judgments produce human conflicts *(actions)*.   And human conflicts produce human miseries *(outcomes)*.

Of course, there are many other causes of human conflicts and miseries in addition to unsound methods of decisionmaking. But adopting the CBA methods, including their patterns of thought and speech, would produce substantial improvements in the quality of human performance and in the quality of human life.

THE NEW STANDARD: BASING DECISIONS ON RELEVANT FACTS

Ginger Brown is a teacher at Bates Elementary School, in North Ogden, Utah. In a series of CBA lessons she developed for her master's degree from Weber State University, she introduces CBA to her third-grade students. In one of the lessons, she explains to her students that the Pygmies of Central Africa have light-colored skin and are only four-and-a-half feet tall (1993: 36). Then, she tells her students that the Watusis are neighbors of the Pygmies. They have dark-colored skin and are sometimes over seven feet tall.   After showing them how to choose from two alternatives by listing advantages versus advantages, she asks the following questions:

- For those who want to be horse racing jockeys, which tribe members have the advantage in tallness? (The Pygmies.)

- Which tribe members have the advantage in skin color? (Neither. Skin color has nothing to do with horse racing.)

- For those who want to be basketball players, which tribe members have the advantage in tallness? (The Watusis.)

- Which tribe members have the advantage in skin color? (Neither.)

Think about what Ginger Brown teaches concerning skin color. Compare what she teaches with what Adolph Hitler taught. Using high-order abstractions and the old standard patterns of thought, Hitler taught hatred and conflict. Using low-order abstractions and the CBA patterns of thought, Brown teaches unity and harmony. Using CBA truly is a matter of semantics. But it isn't "just" a matter of semantics.

Please discourage everyone from teaching unsound methods to anyone—including children, students, and adults. They would need to unlearn what they were taught, and unlearning is the most difficult step in the five-step skill-learning process. Therefore, wherever and whenever possible, the teaching of unsound methods, including teaching by example, needs to be prevented.

16

Sound Methods
Do Not Weigh Factors

A leader in a business organization that teaches the old standard methods, which they call "The Rational Methods" and we call "Weighting-Rating-and-Calculating," made the following statement: "Unless our customers complain, we won't change to CBA." He then said, "And we don't see any need to change. In effect, what we are teaching and CBA are the same. While our methods weigh factors explicitly, the CBA methods weigh factors implicitly." He then said, with conviction, "It's impossible to make decisions without weighing factors."

Many others have made that same false statement, probably without realizing that it is false. During the first part of CBA workshops, during decision meetings, and in other circumstances we have heard it over and over again. Many people—especially authorities in the field of decision-making—have argued that it is impossible to make decisions without weighing factors. This chapter will show that it is actually impossible to weigh factors.

When people talk about "weighing factors," what do they mean? Usually, the phrase *weighing a factor* means assigning an individual number, or weight, to represent the importance of an individual factor. This common definition is the one we have in mind when we say that CBA absolutely does not weigh factors—explicitly or implicitly. Instead, CBA takes into account, in each factor, the relationships between attributes, advantages, and importance of advantages. And these relationships are not factor weights. In some factors, in some decisions, preference charts or preference curves are used to display these relationships.

THE CANOE DECISION, REVISITED

The canoe decision demonstrates that CBA does not explicitly or implicitly weigh factors. To set the stage, the following display of rationale shows that the advantage in color has an importance of 100. And it shows, in bold type because it is the focus of this chapter, that the 10 pound advantage in weight has an importance of 70.

Display of Rationale for the Canoe Decision

Advantages of Canoe C		Advantages of Canoe K	
• **10 Pounds Lighter**	70	• Moderately Smoother Finish	5
• Slightly Greater Stability	75	• Much Nicer Color	100
		• Slightly Better Keel Depth	10
Total Importance:	145	Total Importance:	115
Both Alternatives Have the Same Total Cost.			

TRUE STATEMENTS VERSUS FALSE STATEMENTS

Those who defend the old standard methods of decisionmaking argue that, "According to your own display, color is the most important factor in this decision." "Furthermore," they argue, "the first factor, canoe weight, has an importance of 70." As you know, both of these arguments are false. The canoe decision gives you a way to prove that they are false. (Of course, some will continue defending the old standard methods, even in the face of overwhelming evidence that they are unsound.)

Compared with showing that color doesn't have an importance of 100, it is a little easier to show that weight doesn't have an importance of 70. So, that is what we do. To demonstrate that the canoe weight factor does not have an importance of 70, we revisit the preference curve in this factor. Based on the curve, extended, we present a series of true and false statements. These statements show that it is absolutely impossible to weigh factors. Following is this curve:

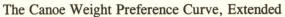

The Canoe Weight Preference Curve, Extended

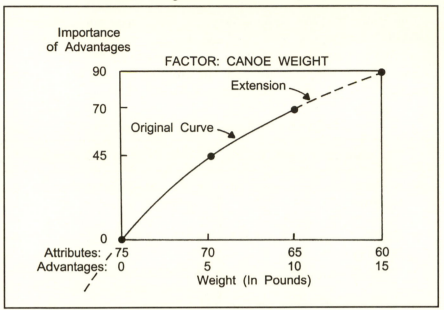

In the following pairs of true and false statements, the true statements are not precisely true. Nevertheless, they are sufficiently true for the purpose of choosing a canoe. They adequately represent the viewpoint of the stakeholders, which is adequately represented by the preference curve. In contrast, the false statements are totally false.

True: The zero *difference* between 75 pounds and 75 pounds is a non-advantage. And obviously, it has no importance. (This is shown in the preference curve as a zero importance.)

False: The *factor*, canoe weight, has a zero importance.

True: The 5 (= 75 - 70) pound *difference* in canoe weight has an importance of 45.

False: The *factor*, canoe weight, has an importance of 45.

True: The 5 (= 65 - 60) pound *difference* in canoe weight has an importance of 20 (= 90 - 70).

False: The *factor*, canoe weight, has an importance of 20.

Notice that the 5 pound difference between 65 and 60 pounds is a lot less important than the 5 pound difference between 75 and 70 pounds. This demonstrates why it is that, in addition to knowing the magnitude of the advantage (5 pounds), we must also know the magnitudes of its associated attributes. (The importance of a 5 pound advantage at one location on the preference curve is not the same as the importance of a 5 pound advantage at a different location.) Now, let's continue comparing true versus false statements.

True: The 10 (= 75 - 65) pound *difference* in weight has an importance of 70.

False: The *factor*, canoe weight, has an importance of 70.

True: The 15 (= 75 - 60) pound *difference* in weight has an importance of 90.

False: The *factor*, canoe weight, has an importance of 90.

The following true statement is based on extending the preference curve to the left, beyond what is shown in the display. Therefore, it is only a very rough approximation. But, as someone said, "It is better to be approximately right than precisely wrong."

True: The 20 (= 80 - 60) pound *difference* in weight has an importance of 160.

False: The *factor*, canoe weight, has an importance of 160.

In formulating each of the true statements, here is what we did: When we measured importance, we measured vertically between two specific points on the preference curve. That is, we measured the importance of a difference between two attributes. Therefore, in each case we measured the importance of an advantage. We absolutely did not measure the importance of the entire factor.

If it were possible to extend the curve all the way to an attribute of zero in the one direction, and all the way to an attribute of infinity in the other direction, we could say, conceptually, that the entire curve—including its shape—would represent the importance of the entire factor. But it would be more accurate and more useful to say that the entire curve would display the relationships, in the entire factor, between attributes, advantages, and importance of advantages.

Clearly, the importance of an entire factor cannot be represented by an individual point on a preference curve or by an individual number. Likewise, it cannot be represented by a pair of points on a curve or by a pair of numbers. Obviously, it cannot be represented by an entire curve, because it is impossible to extend a curve all the way to zero in the one direction and all the way to infinity in the other, except in concept. Furthermore, even if we could construct the entire curve, extending from zero to infinity, we would not be including all of the contents of the factor. For example, we would not be including the criteria.

In review: Using a preference curve, coupled with pairs of true and false statements, we demonstrated that the canoe weight factor does not have an importance of 70. Similarly, using a preference chart, we can demonstrate that the color factor does not have an importance of 100.

These demonstrations bring to light the following principles of sound decisionmaking: First, it is impossible to correctly weigh factors. Second, as stated before, when people think they are weighing a factor, they are actually assigning a numerical weight to a low-order assumption—to an assumed difference between two attributes. Third, it is not only impossible to weigh factors; it is also unnecessary. On the other hand, it is not only possible to weigh advantages; it is essential.

This chapter has shown that the CBA methods do not weigh factors. Chapter 17 shows that they also do not rate attributes. Then, chapter 18 compares CBA with the old standard (WRC) methods, which supposedly do weigh factors and rate attributes. The comparison demonstrates that the WRC methods are not only unsound; they are too complex, as well.

17

Sound Methods
Do Not Weigh Attributes

Choosing By Weighing Attributes—also called Choosing By Pros and Cons—is one of the many unsound methods in common use today. This method is a simplification of Choosing By Weighting-Rating-and-Calculating. When decisionmakers use this method, they sometimes state that, "All the factors have the same importance." Then, they simply assign numerical weights, or ratings, to the attributes. Following is an example of this method:

Choosing By Weighing Attributes

"Pros and Cons" (Attributes) of Canoe C		"Pros and Cons" (Attributes) of Canoe K	
Weighs 65 Pounds	70	Weighs 75 Pounds	30
Mod. Smooth Finish	75	Very Smooth Finish	90
Starry-Brown Color	30	Kelly-Blue Color	95
Excellent Stability	90	Very Good Stability	70
7/8–Inch Keel	50	5/8–Inch Keel	65
Total Importance:	315	Total Importance:	350

It is not only impossible to correctly assign numerical weights, ratings, or scores to factors; it is also impossible to correctly assign numerical weights, ratings, or scores to attributes. Therefore, the mistake in the Choosing By Attributes Method is not that *incorrect* weights are assigned to the attributes. The mistake is that weights—at all—are assigned to the attributes.

People realize that importance is a comparison concept, as shown by the following exchange: "How important is the 75 pound weight of K?" "Compared with what?" CBA takes us beyond this exchange. It recognizes that the concept of importance does not apply to attributes; it applies only to differences between attributes.

In the preceding example of Choosing By Attributes, the 65 pound weight supposedly has an importance of 70, and the 75 pound weight has an importance of 30. This inverse direction of change implies that there is a greater weight, greater than 75 pounds, that has an importance of zero. Obviously, however, there is not a canoe weight greater than 75 pounds that has an importance of zero. With this in mind, let's use the canoe weight preference curve to demonstrate why the concept of importance doesn't apply to attributes.

The Canoe Weight Preference Curve, Revisited

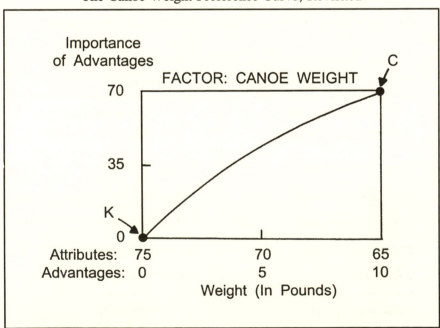

TRUE STATEMENTS VERSUS
FALSE STATEMENTS

To see why the concept of importance does not apply to attributes, although it does apply to advantages, carefully examine the following comparisons of true statements versus false statements. Again, the true statements are based on the preference curve.

True: The *non-advantage* of Canoe K has no importance.

False: The 75 pound *attribute* of Canoe K has an importance of zero.

True: The 5 pound *advantage* (= 75 - 70) has an importance of 45.

False: The 75 pound *attribute* has an importance of 45.

False: The 70 pound *attribute* has an importance of 45.

True: The 10 pound *advantage* (=75 - 65) has an importance of 70.

False: The 75 pound *attribute* has an importance of 70.

False: The 65 pound *attribute* has an importance of 70.

THE INSTINCTIVE METHOD, REVISITED

Methods that supposedly weigh attributes not only produce unsound decisions, they also produce conflicts. For example, suppose we asked two people the same question: "How important is an attribute of 70 pounds, in the canoe decision?"

The instinctive response, as you know, is to fill in data gaps with assumptions, and then to jump to a conclusion. In this case, one person might assume a corresponding attribute of 75 pounds, and would say that the 70 pound weight has an importance of 45. And that would be false. In reality, this person would be assigning an importance of 45 to an assumed 5 pound difference—specifically, the difference between 75 pounds and 70 pounds. The other person might assume a corresponding attribute of 65 pounds, and would say that the 70 pound weight has a negative importance of 25 (= 45 - 70). That, too, would be false.

Someone else might assume a corresponding attribute of zero, and would say that a weight of 70 pounds has a very large negative importance. That, also, would be false. It would be the 70 pound increase from zero to 70 that would have a large negative importance. Exactly the same 70 pound difference would have a large positive importance if viewed as a decrease from 70 pounds to zero.

In either case (positive or negative), it would be difficult, if not impossible, to judge the importance of the difference between the 70 pound attribute of a real canoe and the zero-pound attribute of an imaginary weightless canoe. Furthermore, we don't need to judge the importance of this difference. In a choice between two actual canoes, in the real world, this difference is irrelevant.

Without becoming aware of his or her assumption, each person trying to judge the importance of the 70 pound attribute would be assuming a second attribute, to form a pair of attributes. Because the assumed attribute would be specific, it would be a low-order assumption. Remember, decisions must be based on relevant facts, not on low-order assumptions. In cases where two persons make different assumptions, they each argue that the other person's rating is wrong; when in fact, they both are wrong. In cases where they both make the same assumption, they don't argue. Because they are in agreement, they are unable to discover that they both are wrong.

Some have incorrectly concluded from examples such as those given in this chapter that it is a mistake to use numbers to represent importance. But it is not the use of numbers that is wrong, it is their misuse that is wrong. The following chapter demonstrates how to transform Choosing By Weighting-Rating-and-Calculating to Choosing By Advantages. This will demonstrate the difference between misusing numbers versus correctly using numbers to disclose viewpoints about importance.

18

Sound Methods
Weigh Advantages

Question: How can we consistently make sound decisions?

Answer: Decisions must be anchored to the relevant facts.

Question: How can we anchor our decisions to the relevant facts?

Answer: *Decisions must be based on the importance of advantages.*

Question: How can we correctly base our decisions on the importance of advantages?

Answer: Different decisions call for different methods of Choosing By Advantages.

The three answers listed above are the principle of anchoring, the fundamental rule of sound decisionmaking, and the methods principle. When these three cornerstone principles converged, the CBA system was born. The event that brought about this convergence was the discovery of the fundamental rule—the topic of this chapter.

One of the best ways to review, relearn, and learn more about the fundamental rule is by walking through its history. We begin by outlining the evolution of the fundamental rule, from 1776 to the present. Then details are added by reviewing:

- The old standard

- The transition from the old standard to Choosing By Advantages

- Choosing By Advantages

THE OLD STANDARD

The diamonds/water paradox: Why are diamonds worth more than water? The traditional response: Due to the scarcity of diamonds and the abundance of water. Adam Smith's response: Due to value in exchange, versus value in use.

(Smith 1776)

TRANSITION FROM THE OLD STANDARD TO CHOOSING BY ADVANTAGES

No increase of expenditure over the unavoidable minimum is expedient or justifiable, however great the probable profits and value of the enterprise as a whole, unless the INCREASE can with reasonable certainty be counted on to be, in itself, a profitable investment.

(Wellington 1887)

It is prospective *differences* between alternatives which are relevant to their comparison.

(Grant 1938)

Decisions must be based on
the differences among alternatives.

(Bishop 1969)

Decisions must be based on the importance of
the differences among alternatives.

(Suhr and Bishop 1976)

CHOOSING BY ADVANTAGES

Decisions must be based on the importance of
advantages.

(Suhr 1981)

THE OLD STANDARD

Let's go back to 1776, to the publication of *The Wealth of Nations*—written by economist Adam Smith. *The Wealth of Nations* sharpened the world's understanding of economics. Smith gave an insightful (but incorrect) response to the following type of question: Why are diamonds, which are beautiful but not essential for survival, worth more than water, which is both beautiful and essential?

For centuries, philosophers, economists, and others have responded to this question by saying that diamonds *are* worth more than water, due to the scarcity of diamonds and the abundance of water. Smith responded by saying that water has a higher "value in use" but a diamond has a higher "value in exchange" (1986 [1776]: 131). Now, based on the principle of anchoring, how would you respond to the diamonds/water question: Why are diamonds worth more than water?

I hope you recognized, instantly, that this is an unanchored question, and that both the traditional response and Smith's response are unanchored judgments. Why? Because the words *diamonds* and *water* are high-order abstractions. What happened for centuries is that each person assumed specific meanings of these high-order abstraction words. At the same time, each assumed a specific purpose and a specific set of circumstances associated with the question. Then, each person answered his or her assumed question. Because most people made similar assumptions, they convinced one another that they had correctly responded to the question.

When we think carefully about the diamonds/water paradox, three things become obvious: First, diamonds, in general, are not worth more than water, in general. Anyone can easily think of many specific quantities and qualities of water and diamonds, in particular circumstances, where the water would be worth more than the diamonds. Second, water, in general, is not worth more than diamonds, in general. And third, they do not have the same worth. Again, the terms *diamonds* and *water* are high-order abstractions. Remember, concepts such as worth and importance do not apply to high-order abstractions.

In 1776, however, this principle wasn't widely known (perhaps, it wasn't known at all). At that time, responding to unanchored questions by making assumptions and jumping to conclusions was the standard method. Unfortunately, this same way to make decisions is built into what we call the old standard, or Weighting-Rating-and-Calculating (WRC). As stated earlier, some call the old standard methods "The" Rational Methods. But they are not truly rational. They make too many mistakes. In particular, many of the methods in common use today require activities such as those in the following outline:

The Central Activities of Weighting-Rating-and-Calculating (WRC)

---

1. Assign numerical WEIGHTS to the factors. (Some WRC methods assign weights to criteria or objectives—or to goals, categories, or other high-order abstractions. Typically, one of the factors that is assigned a numerical weight is cost.)

2. *Summarize the attributes of each alternative.* Then, in all the factors, assign numerical RATINGS to the alternatives or their attributes.

3. CALCULATE individual scores—one for each attribute of each alternative—by multiplying the weights times the ratings.

4. Choose the alternative with the greatest total of weights times ratings.

As shown in chapter 16, sound methods do not weigh factors. Therefore, the first activity in the WRC methods is a critical mistake. Also, as shown in chapter 17, sound methods do not rate attributes. Therefore, the second part of the second activity is also a critical mistake. The third activity multiplies mistakes times mistakes, and the fourth selects the alternative with the greatest total of mistakes times mistakes. (There are many variations of the WRC process—many WRC methods—with these same mistakes.)

How can we transform the WRC process from unsound to sound? Simply throw away and replace the entire WRC process—except for the following activity: *Summarize the attributes of each alternative.* For simple decisions, even this activity isn't required, in writing. But for complex decisions, it is essential; and it must be performed at the right time—for the right purpose—as in the Tabular Method. In WRC, the purpose is to provide data for rating the attributes. In CBA, the purpose is to provide data for deciding and weighing the advantages.

Now, let's use the above WRC method to choose between Canoe C and Canoe K. Then, let's compare the WRC results with the CBA results, from chapter 9. The WRC process will use the same viewpoint and the same objective data that were used in the CBA process. The result will be different, however, because the method will be different.

In their first activity, the WRC methods require weighing the factors. So, let's pretend to weigh the factors (we will actually be assigning weights to low-order assumptions).

An Example of Weighing Factors

FACTORS	WEIGHTS	RATIONALE
Canoe Weight	7	Canoe weight is very important, especially when making portages.
Stability	8	If a canoe isn't stable, it isn't safe. And safety is a very important factor.
Flotation	6	Although flotation and stability both affect safety, flotation is not quite as important as stability.
Finish	1	If a smoother finish is desired, the canoe can be sanded.
Color	10	The selected canoe will be stored, all year, where the stakeholders will be able to see it.
Keel Depth	1	Keel depth has very little importance. Any standard keel is acceptable.

The above factor weights might seem to be consistent with the weights that were assigned to the advantages, in the CBA example. And the statements of rationale for these weights might seem to make sense. But if you will closely examine these weights and rationale, you will discover that they make no sense at all. They were, in effect, pulled right out of the blue sky. They are not anchored to relevant facts.

What should be emphasized is that it is impossible to select factor weights that make sense. Factor weights are unanchored judgments. Names of factors are high-order abstractions; they do not have specific meanings. Therefore, factors do not have specific amounts of importance. Remember: Factors are not data, they are containers of data.

The mistakes in the WRC methods are not easy to see, and their number-mumbo-jumbo makes them very attractive, to some. Some have even computerized them. In fact, they have developed computer programs that are easy to use and produce colorful displays. Nevertheless, the WRC methods are not only too slow and too complex; they are unsound, as well. Therefore, methods that weigh factors and those that rate attributes should no longer be used. The following display is the result from Weighting-Rating-and-Calculating:

Choosing By Weighting-Rating-and-Calculating

FACTORS	FACTOR WEIGHTS	ALTERNATIVES			
		CANOE C		CANOE K	
CANOE WEIGHT Attributes:	7	65 Pounds		75 Pounds	
Ratings/Scores:		7	49	5	35
STABILITY Attributes:	8	Excellent		Very Good	
Ratings/Scores:		9	72	7	56
FLOTATION Attributes:	6	Very Good		Very Good	
Ratings/Scores:		8	48	8	48
FINISH Attributes:	1	Mod. Smooth		Very Smooth	
Ratings/Scores:		6	6	9	9
COLOR Attributes:	10	Starry-Brown		Kelly-Blue	
Ratings/Scores:		4	40	9	90
KEEL DEPTH Attributes:	1	7/8 Inches		5/8 Inches	
Ratings/Scores:		5	5	7	7
TOTAL SCORES:			220		245

This modern method is based on a very old concept of how to make decisions. Although this method probably didn't exist in Adam Smith's time, the concept did—as demonstrated by the diamonds/water question. Now, compare Weighting-Rating-and-Calculating, above, with Choosing By Advantages, which follows:

Choosing By Advantages

Advantages of Canoe C		Advantages of Canoe K	
• 10 Pounds Lighter	70	• Moderately Smoother Finish	5
• Slightly Greater Stability	75	• Much Nicer Color	100
		• Slightly Better Keel Depth	10
Total Importance:	<u>145</u>	Total Importance:	115
Both Alternatives Have the Same Total Cost.			

In what ways are these methods the same? And in what ways are they different?

As you can see, there are several similarities. For example, they both recognize that all decisions are subjective. If the decision is complex, both methods require disclosing—in writing—intensities of preferences, or weights. Another similarity (if the decision is complex) is that both methods divide the decision into factors. However, for typical day-to-day decisions, CBA does not require the step of writing down intensities of preferences and does not divide the decision into factors.

A difference that stands out, perhaps more than it should, is the difference in format. Obviously, the Two-List Format is much simpler than the WRC Format. This difference in complexity is a major advantage of the Two-List Method. But the Two-List Method can be used only for choosing from two alternatives at a time. The Tabular Method for choosing from several alternatives is only slightly less complex than the WRC Method. But the CBA methods for very simple decisions are enormously less complex than the WRC methods.

The most significant difference between these two methods is that, in many cases, they produce opposite decisions. Of course, in either method the decision can sometimes be changed, by simply changing the weights. In the WRC example, the choice could be changed—from K to C—by arbitrarily decreasing the factor-weight of color. In CBA, changes are not arbitrary, because the CBA displays help decisionmakers to see if decisions should be changed. But the WRC displays provide very little help, if any, because they display unanchored judgments.

As previously stated, the typical WRC methods require two unanchored judgments: First, they weigh factors; second, they rate attributes. Many have said that, at first, they didn't agree that weighing factors and rating attributes were mistakes. But others have said, "I knew that what they were telling us to do didn't make sense. I just wasn't able to explain why it didn't make sense."

One of the participants in a CBA workshop said that in every class he had taken in college he had received a grade of either an A or a B, except in one class. In that class, he received a C because he was unwilling to assign weights to factors. He told his instructor that weighing factors isn't logical. But instead of listening and learning, the instructor lowered the student's grade. After attending the CBA workshop, the student said that now he will be able to go back to his instructor and explain why weighing factors isn't logical.

TRANSITION FROM THE OLD STANDARD TO CHOOSING BY ADVANTAGES

An economist at the University of Utah said there is some evidence that the transition from the old concept of how to make decisions to the CBA concept was already taking place in France, in civil engineering, before 1776 (before Adam Smith published *The Wealth of Nations*). Whether that is true of not, a milestone in the transition was a seemingly complex statement made by a railroad economist named Arthur Wellington. In 1887, he said: "No increase of expenditure over the unavoidable minimum is expedient or justifiable, however great the probable profits and value of the enterprise as a whole, unless the INCREASE can with reasonable certainty be counted on to be, in itself, a profitable investment" (1887: 15).

In 1938, Eugene L. Grant, at Stanford University—building on Wellington's rule—emphasized the following, in *Principles of Engineering Economy:* "It is prospective *differences* between alternatives which are relevant to their comparison" (1938: iii).

In the fifth edition of *Principles of Engineering Economy,* Grant and Ireson restated the rule as follows: "It is only prospective *differences* among alternatives that are relevant in their comparison." They go on to say, "Over the years, many published formulas for the solution of problems in engineering economy have given dangerously misleading guidance to decision makers because the authors of the formulas have not recognized this concept" (1970: 227). Today, unfortunately, many authors and decisionmakers in all fields—not only in the field of engineering economy—have still not recognized this concept.

It seems to me that Grant and Ireson's rule describes how people naturally make decisions: They base decisions on *prospective differences* among alternatives. Apparently, however, they are usually unaware that they are basing decisions on differences. Therefore, what often happens is that they subconsciously base decisions on assumed differences, rather than consciously basing them on the best available measurements, or estimates, of actual differences. Because the assumed differences are low-order abstractions, they are called low-order assumptions.

In 1972, during a discussion I had with a group of engineers in the Forest Service about basing decisions on differences, one of them suggested that I get together with Bruce Bishop. He said, "You and Dr. Bishop seem to be on the same track." It turned out that getting together with Bishop, who is now the Dean of Engineering at Utah State University, was one of the best things that ever happened to the CBA system. In addition to his own participation in the development of CBA, Bishop selected Mac McKee, who was then a graduate student, as a research assistant for the CBA project. In addition to his many other contributions, McKee, with the participation of professors in various departments in the university, found ways to validate and explain many of the CBA principles and methods. McKee helped both in the design of CBA and in bringing it to life.

Another person whose contributions were vital at that time was Ross Carder, a research scientist in the Forest Service. Carder was the project leader of the Beaver Creek Project at Flagstaff, Arizona. A purpose of the Beaver Creek Project was to find better ways to make complex, controversial, resource management decisions. Without Carder's contributions, the CBA system couldn't have been developed. Carder and scientists from several universities who were involved in the Beaver Creek Project—both physical scientists and behavioral scientists—made many contributions to the CBA system.

Bishop and I truly were on the same track. While at Stanford University, Bishop wrote *Socio-Economic and Community Factors in Planning Urban Freeways*. This highway research report was selected by the U.S. Highway Research Board as the one with the greatest merit of all those that were written in the United States in 1969. In his report, Bishop elegantly restated Grant and Ireson's rule, as follows: "Decisions must be based on the differences among alternatives" (1969: 113). He also presented what he called factor profiles to clearly display the differences.

Bishop emphasized that all decisions are value-laden. That is, they depend on the viewpoints of people. Therefore, after determining the differences among the alternatives, the participants in the decisionmaking process must decide the relative importance of each difference.

In 1976 (unpublished), to emphasize that decisionmaking is subjective, we added three words to Bishop's rule, as follows: Decisions must be based on *the importance of* the differences among alternatives. Basically, this 1976 rule is sound; it would consistently produce sound methods, except for one thing: A particular difference between two alternatives can be viewed as positive (as an advantage of the one alternative) or as negative (as a disadvantage of the other). Therefore, this rule doesn't discourage the use of Choosing By Advantages *and* Disadvantages.

At least two of the decision methods that consider both advantages and disadvantages almost qualify as sound methods. One of them is similar to the Tabular Method. The other (Choosing By Advantages *Versus* Disadvantages) is similar to the Two-List Method:

Choosing By Advantages Versus Disadvantages

Advantages of Canoe K, Compared with Canoe C		Disadvantages of Canoe K, Compared with Canoe C	
• Moderately Smoother Finish	5	• 10 Pounds Heavier	90
• Much Nicer Color	100	• Slightly Less Stability	95
• Slightly Better Keel Depth	10		
Total Importance:	115	Total Importance:	185
Both Alternatives Have the Same Total Cost.			

On the surface, this method appears to be the same as the Two-List Method, and they are the same in a very important way: They both base decisions on the importance of the differences between the two alternatives. But, as you can see, they are not quite the same. What are the most significant differences between the Two-List Method and Choosing By Advantages Versus Disadvantages?

In actual decisionmaking situations, one of the differences between this method and the Two-List Method is that when some of the differences between two alternatives are labeled as disadvantages, many tend to magnify the importance of those particular differences. (In the example, the disadvantages incorrectly received scores of 90 and 95, instead of 70 and 75.) Another difference, in actual decisionmaking situations, is that those who haven't been taught the CBA vocabulary and methods very often include attributes in their displays, as if they were advantages and disadvantages. Also, double-counting is very common.

In response to the 1976 rule, we began developing a set of methods that based decisions on the importance of differences among alternatives. This set of methods was called TEP: A Tradeoff Evaluation Process. In pilot tests, these methods were quite successful. Adam Smith's response to the diamonds/water paradox, Wellington's rule, Grant's rule, the Grant and Ireson version of this same rule, Bishop's version, the 1976 version, and the TEP methods moved us closer and closer to the fundamental rule of sound decisionmaking. They paved the way for CBA.

CHOOSING BY ADVANTAGES

In 1981, while I was driving back to my office in Ogden, Utah, after a meeting in Provo, I found myself thinking about something I had noticed during the meeting: A difference between two alternatives had been listed as a disadvantage of one alternative, when it could have been listed as an advantage of another. I wondered, "How often does this happen?" A few months later, after we had challenged the idea in every way that we could, it became clear that a disadvantage of one alternative is an advantage of another. And there are no exceptions.

Think of what this discovery means. It means that when we have listed all the advantages of each alternative we have listed all the disadvantages— because advantages are disadvantages. To list them again would be double counting. And, as you saw before, that would be a critical mistake. Therefore, the rule was rewritten, once more (unpublished), as follows: *Decisions must be based on the importance of advantages.*

Now we know how to anchor decisions to the relevant facts: We must base decisions on the importance of advantages. This rule is simple; it is valid; it works. It truly is the fundamental rule of sound decisionmaking. Once this rule had been validated, the Tradeoff Evaluation Process was modified accordingly, and CBA came to life. The next challenge was to find out how to correctly include money in the decisionmaking process. In 1986, when that had been accomplished, the name of the process we were developing was changed from TEP to CBA.

One of the major advantages of using the CBA methods, compared with other methods, is that the CBA methods are positive, while others are both positive and negative. It should be pointed out, however, that CBA doesn't see the world through rose-colored glasses. It is realistically positive. It doesn't magnify the positives, and it doesn't leave out the negatives. Instead, it transforms the negatives into positives and includes them in the right way.

Because the CBA methods are positive, they are effective, not just sound. After deciding, and after reconsidering the decision, a CBA decisionmaker forms strong, sensory-rich, motivational perceptions of the advantages of the selected alternative. These positive perceptions substantially increase one's ability to successfully implement the decision. Because the CBA methods are sound, clear, simple, and positive, they produce wise choices: mental choices (decisions), emotional choices (motivations), and physical choices (actions and outcomes).

19

Arithmetic, Reading, Writing, and Choosing By Advantages

There are many close ties and parallels between arithmetic skills, reading and writing skills, and CBA skills. A very significant parallel is that all of these skills must be taught. People seldom, if ever, acquire them simply from experience.

ARITHMETIC

Suppose you gave a pencil and a sheet of paper to someone with at least an average level of arithmetic skill and asked that person to divide the number twelve by the number four. What would happen? Of course, she or he would give you the correct answer, immediately, without using the pencil and paper. Now, suppose you asked that same person to divide 1,363 by 29. In this case, she or he would probably use the following long-division process:

$$29 \overline{)1{,}363} \begin{array}{r} 47 \\ \hline \end{array}$$

$$
\begin{array}{r}
47 \\
29 \overline{)1{,}363} \\
116 \\
\hline
203 \\
203 \\
\hline
\end{array}
$$

Of course, many would use their pocket calculators, rather than performing the long-division process. Nevertheless, long division simplifies complex problems by displaying the data in writing and by dividing the process into bite-size steps. That is how CBA simplifies complex decisions. The CBA methods for difficult, complex decisions are like the methods for difficult, complex arithmetic: They always require writing. The CBA methods for simple decisions are like the methods for simple arithmetic: Sometimes they require writing, and sometimes not. Those for very simple decisions are like the methods for very simple arithmetic: They never require writing.

Although there are parallels between CBA and mathematics, CBA is not a mathematical process. Mathematics is more objective than CBA. For example, there is only one correct answer to an arithmetic question. When using the long-division process, you can go in a straight line, step-by-step, from the question to the answer. And if you do every step correctly, your first answer will be the correct answer. That is why arithmetic can be performed by a machine.

In contrast with arithmetic, decisionmaking is partly subjective, which is why, in the CBA process, we sometimes initially prepare a rough draft, rather than a final decision. Then, we reconsider the decision.

READING AND WRITING

Before writing was invented, people didn't know they didn't know how to read and write. Before CBA was invented, people didn't know they didn't know how to choose by advantages.

For complex decisions, the CBA process is like writing a book: We start with a rough draft and then make improvements. During Phase III, we put our initial thoughts on paper—where we can see them. Then, during Phase IV, we study them, discuss them, and revise them. For exceptionally complex or difficult decisions, several revisions are sometimes required.

When CBA is used correctly—especially for difficult, complex, controversial decisions—it is definitely not a straight forward, linear process. It is a turbulent, muddy, dynamic, searching–discovering, negotiating–bargaining, creative–decisionmaking process. *In many cases, even if you do every step of Phase III perfectly, your initial decision will not be a sound decision.* That is why CBA cannot be performed by a machine. It is also one of the reasons displaying the process in writing is so helpful. You can see what you wrote, study it, and make improvements.

Where is the line between decisions that require writing and those that do not? For most people, the canoe decision is near the line. In a laboratory situation, most of us can store, retrieve, and use in active memory—without the aid of a pencil and paper—about seven chunks of information at a time. But in a real-world decisionmaking situation, we can easily remember only about five chunks. (That is how many there are in the canoe decision—there are five advantages.) Someone who is highly skilled in using CBA can mentally weigh the two advantages of Canoe C against the three advantages of Canoe K without using a pencil and paper. But someone who is just learning CBA would need to display all five advantages in writing.

Obviously (especially in a complex, rapidly changing, modern society), reading and writing skills are essential in the decisionmaking process. Unfortunately, many decisionmakers do not have adequate reading and writing skills. On September 9, 1993, in *USA Today,* in an article titled "90 Million Can Barely Read, Write," Tamara Henry revealed that nearly 80 percent of American adults have inadequate reading and writing skills. The article was based on a Department of Education survey of more than 26,000 American adults, 16 and older, scientifically selected to represent the population as a whole. The survey found that:

- Nearly 50 percent—90 million at the time of the survey—are unable to handle text that should be non-challenging. For example, they are unable to find an error in a credit card bill and write a letter explaining it. Nearly 15 million in this group are illiterate—unable to complete the survey. The other 75 million can barely read and write.

- Those who are barely able to read and write don't know they don't know how to skillfully read and write. They said they are able to read and write "well" or "very well," the survey revealed.

- Nearly 80 percent—151 million—are unable to handle challenging text. Therefore, according to the survey, they have inadequate reading and writing skills.

Questionnaires, the bridge design experiment, observations of decisionmakers in action, and examinations of decision documents have all shown that considerably more than 80 percent of American adults have inadequate decisionmaking skills.

- Many people throughout the world use primitive methods of decisionmaking—methods that are severely inadequate in a complex, rapidly changing, modern society.

- Many others use modern methods that are too slow, too complex, or unsound.

- More than 80 percent of American adults don't know how to skillfully use sound methods, ***and they don't know they don't know.***

As I stated before, I am convinced that unsound decisions are more often methods-caused than people-caused. I believe, also, that expert decision-makers can make better decisions by simply using good intuition and well-informed, facts-based judgments, rather than by using the typical modern methods. Why? Because many of the modern methods that supposedly base decisions on facts do not.

CHOOSING BY ADVANTAGES

CBA doesn't replace using good intuition and good judgment. Instead, it enhances good intuition and good judgment. And it doesn't replace modern methods that are too slow, too complex, or unsound; it transforms them from unsound to sound.

As explained in chapter 6, simply perceiving the advantages of two alternatives and choosing the one that is preferred is called the Instant CBA Process. Because Instant CBA requires a higher level of skill than the Two-List Method, Mark Wilcox, president of The Brain Connection, suggested changing the name from "Instant CBA" to "Expert CBA." His suggestion reminds us that learning a valuable set of skills, such as CBA skills, requires both study and practice.

Using good intuition and good judgment requires an even higher level of skill than the level required by the Instant CBA Process. In CBA, intuitively using correct data is good intuition, and intuitively using data correctly is good judgment. Therefore, simply using good intuition and good judgment is the very best CBA method—for some types of decisions. But in many cases, when decisionmakers perceive that they are using good intuition and good judgment they are actually using the Instinctive Method. That is, they are making assumptions to fill in data gaps and jumping to conclusions. And, as chapter 15 describes, the Instinctive Method has been the root cause of many human conflicts and miseries.

Again, primitive methods might have been adequate in primitive societies. But they are severely inadequate for many of the decisions we face in a complex, rapidly changing, modern society. Nevertheless, they often produce better decisions than those produced by modern methods that are unsound. Obviously, major improvements in reading, writing, and decisionmaking skills are urgently needed. Decisionmakers need to select, learn, and skillfully use modern methods that are sound and simple. How can we improve the reading, writing, and decisionmaking skills of both children and adults?

The answer, of course, is education. The field of education needs CBA, and CBA needs the field of education. CBA will help educators make better decisions about what and how to teach, and it will help students make better decisions about what and how to learn—including better decisions about learning to read and write. By using and teaching CBA, educators will be able to improve reading, writing, and other skills of students in all levels of the educational system. Therefore, educators need to include CBA as a vital subject in an already crowded curriculum. But first they need to learn and use CBA themselves.

The Instinctive Method could be the number one barrier to including CBA in the curriculum. Most people are comfortable with the Instinctive Method—with basing decisions on low-order assumptions. Therefore, they use the Instinctive Method to decide how to make decisions. And when they make assumptions about CBA, their assumptions are usually false.

False Assumption: Choosing By Advantages Is a Tool

The assumption that CBA is a tool produces methods of teaching and learning that are unsuccessful when applied to CBA. Think about teaching the Two-List Method, for example. It doesn't work to just show someone the activities and tasks of the Two-List Method, as if they were learning how to use a tool. Before individuals or groups can skillfully use the Two-List Method, they need to be skillfully and automatically using the CBA patterns of thought and speech. When CBA is taught to others, the CBA definitions, principles, and models must be included—not just the mechanics of the methods.

For example, those who want to skillfully use the Two-List Method will need to study most of the chapters in this book. They need to understand such things as the fundamental rule of sound decisionmaking and the principle of anchoring; they need to understand why decisions must be based on the relationships between attributes, advantages, and importance of advantages, not on factor weights; and they need to know when to not use the Two-List Method.

False Assumption: Choosing By Advantages Is Too Complex

CBA can seem very complex, at first, while it is still unfamiliar. Nevertheless, as you know, side-by-side comparisons with several methods that are commonly used today show that the CBA methods are simpler and faster.

- As demonstrated in chapter 5, Choosing By Advantages is much simpler than Choosing By Advantages and Disadvantages.

- As shown in chapter 18, CBA is also much simpler than Choosing by Weighting-Rating-and-Calculating—especially for very simple decisions.

- Instant CBA and the Instinctive Method both require the same number of tasks. And neither requires writing. But when used by expert decisionmakers, Instant CBA is faster, because it quickly clarifies the situation.

False Assumption: CBA Is Only for Major Decisions

Virtually all decisions, not only major ones, call for CBA. About two-thirds of America's economic activity is in the household sector, and much of that activity is in response to decisions that are not major decisions. But they are important decisions, and they call for sound methods. Collectively, our small decisions could be our most important decisions.

False Assumption: CBA Is Too Slow

While people are learning how to use the CBA process, it is definitely slower than the Instinctive Method. This causes some to assume that CBA is too slow. But in fact, whenever CBA is taking too long, it is not being used correctly.

False Assumption: Choosing By Advantages Is Confusing

This assumption reminds me of a conversation I listened to between a university professor and the leader of a small work group in an organization. The group leader had asked the professor for information about CBA. After a lengthy discussion, the leader said, "I can see that what we are doing is wrong. But we just recently taught our group members to use what you call Weighting-Rating-and-Calculating. If we changed, they would become confused." After the meeting, as we walked toward the professor's car, he said, "I guess he thinks it's better to be wrong than confused."

It is true that there is a short-term price to pay when individuals or groups change to CBA. At first, it can cause confusion. But in the long run, CBA simplifies, clarifies, and unifies. It simplifies the decision, clarifies the decisionmaking process, and unifies those who participate in the process. And it feels so good—so very good—when you know that you are using sound methods of decisionmaking.

Part IV

The Methods Principle

The pivotal cornerstone principle (presented in part I) and the methods principle (presented in part IV) go hand-in-hand. The pivotal cornerstone principle is what stimulated the evolution of decisionmaking methodology from primitive decisionmaking to Choosing By Advantages. The evolution of decisionmaking methodology is what brought to light the methods principle. Following are the first and fourth cornerstone principles, side by side. Principle No. 4, the methods principle, is the focus of part IV.

- Principle No. 1: Decisionmakers Must Learn and Skillfully Use Sound Methods.

- Principle No. 4: *Different Types of Decisions Call for Different Sound Methods.*

Chapters 20 and 21 detail the need for using sound methods. Chapters 22 through 26 present a family of sound methods. Chapter 22 presents the Tabular Method for more than two alternatives. Chapter 23 presents special methods for complex decisions—including the Prior Anchoring Method, which is for choosing from contract proposals and for similar decisions. (The Prior Anchoring Method uses preference charts and curves to anchor decisions about importance to the relevant facts.) Chapter 24 provides the basic sound-decisionmaking concepts and methods for money decisionmaking. To set the stage, it reviews the evolution of money-decisionmaking methodology. Chapters 25 and 26 present simple methods for simple decisions and very simple methods for very simple decisions.

THE PIVOTAL CORNERSTONE PRINCIPLE, REVISITED: DECISIONS DO MATTER

Choosing By Advantages was developed in response to three vital questions. By presenting a model called the sound-decisionmaking model, chapter 20 responds to the first two: "How can we consistently make sound decisions?" and "How can we clearly show that our decisions are sound?" You know the answer: Decisions must be anchored to the relevant facts, and this requires basing decisions on the importance of advantages. The sound-decisionmaking model will help you explain this requirement. Chapter 21 responds to the third question: "How can we simplify sound decisionmaking?" Chapters 22 through 26 respond to all three questions by presenting a family of sound methods.

A few people (fortunately, very few) argue that we do not have free will, or free agency, or that decisions do not matter. Some say that decisionmaking is just an illusion. They argue that human performance is entirely the product of only two factors: nature, and nurture. Following are comparisons between nature/nurture concepts and CBA concepts.

Concepts Pertaining to the Importance of Making Sound Decisions

Nature/Nurture Concepts	CBA Concepts
The quality of our lives depends on what happens to us.	The quality of our lives depends on the quality of our decisions.
The future course of events is predetermined. Decisionmaking is just an illusion.	We are shaping our future by our mental, emotional, and physical choices.
Human performance is the result of nature and nurture.	Human performance is the result of nature, nurture, and choice.
	Human performance is a decisionmaking process.

DECISIONMAKING METHODS, ALSO, DO MATTER

Although few people say that *decisions* do not matter, many say that *decision methods* do not matter. "Therefore," they say, "there is no need for decisionmaking training." Following are comparisons between traditional concepts, apparently believed by many, and CBA concepts.

Concepts Pertaining to the Importance of Using Sound Methods

Traditional Concepts	CBA Concepts
Methods of decisionmaking don't really matter. "Just use whatever works for you."	To consistently make sound decisions, decisionmakers must learn and skillfully use sound methods.
There are dozens of methods, and "on average they will all produce the same results."	There are very few sound methods, and different methods will often produce different results.
Unsound decisions are usually people-caused.	Unsound decisions are usually methods-caused.
Sound decisionmaking is like crawling and walking, and talking. It is a skill that is naturally acquired.	Sound decisionmaking is like reading and writing, and mathematics. It is a set of skills that are not naturally acquired.
The purpose of the educational system is to provide essential KSAs: Knowledge, Skills, and Attitudes. The system emphasizes such skills as reading, writing, mathematics, and computer literacy. But sound decisionmaking skills are seldom emphasized.	The purpose of the educational system is to improve the quality of human choices, to improve the quality of life. Therefore, in addition to reading, writing, and other skills that are vital in a modern society, sound decisionmaking skills must also be emphasized.
	Parents, educators, and leaders in organizations need to be teaching how to make decisions, instead of just telling what decisions to make.

Somewhat surprising, to me, is that of all the CBA concepts, the concept that methods do matter has been one of the most controversial. Some say that methods are unnecessary. One person said, emphatically, "I *don't* use *methods* of decisionmaking."

Now, before presenting the family of sound methods, let's look at details of how to consistently make sound decisions, how to clearly show that our decisions are sound, and how to simplify sound decisionmaking.

20

How Can We Consistently Make Sound Decisions?

To consistently make sound decisions, decisionmakers must learn and skillfully use methods of decisionmaking that anchor subjective data to objective data—that anchor viewpoints to relevant facts.

There is no such thing as a totally objective decision, and there never will be. Furthermore, there is no such thing as a totally objective method of decisionmaking, and there never will be. If a totally objective method could exist, which is an impossibility, it would be an unsound method. Subjective soundness is just as important as objective soundness. Methods that qualify as sound methods are both objectively sound and subjectively sound. Remember: The CBA methods are sound, not merely objective. They anchor the subjective data to the objective data.

To show that sound methods of decisionmaking are both objectively sound and subjectively sound, this chapter progressively constructs a model of the decisionmaking process, called the sound-decisionmaking model. This CBA model is so useful in explaining the decisionmaking process that expert CBA facilitators and instructors are able to construct it and explain it, entirely from memory.

To construct the sound-decisionmaking model, a good way to begin is by modifying the cause-effect model that was presented in chapter 1, and again in chapter 15. Details are added until the sound-decisionmaking model is completed, as shown at the end of this chapter. Following is the cause-effect model:

Methods ⟶ Decisions ⟶ Actions ⟶ Outcomes

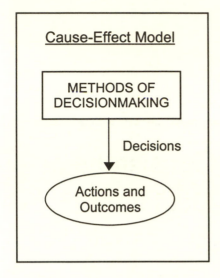

As shown by this version of the model, our outcomes are caused, in large measure, by our methods of decisionmaking. Therefore, we can improve our outcomes by improving our methods.

Of course, every link in the chain must carry the full load. Our *methods* produce our decisions. Our *decisions* guide our actions. And our *actions* produce our *outcomes.*

The next model adds data, sources of data, and feedback to the cause-effect model. Shown with the model are three requirements for sound decisionmaking.

First, decisionmakers must use correct data. Second, they must use data correctly; that is, they must use sound methods. And third, they must be responsive to feedback. By including feedback, the model shows that decisionmaking is a continuous, dynamic process. Typically, the implementation of one decision creates the need for another.

Three Requirements for Sound Decisionmaking

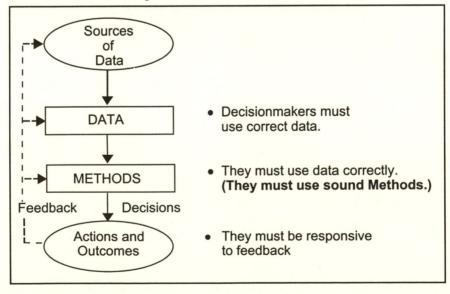

TWO PRIMARY SOURCES OF DATA

The diagram that follows shows that all methods of decisionmaking, both sound and unsound, use data from two primary sources: the objective universe and the subjective person, or persons, whose viewpoints the decision will be based on. Items of data that pertain to the objective universe are labeled as *facts,* or as objective data. Items that pertain to preferences and those that pertain to intensities of preferences are labeled as *viewpoints,* or as subjective data. (When you are teaching CBA, this model will help you explain the difference between objective and subjective data.)

The left-hand side of the model represents the objective side of the decisionmaking process. The right-hand side of the model represents the subjective side of the process. To continuously make sound decisions, there must be feedback to both sides.

Due to our *mental filters,* no items of data—objective or subjective—are totally accurate. What happens is that we filter new data through old perceptions and old models. In extreme cases of unsound decisionmaking, the filters, not the valid primary sources, provide the data. That is why the Instinctive Method so very often produces unsound decisions. Remember, it is usually the method, not the person, that is the cause of an unsound decision.

The Two Primary Sources of Data

THE THREE TYPES OF DATA, REVISITED

Before we continue constructing the sound-decisionmaking model, let's review what has been constructed, so far. The left-hand side of the model shows the use of objective data. The right-hand side shows the use of subjective data. Both types are filtered, in our minds, through our memories of past experience and our models that explain past experience. Filtering is natural, and it is essential, but it does cause distortions of facts and it does cause distortions of viewpoints. One of our challenges, as decisionmakers, is to minimize these distortions.

In addition to objective data, the left-hand side of the model also includes a third type of data—subjectively colored data. The three types of data are illustrated by the following questions and answers, which were first presented in chapter 4:

Objective Data (Facts)

    Q. What is the color of Canoe C?

    A. Starry-brown.

Subjective Data (Viewpoints)

    Q. Which do you prefer, the color of Canoe C (starry-brown) or the color of Canoe K (kelly-blue)?

    A. I strongly prefer the kelly-blue color.

Subjectively Colored Data (Subjectively Colored Facts)

    Q. How stable is Canoe C? (This is an objective question.)

    A. Canoe C has excellent stability. (This is a subjectively colored response.)

TWO TYPES OF DECISIONS

The next addition to the model shows that our methods of decision-making produce two types of decisions: criteria and action decisions. *Criteria* are decisions that guide further decisionmaking. *Action decisions* are decisions that steer the course of action. Everyone produces a continuous flow of action decisions all day, every day. Individually, action decisions are usually not very important. Collectively, however, they are extremely important. Therefore, action decisionmaking—not only criteria decisionmaking—calls for the continuous use of sound methods.

Criteria Versus Action Decisions

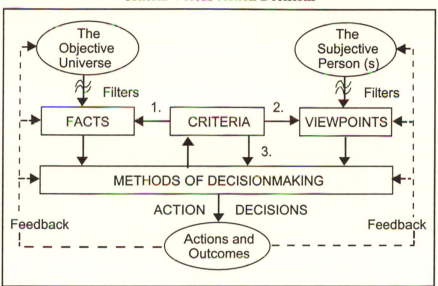

The model shows three types of criteria:

1. Those that guide the selection and organization of objective data

2. Those that guide the selection and organization of subjective data

3. Those that directly guide further decisionmaking

Examples of criteria include laws, regulations, policies, guidelines, and preferences. Additional examples include long-range plans, mid-range plans, short-range plans, and very short-range plans (which guide action decisionmaking). Because beliefs can strongly influence decisionmaking, they too are criteria. They range from opinions, which are lightly-held beliefs, to values, which are deeply-held beliefs. Between these extremes are attitudes.

The next addition to the model shows that facts are data pertaining to what is objectively true versus false. Viewpoints are data pertaining to what is subjectively good versus bad. Criteria are decisions, based on facts and viewpoints, about what is right versus wrong. Many criteria come from outside sources. For example, both secular laws and religious commandments are typically from outside sources, such as scriptures. Following are examples of criteria from outside sources:

- Do unto others as you would have them do unto you.

- Do unto others as they would have you do unto them. (This criterion was presented in a Total Quality Management workshop.)

A ***Descriptive*** Model of the Decisionmaking Process

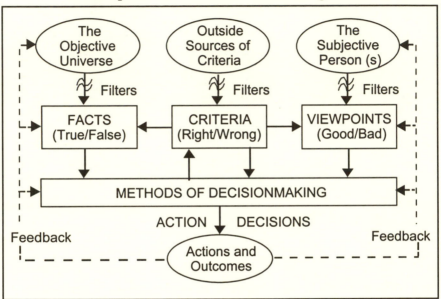

Values are not shown explicitly in the model, but they are implicitly included. And they are very significant. In the CBA vocabulary, *values* are defined as deeply-held beliefs about what is true versus false, good versus bad, and right versus wrong—especially right versus wrong. As everyone knows, values strongly influence people when they make decisions, including decisions about how to make decisions. For example, those who strongly value power are likely to base their decisions on power, rather than using sound methods. Therefore, one of the major goals in the CBA training process is to establish the high value of using sound methods.

THE SOUND-DECISIONMAKING MODEL

By adding a qualifying word in each of the four boxes, the model is transformed from descriptive to prescriptive. The preceding model *describes* how people naturally make decisions. The sound-decisionmaking model *prescribes* how to make sound decisions.

The Sound-Decisionmaking Model
A *Prescriptive* Model of the Decisionmaking Process

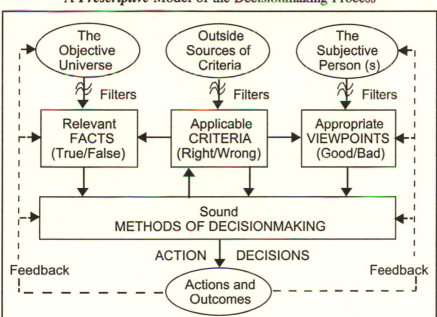

The four boxes represent the four essentials for producing sound decisions. The first three—which represent criteria, facts, and viewpoints—are like the ingredients of a cake. In the same way that a cake must have correct ingredients, a decision must be based on correct data. The CBA recipe calls for

- the applicable criteria,

- the relevant facts, and

- the appropriate viewpoints.

The fourth box represents combining and using the criteria, the facts, and the viewpoints to make a decision. This is like mixing and baking a cake. Improper mixing and baking can produce a wide variety of bad outcomes, ranging from a ball of dough to a pile of ashes. But proper mixing and baking of the correct ingredients will nearly always produce an excellent cake.

The completed sound-decisionmaking model, shown on page 181, reminds us that *using correct data* (represented by the three small boxes), *using data correctly* (represented by the one large box), and *responding to feedback* (represented by the dashed lines) will nearly always produce excellent decisions. The large box reminds us of the pivotal cornerstone principle: To consistently make sound decisions, decisionmakers must learn and skillfully use sound methods of decisionmaking.

The model emphasizes feedback. Without feedback, actions and outcomes would be final products, at the end of the process. But when feedback is emphasized, actions and outcomes are placed at the beginning, in the middle, and at the end. At the beginning, our actions change both the objective universe and the subjective person or persons whose viewpoints guide the process. In the middle, they change the criteria, the facts, and the viewpoints. And sometimes, they change the way decisions are made. At the end, each outcome is a new beginning.

The completed model provides vital details about how to make sound decisions. It shows that sound decisionmaking moves back and forth between the objective and subjective sides of the process and that the key words for remembering the central activities of the sound-decisionmaking process are: *attributes, advantages, importance,* and *total importance.* (Selecting the *least-preferred attributes* is a key task in the second central activity.)

HOW CAN WE CLEARLY SHOW THAT
OUR DECISIONS ARE SOUND?

In a request for a CBA facilitator, for a meeting about an important decision, the person who made the request said, "We evaluated seven alternatives, and we selected the fourth as the preferred alternative." So I asked, "If you have already selected the preferred alternative, why do you need CBA?" And he said, "To show that we made the right decision."

Sometimes, CBA displays are correctly used simply to explain the rationale for a decision. But in this case, it turned out that the fourth alternative was not the preferred alternative. Therefore, in this case, displaying the rationale helped the decisionmaking team to correct their decision, in addition to showing that the corrected decision was a sound decision. In many cases, especially for simple decisions, a skilled CBA decisionmaker can easily select the best alternative without displaying the rationale, but cannot easily explain why the best alternative is the best alternative without displaying the rationale.

So, use CBA not only to make sound decisions, but also to clearly show that your decisions are sound. For example, CBA provides a way for parents to respond when their children ask, "Why?" or, "Why not?"

The Sound-Decisionmaking Model

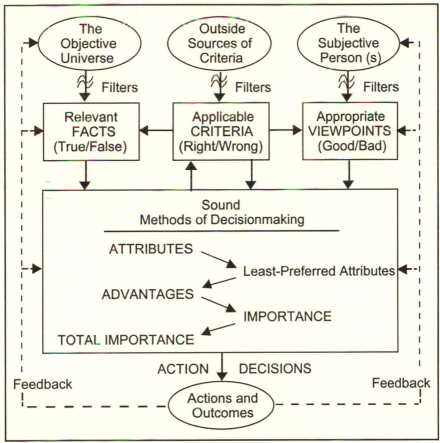

CBA uses three tools to show that a decision is sound: education, participation, and documentation. First, to show others that you have made a sound decision, they will need to understand the *process* that produced the decision. Therefore, you will need to teach them at least the basic CBA concepts (definitions, principles, and models) and the basic CBA methods. And in some cases, you will need to teach them additional CBA concepts and methods—those pertaining to the particular decision.

Second, they will need to understand the *content* of the decision—the data that produced the decision. The most effective tool for learning the content is participation. Compared with those who don't participate in making a decision, those who do participate are far more likely to understand and accept the decision's rationale (if they have been taught the CBA process).

The third tool for explaining the decision's rationale is documentation. To document the decision, accurately use the applicable format—usually either the Two-List Format or the Tabular Format. For clarity, use each format precisely. For example, use solid lines where the format calls for solid lines, and use dashed lines where it calls for dashed lines. Use the CBA formats to guide you through the process, as well as to disclose the rationale for the decision. Also, use supplemental documentation, if necessary, to fully disclose the rationale.

Each of the three tools—education, participation, and documentation—is a double-edged sword. After you teach the CBA concepts and methods to others, they will expect you to skillfully, and consistently, use CBA. And it's the same when they participate, or when they study your documentation. They will be able to recognize when you haven't used CBA, or when you haven't used it correctly. So, always use CBA, correctly.

21

How Can We Simplify Sound Decisionmaking?

We must simplify decisionmaking. At the same time, we must make sound decisions. How can we do both?

CBA SIMPLIFIES THE ART OF DECISIONMAKING

Before CBA was developed, decisionmakers faced, as their only option, *a disjointed collection of methods*—sound and unsound—each with its own philosophy, its own vocabulary, and its own models of the decisionmaking process. Taken together, the methods in common use today are incomprehensible and unworkable. In contrast, CBA is a decisionmaking *system*. It includes a variety of tools, techniques, and methods—unified by just one set of definitions, principles, and models. It is much simpler to learn and use the CBA system than it is to learn and use the disjointed collection of methods that CBA will replace. Because CBA is not just a method and not just a collection of methods, it simplifies the art of decisionmaking.

The relationship between the CBA system and an individual CBA method is similar to the relationship between the United States of America and an individual state. In the same way that the United States is not an individual state, CBA is not an individual method. And in the same way that the United States is one nation, CBA is one system.

Choosing CBA doesn't need to be an all-or-nothing decision. Now that you are familiar with the basic CBA definitions, principles, and models, choose only those CBA methods that you will need for your decisions.

Chapters 22 through 26 provide a variety of methods for you to choose from. Of course, you could decide not to use the CBA methods, at all. But I hope you will decide to use them for virtually all your decisions.

The art of decisionmaking is a broad field of study, too broad to be studied all at once. So that one area can be studied at a time, the CBA system organizes the art of decisionmaking into three overlapping areas, as follows:

- *Sound decisionmaking* (making decisions that are anchored to the relevant facts) is the foundation of the CBA system. (This is where the CBA training process begins, and it is the topic of this book.)

- *Congruent decisionmaking* (making sound decisions that have unity, harmony, and integrity—in addition to accomplishing, on schedule, the highest-priority activities, projects, and programs of an individual or an organization) is the foundation and framework.

- *Effective decisionmaking* (making sound, congruent decisions that are willingly, or grudgingly, accepted and implemented) is the total CBA system.

The CBA System

EFFECTIVE
Decisionmaking

The Total
CBA System

CONGRUENT
Decisionmaking

The Foundation
and the Framework

SOUND
Decisionmaking

The Foundation
of the CBA System

Source: U.S. Forest Service

In 1970, after several of the congruent-decisionmaking methods had been developed, validated, and organized into a system, I began adding new methods to the system. It soon became obvious that the total system was becoming too complex, so I struggled with the question of how to simplify. One of the answers came to me while my wife and I were walking through the women's fashion area in a department store in Ann Arbor, Michigan. I noticed a sign that advertised *"coordinated separates."* That led to changing the goal from developing a fully-integrated system to developing a set of simple, coordinated but separate components. Due to this change, you and others will be able to learn and adopt one component of the CBA system at a time.

However, it is best, if not essential, to learn the components in sequence. For example, the CBA methods that you will probably use most often are the very simple CBA methods for very simple decisions. My guess is that expert CBA decisionmakers use these methods for at least 90 to 95 percent of their decisions. Except for the Recognition–Response Process, which was introduced in chapter 6, the very simple CBA methods are not presented until chapter 26, the final chapter of this book. So, why are these methods not presented until chapter 26?

In many cases, the simplest of all the decisions that people make, those that call for the very simple CBA methods, require the highest level of skill. Why? Because our very simple, day-to-day and minute-to-minute decisions happen so rapidly—one after another. Only those who practice and become skilled in using the other CBA methods will be able to use the very simple CBA methods, instead of the Instinctive Method, for their very simple decisions.

Like the other chapters in this book, chapter 26 builds on many of the concepts and methods that are presented in earlier chapters. Therefore, to be fully successful in learning and using the very simple CBA methods, decisionmakers must first learn and *practice* the definitions, principles, models, and methods presented in the first twenty-five chapters.

This section has shown that Choosing By Advantages is a decision-making *system,* and that CBA simplifies the art of decisionmaking by organizing it into three overlapping areas. The following section shows that CBA is also a decisionmaking *process,* and that for complex decisions CBA simplifies decisionmaking by dividing the process into five phases. The methods in this book are used, primarily, in Phase III: the decisionmaking phase.

CBA SIMPLIFIES THE DECISIONMAKING PROCESS

In laboratory demonstrations, most people can memorize (store, recall later, and use in active memory) about seven chunks of information at a time. But in real-world decisionmaking situations, the number is only about five. Therefore, the entire CBA process is divided into only five chunks, or phases, so the entire process can easily be memorized.

Within each large chunk of information, most people can easily memorize about five smaller chunks at a time. Therefore, each phase of the CBA process is divided, as necessary, into no more than five major activities. And each activity is further divided, as necessary, into bite-size tasks and steps. In the model that follows, the five phases of the CBA process are superimposed on the three areas of the CBA system. As stated earlier, the five phases are:

Phase I: The Stage-Setting Phase

Phase II: The Innovation Phase

Phase III: The Decisionmaking Phase (the topic of this book)

Phase IV: The Reconsideration Phase

Phase V: The Implementation Phase

The CBA System and the CBA Process

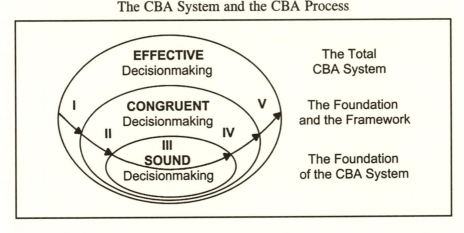

The CBA training process begins in the sound-decisionmaking area of the system, where it emphasizes the decisionmaking phase of the process. Congruent-decisionmaking training emphasizes Phases II and IV (it also emphasizes some aspects of Phase V). Effective-decisionmaking training emphasizes Phases I and V. Learning the entire CBA system and process is like climbing higher and higher on a mountain slope. The training process begins at the bottom and climbs to the first level—sound decisionmaking. This level provides an excellent, partial view of the art of decisionmaking. As one climbs to congruent decisionmaking and then to effective decisionmaking (which I hope will be the topics of future books) more and more of the art of decisionmaking comes into view.

The CBA System, the CBA Process, and the CBA Training Process

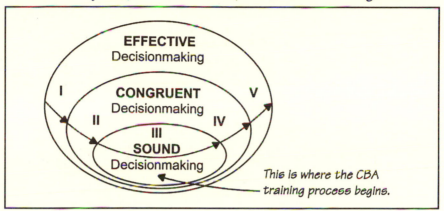

The first area in the training process (sound decisionmaking) is, in itself, a broad field of study, too broad to be studied all at the same time. Nevertheless, this book covers much of this first area. Therefore, once you have studied and practiced the definitions, principles, models, and methods presented in this book, you will be able to use the sound-decisionmaking methods in a wide variety of your decisionmaking situations to quickly—in most cases, instantly—make sound decisions.

In review: For complex decisions *(but not for simple decisions)*, CBA divides the decisionmaking phase of the process into four major activities:

1. Summarize the *attributes* of each alternative.

2. Decide the *advantages* of each alternative.

3. Decide the *importance* of each advantage.

4. If the costs of the alternatives are equal, choose the one with the greatest *total importance* of advantages.

The chart on the following page shows that most CBA methods do not require all four of these activities, and that some of the required activities are not displayed in writing (the key words in parentheses represent activities that do not require writing). As shown, the CBA system includes:

- Special methods for complex and very complex decisions

- Special methods for money decisions

- Simple methods for simple decisions

- Very simple methods for very simple decisions

Methods in the Sound-Decisionmaking Area of the CBA System

SPECIAL METHODS FOR COMPLEX AND VERY COMPLEX DECISIONS	SIMPLE METHODS FOR SIMPLE DECISIONS					VERY SIMPLE METHODS FOR VERY SIMPLE DECISIONS
	The Tabular Method	**The Two-List Method**	Simplified Tabular Method	Simplified Two-List Method	Instant CBA	
Attributes	Attributes	—	Attributes	—	—	
Advantages	Advantages	**Advantages**	(Advantages)	Advantages	(Advantages)	
Importance	Importance	**Importance**	—	—	—	
	Total Importance	**Total Importance**	(Total Importance)	(Total Importance)	(Total Importance)	
SPECIAL METHODS FOR MONEY DECISIONS						

Source: U.S. Forest Service

As in this chart, the Two-List Method is near the middle-level of complexity in the CBA system. Moving toward the left and then toward the right from the Two-List Method:

- CBA simplifies complex decisions by taking smaller steps.
- CBA simplifies simple decisions by taking fewer steps.
- CBA simplifies all decisions by using correct data, and by using data correctly.

CBA can do only its part in simplifying sound decisionmaking. Decisionmakers must do the rest. To simplify sound decisionmaking,

LEARN: Learn the sound-decisionmaking concepts and methods, one set at time.

UNLEARN: Learn to not use unsound methods—including those that weigh the advantages and disadvantages of each alternative and those that weigh factors, goals, roles, objectives, categories, criteria, or attributes. To "unlearn" unsound methods, transform them from unsound to sound.

RELEARN: No one can *simplify* sound decisionmaking without *understanding* sound decisionmaking. And understanding usually requires relearning. For example, to understand the Two-List Method, you might need to relearn this method, several times.

PRACTICE: *The more you practice the CBA methods, the simpler they will become.* Practice the CBA vocabulary and methods until you can use them almost without thinking about them. Then, you will be able to focus on the *content* of your decisions, instead of the *process*.

TEACH: By teaching CBA, you will not only be providing a service to others, you will also be strengthening you own understanding of the CBA process.

When teaching CBA, remember that it is important for you to *not* use complex or critical real-world examples too soon in the training process. At first, the participants need to focus their attention on the decisionmaking *process,* not on the *content,* of a particular decision. That is, they need to focus on the CBA definitions, principles, models, and methods.

Initially, we thought we should be using relevant, real-world examples early in the training process; so that is what we did, several times, and the results were disappointing. Due to their lack of CBA skills, the participants were too often unhappy with their decisions. And, because they were focusing on their decisions, they didn't adequately learn the process. To make matters worse, they formed habits that had to be unformed later. This is why, especially for complex, difficult, or controversial decisions, the rule is: *First, learn CBA; then, use CBA.* This rule should not be surprising. There are numerous situations where learning-while-doing is not a good way to begin learning:

- You would never allow a prospective surgeon to begin learning surgery by performing a delicate operation on your brain.

- You would never ask a prospective engineer to design a new airplane while learning the basic principles and methods of engineering.

- You wouldn't even consider learning how to drive an automobile by competing in a stock-car race.

Ideally, we would never ask someone to make an important decision until after she or he has acquired the necessary sound-decisionmaking skills. When we need vital skills—such as CBA skills—we should expect to learn them, and practice them, before using them in critical real-world situations. Therefore, when you practice the CBA methods, start with simple, hypothetical decisions or with real-world decisions that don't matter. Also, start with the simple methods for simple decisions and the special methods for complex decisions, rather than starting with the very simple methods for very simple decisions. The methods for simple and complex decisions base decisions *explicitly* on the importance of advantages. The very simple methods for very simple decisions base decisions *implicitly* on the importance of advantages. Therefore, the very simple methods require the highest level of skill.

CBA ADDS SELECTION TO THE CREATIVE PROCESS

The previous section described CBA as a five-phase decisionmaking process. This same process can be viewed as a seven-stage creative process. We are creating our future by the choices we are making, day-by-day and minute-by-minute.

Choosing By Advantages

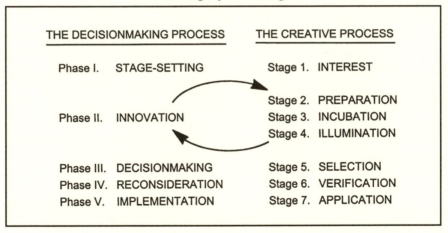

THE DECISIONMAKING PROCESS	THE CREATIVE PROCESS
Phase I. STAGE-SETTING	Stage 1. INTEREST
	Stage 2. PREPARATION
Phase II. INNOVATION	Stage 3. INCUBATION
	Stage 4. ILLUMINATION
Phase III. DECISIONMAKING	Stage 5. SELECTION
Phase IV. RECONSIDERATION	Stage 6. VERIFICATION
Phase V. IMPLEMENTATION	Stage 7. APPLICATION

Many years ago, a researcher named Graham Wallis (some say it was Henri Poincaré) identified *preparation, incubation, illumination,* and *verification* as the four stages of the creative process. Ned Herrmann added *interest* and *application* (1988: 191). Without interest, the preparation stage wouldn't happen. And without application, the creative process wouldn't be complete.

In the innovation phase, CBA repeats the preparation, incubation, and illumination stages, as many times as necessary, to create a full range of alternatives. Of course, after creating a set of alternatives, it becomes necessary to select one of them. Therefore, CBA adds *selection* to the creative process, as stage five. CBA recognizes that creativity is a vital part of the sound-decisionmaking process, and that sound decisionmaking is a vital part of the creative process.

Congruent-decisionmaking training emphasizes the innovation phase of the CBA process. We have all experienced the three stages of the innovation phase. Sometimes we struggle for hours, or days, or years, trying to formulate a concept, design a course of action, or answer a question. That is the preparation stage. In the next stage, we sleep-on-it, go to a concert, or just take a break. But our subconscious doesn't take a break. It keeps looking for an answer. That is the incubation stage. Finally, while we are taking a shower, or a walk—or watching the stars—the answer comes to the surface of the mind. And that is the illumination stage.

Too many people stop right there. But in the CBA process we ask ourselves, as many times as necessary, "What other possibilities can we create?" And we keep reminding ourselves, "Don't fall in love with your first idea." To find a full range of possibilities, sometimes it is necessary to repeat the preparation-incubation-illumination process many times (this is how the CBA system was created). Keep in mind the following congruent-decisionmaking principle: We can never select the best alternative if we never formulate the best alternative.

CBA can be viewed as a problem-solving process. However, it is more accurate to view it as a creative decisionmaking process. The difference is that in typical problem-solving methods, people look into the past to discover how they did things wrong. In CBA they look into the future to decide how to do things right. Nevertheless, problem solving—identifying a problem and finding its root cause—is sometimes a necessary activity in the CBA process. And very often, the root cause turns out to be the use of an unsound method of decisionmaking. Human performance is a cause-effect chain, which tells us, again, that methods do matter:

Methods ⟶ Decisions ⟶ Actions ⟶ Outcomes

So, as soon as you are reasonably comfortable with the CBA concepts and methods that you have learned, so far, learn and practice those that are presented in the following chapters.

22

The Tabular Method

The following display reminds us that, compared with decisions that call for the Two-List Method, CBA simplifies complex decisions by taking smaller steps. In particular, the Tabular Method and the methods for complex decisions require four central activities, instead of three.

Sound Methods

SPECIAL METHODS FOR COMPLEX AND VERY COMPLEX DECISIONS	SIMPLE METHODS FOR SIMPLE DECISIONS					VERY SIMPLE METHODS FOR VERY SIMPLE DECISIONS
	The Tabular Method	**The Two-List Method**	Simplified Tabular Method	Simplified Two-List Method	Instant CBA	
	Attributes	—	Attributes	—	—	
	Advantages	**Advantages**	(Advantages)	Advantages	(Advantages)	
	Importance	**Importance**	—	—	—	
	Total Importance	**Total Importance**	(Total Importance)	(Total Importance)	(Total Importance)	
SPE CIAL METHODS FOR MONEY DECISIONS						

Smaller Steps

◄———————●———————————|

The display of sound methods shows that the next one to learn, after the Two-List Method, is the Tabular Method. This method has been successfully used many times, for many decisions. Although some decisionmakers will often need to use the Tabular Method, others will seldom need to use it. However, even those who will seldom need to use it need to carefully study it. It illustrates several of the basic CBA concepts, and it sets the stage for the additional CBA concepts and methods that are presented in chapters 23 through 26.

As shown in chapter 8, the Tabular Method can be used for choosing from only two alternatives. However, as shown in this chapter, it is designed, primarily, for choosing from several alternatives (three or more, but not a large number). For choosing from a large number of alternatives and for choosing from an infinite number of possibilities, special methods are required—these are shown in chapter 23.

To demonstrate the Tabular Method, let's assume that we are planning to camp overnight in Colorado, in a National Forest campground. Within the campground, we need to choose from the available campsites. Because it's late in the camping season, the Forest Service has discontinued collecting a user fee. Therefore, this will be a nonmoney decision.

Let's assume that we have narrowed the choice to the following alternatives: Sites Number 8, Number 19, and Number 23. We have the purpose and circumstances of the decision in mind, and we are the stakeholders. For this decision, due to its simplicity, we don't need to use the Tabular Method. However, this is an excellent opportunity to practice it. Because this decision is simple and unimportant, we will be able to focus on the process; we won't need to worry about the content of the decision. If we make the wrong decision, it won't matter.

THE DECISIONMAKING PHASE
OF THE TABULAR METHOD

The following is an outline of the entire CBA process for moderately complex decisions. This is followed by an outline of Phase III of the Tabular Method, which is followed by the campsite example. In the outline of the entire process, three things are highlighted: First, it is essential to provide CBA training to the decisionmaking participants, and the best time to provide it is during Phase I. Second, the initial focus of the training needs to be Phase III. Third—in Phase III to make the right mental choice, and in Phase IV to make the right emotional choice—the participants need to form clear, accurate, sensory-rich perceptions of the advantages of the alternatives.

PHASE I. THE STAGE-SETTING PHASE

1. Define the purpose and circumstances of the decision.
2. Where applicable, define the "problem," and find its root cause.
3. Identify the participants, the customers, and other stakeholders.
4. **Provide CBA training to the participants.**
5. Identify the laws, regulations, and other criteria for the decision.

PHASE II. THE INNOVATION PHASE

1. Formulate/create a full range of alternatives.
2. Determine the relevant attributes of each alternative. (The relevant attributes are those that reveal the differences among the alternatives.) In this same activity, identify the factors containing the attributes.
3. If necessary, construct a detailed comparison display, to fully disclose the attributes of the alternatives.

PHASE III. THE DECISIONMAKING PHASE (Mentally Choosing)

1. **Summarize the attributes of each alternative.**
2. **Decide the advantages of each alternative.**
3. **Decide the importance of each advantage.**
4. **If the costs are equal, choose the alternative with the greatest total importance of advantages.**

PHASE IV. THE RECONSIDERATION PHASE (Emotionally Choosing)

1. Reconsider the decision.
2. If it should be changed, change it.
3. **Form clear, accurate, sensory-rich, motivational perceptions of the advantages of the selected alternative.**
4. Make a strong commitment to successfully implement the final decision. Also, remove any barriers to its implementation.

PHASE V. THE IMPLEMENTATION PHASE (Physically Choosing)

1. Implement the decision—adjusting it, if necessary, during implementation.
2. Evaluate the process and the results.

PHASE III. THE DECISIONMAKING PHASE

1. Summarize the **ATTRIBUTES** of each alternative.

2. Decide the **ADVANTAGES** of each alternative.

   a. Underline the Least-Preferred Attributes. (Underline only one in each factor, even if there are two the same.)

   b. Summarize the differences from the least-preferred attributes. These differences are the advantages of the alternatives.

3. Decide the **IMPORTANCE** of each advantage.

   a. *Circle* the most important advantages—only one in each factor. (When choosing from only two alternatives, this task is optional, because there is only one advantage in each factor. However, even when there are only two alternatives, this task is highly recommended. It instantly reveals the advantages.)

   b. *Select* the paramount advantage (the most important of the most important advantages). To identify the paramount advantage and to establish a scale of importance for the decision, assign an importance-score of 1, 10, or 100—or any convenient number— to the paramount advantage.

   c. *Weigh* the importance of each remaining most important advantage, compared directly or indirectly with the paramount advantage. (All the advantages must be weighed on the same scale of importance.)

   d. *Decide* the importance of each remaining advantage, compared directly or indirectly with the paramount advantage. Preference charts and preference curves, described in chapter 10, are sometimes used in this task. (When choosing from only two alternatives, this task is not applicable—because there are no remaining advantages.)

4. When the costs of the alternatives are equal, and sometimes when the costs are unequal, choose the alternative with the greatest **TOTAL IMPORTANCE** of advantages.

Activity No. 1: Summarize the Attributes of Each Alternative

In the first central activity of the Tabular Method, we summarize the attributes of the alternatives. When using the Tabular Method, it is important to accurately use the Tabular Format. For example, use both dashed lines and solid lines as shown in the example. Using this format will help both in making a sound decision and in explaining its rationale—especially to those who are familiar with this format.

The Tabular Format organizes the sound-decisionmaking thought process. Only a few words or numbers are used to summarize the attributes. The summaries simply remind us of details we already know—details that we have described in a separate display of attributes, if necessary. For example, in the second factor, tent spot, we know exactly what we mean by "Quite Sloping," because we have carefully examined each site.

Summarize the Attributes

FACTORS	ALTERNATIVES		
	SITE NO. 8	SITE NO. 19	SITE NO. 23
1. WATER Attributes:	60 Ft. Away	260 Ft. Away	150 Ft. Away
Advantages:			
2. TENT SPOT Attributes:	Moderately Level	Almost Level	Quite Sloping
Advantages:			
3. TABLE Attributes:	Without	Without	With
Advantages:			
4. PRIVACY Attributes:	Not Very Private	Very Private	Moderately Private
Advantages:			
TOTAL IMPORTANCE :			

Activity No. 2: Decide the Advantages of Each Alternative

This activity is divided into the following bite-size tasks:

    a.   Underline the least-preferred attribute in each factor. (If there are two that are the same, underline only one. It doesn't matter which one.)

    b.   Summarize the differences from the least-preferred attributes. These differences are the advantages of the alternatives.

The following display is the result of this second central activity. Notice that when there is no advantage, the space for showing an advantage is left blank (there is no such thing as a zero advantage). In the third factor, for example, Site Number 23 is the only alternative that has an advantage.

Decide the Advantages

FACTORS	ALTERNATIVES		
	SITE NO. 8	SITE NO. 19	SITE NO. 23
1. WATER Attributes:	60 Ft. Away	260 Ft. Away	150 Ft. Away
Advantages:	200 Feet Closer		110 Feet Closer
2. TENT SPOT Attributes:	Moderately Level	Almost Level	Quite Sloping
Advantages:	Mod. More Level	Much More Level	
3. TABLE Attributes:	Without	Without	With
Advantages:			With Versus Without
4. PRIVACY Attributes:	Not Very Private	Very Private	Moderately Private
Advantages:		Much More Privacy	Mod. More Privacy
TOTAL IMPORTANCE :			

Activity No. 3: Decide the Importance of Each Advantage

The third central activity is divided into four tasks—the four central tasks of the CBA process. Following are the first two:

    a.   Circle the most important advantage (only one) in each factor.

    b.   Select the paramount advantage. Then, to establish a scale-of-importance for the decision, assign the paramount advantage an importance score of 1, 10, or 100—or any convenient number. (In this example, a 0-to-100 scale was established.)

When selecting the paramount advantage, it is essential to use the CBA patterns of thought and speech. For example, do not say, "Privacy is the most important factor." That would be an unanchored judgment.

Establish a Scale of Importance

FACTORS	ALTERNATIVES		
	SITE NO. 8	SITE NO. 19	SITE NO. 23
1. WATER Attributes:	60 Ft. Away	260 Ft. Away	150 Ft. Away
Advantages:	(200 Feet Closer)		110 Feet Closer
2. TENT SPOT Attributes:	Moderately Level	Almost Level	Quite Sloping
Advantages:	Mod. More Level	(Much More Level)	
3. TABLE Attributes:	Without	Without	With
Advantages:			(With Versus Without)
4. PRIVACY Attributes:	Not Very Private	Very Private	Moderately Private
Advantages:		(Much More Privacy) 100	Mod. More Privacy
TOTAL IMPORTANCE :			

Following are the third and fourth central tasks:

    c.   Weigh the importance of each most important advantage, compared directly or indirectly with the paramount advantage.

    d.   Decide the importance of each remaining advantage, compared directly or indirectly with the paramount advantage.

I assume you have already memorized the key words in the four central activities (attributes, advantages, importance, and total importance). The key words in the four central tasks are circle, select, weigh, and decide.

As in the first two central tasks, remember that to anchor decisions about importance to the relevant facts, the CBA patterns of thought and speech must be used. For example, do not ask, "How important is water, compared with privacy?" That would be an unanchored question.

Decide the Importance of Each Advantage

FACTORS	ALTERNATIVES		
	SITE NO. 8	SITE NO. 19	SITE NO. 23
1. WATER Attributes:	60 Ft. Away	260 Ft. Away	150 Ft. Away
Advantages:	(200 Feet Closer) 40		110 Feet Closer 30
2. TENT SPOT Attributes:	Moderately Level	Almost Level	Quite Sloping
Advantages:	Mod. More Level 30	(Much More Level) 70	
3. TABLE Attributes:	Without	Without	With
Advantages:			(With Versus Without) 65
4. PRIVACY Attributes:	Not Very Private	Very Private	Moderately Private
Advantages:		(Much More Privacy) 100	Mod. More Privacy 45
TOTAL IMPORTANCE :			

Activity No. 4: Calculate the Total Importance of Advantages

When the costs of the alternatives are equal (and sometimes when they are unequal), simply choose the one with the greatest total importance of advantages. When the costs are equal (but not when they are unequal), identify the preferred alternative by double-underlining the greatest total importance. In the campsite example, Site 19 is the preferred alternative.

In this case, the alternative with the paramount advantage was selected. Sometimes this is what happens, and sometimes not. Sometimes, the alternative with the greatest number of advantages is selected, and sometimes not. (In this case, the one with the greatest number of advantages is not the one that was selected.) Always, when the costs of the alternatives are equal, and sometimes when they are unequal (see ch. 24), choose the alternative with the greatest total importance of advantages.

Choose the Preferred Alternative

FACTORS	ALTERNATIVES					
	SITE NO. 8		SITE NO. 19		SITE NO. 23	
1. WATER Attributes:	60 Ft. Away		260 Ft. Away		150 Ft. Away	
Advantages:	200 Feet Closer	40			110 Feet Closer	30
2. TENT SPOT Attributes:	Moderately Level		Almost Level		Quite Sloping	
Advantages:	Mod. More Level	30	Much More Level	70		
3. TABLE Attributes:	Without		Without		With	
Advantages:					With Versus Without	65
4. PRIVACY Attributes:	Not Very Private		Very Private		Moderately Private	
Advantages:			Much More Privacy	100	Mod. More Privacy	45
TOTAL IMPORTANCE :		70		170		140

THE RECONSIDERATION PHASE

During the reconsideration phase, CBA decisionmakers ask themselves probing questions, such as: Are there any additional alternatives that should be considered? Are there any additional advantages? Are the importance scores consistent with one another? For example, when two advantages have the same importance score, do they truly have the same importance? If one of the scores is twice as large as another, is the one advantage truly twice as important? Do the scores accurately represent the viewpoints of the stakeholders? (To find out, ask them.) This phase needs to be as thorough as the decisionmaking phase. It often discloses and corrects critical mistakes that couldn't be discovered before constructing and reviewing either a Two-List Display or a Tabular Display. Sometimes, for example, reviews reveal that additional factors containing significant advantages need to be included.

People often ask, "What is the maximum number of factors that should be considered in a decision?" There is no maximum. The number of factors depends on the decision. The rule is simple: All the significant advantages of each alternative must be taken into account. Remember that the reason for dividing a decision into factors is to simplify decisionmaking. (Simplify complex decisions by taking smaller steps.) When the decision is difficult, and when accuracy is essential, it is easier to decide the importance scores for a larger number of small advantages, rather than for a smaller number of large advantages. But most decisions call for only small numbers of factors.

What if you *think* you should select one alternative—the one with the greatest total in the Tabular Display—but you *feel* you should select another? Should you base the final decision on your thoughts or your feelings? I suggest that you should postpone the final decision, if possible, because your initial decision isn't congruent.

Your decision isn't internally congruent unless you believe, think, and feel that it is the right decision. And it isn't totally congruent unless it is also in agreement with external realities. If you think you should select one alternative but feel you should select another, it could be either your thoughts or your feelings—or both—that are incorrect. You might have in your mind, at the subconscious level, pertinent information that you didn't think of and didn't include during the decisionmaking phase. On the other hand, your feelings might be based on false assumptions.

To bring about agreement between your mental choice and your emotional choice, use the creative process: Study and restudy the decision. Then, let it incubate for a while. If your feelings are based on false assumptions, they will usually correct themselves, eventually. Or, if your feelings are based on valid facts, those facts will usually come to the surface. If new facts do surface, and if they show that the decision needs to be changed, change it. Don't fall into the trap of defending an unsound decision.

AN UN-SUCCESS STORY

The Tabular Method has produced plenty of success stories. But there have been disappointments, as well. In one case, a large group of participants—too large to be effective—tried, unsuccessfully, to use the Tabular Method in a decision meeting. (Some in the meeting were members of state and federal agencies. Others were from private business organizations. Still others were interested individuals. I was invited to observe the meeting and, as necessary, to serve as a process consultant.)

Although they were dealing with a major, controversial issue, only the facilitator and two or three of the participants seemed to understand the basic principles of sound decisionmaking. (The others had declined an opportunity to attend a free sound-decisionmaking workshop.) After the participants had introduced themselves to one another, the facilitator tried to get them to clarify the purpose of the decision. When that didn't work, he tried to get them to summarize the attributes of the alternatives. But they were not well acquainted with the alternatives, and they didn't know the attributes. After a few minutes one of them said, "This is taking too long. I came here to make a decision." The facilitator asked me to respond.

The participant was right. It was taking too long, because proper preparations hadn't been made for the meeting. But I didn't point that out, because it was too late to do anything about it. Instead, I walked to the back of the room and initiated the following discussion:

Q. What do you have in these three-ring binders? (The binders, containing thousands of pages of data, were stacked on banquet tables.)

A. You already know what's there—the data for the decision.

Q. How long did it take to gather this much data?

A. About four years.

Q. What did it cost?

A. I don't know, but a lot of people worked on it.

Q. If you were willing to spend four years to gather the correct data, shouldn't you be willing to spend a few hours—or even a few days—to organize and use the data correctly?

A. Well, let's go ahead. But we've got to make the decision, right away.

This example demonstrates a common false perception about decisionmaking: "If the decisionmaker had enough data, it would be a foregone conclusion, not a decision." In this case, the participants had far more data than they could use. At the same time, they didn't have enough of the right kind of data. Those who collected the data didn't adequately understand what data to collect or how to organize it to make it useful in choosing the preferred alternative.

An important lesson from this is obvious: Before formulating alternatives and collecting data, be sure to provide CBA training to the participants. In just one major decision, the cost of not providing adequate training can be enormous. Inadequate training can produce a costly, wasteful data collection process. And what's worse, it can produce an unsound decision. Therefore, as a minimum, all of the participants need to study this book.

This same example also demonstrates a natural tendency that is difficult to avoid. It is the tendency to treat both small and large as if they were average. Following are three examples:

- Most decisionmakers tend to overestimate small risks and underestimate large risks. Some researchers say that this tendency is genetic.

- Most decisionmakers tend to overstate the importance of small advantages and understate the importance of large advantages.

- Most decisionmakers spend too much time on minor decisions. And, as in the example above, they don't spend enough time on major decisions.

For a major decision—where it takes several months, or years, to formulate a set of alternatives and to determine their attributes—it wouldn't be unreasonable to spend at least several hours, or days, to identify their advantages and to judge the importance of their advantages. Failing to even identify the advantages is a critical mistake. And it should be obvious that an error in subjectively judging the importance of an advantage is just as serious as a corresponding error in objectively measuring the magnitudes of its associated attributes. Spending years in collecting data and then failing to use the data correctly is not a good way to use human resources.

Some observers have said that because major decisions are stressful, people try to get rid of them, as soon as possible. They say that some people spend more time when shopping for a new bicycle than when shopping for a new home—because buying a new home is so stressful. CBA reduces the stress of decisionmaking. The key is to study and practice the CBA definitions, principles, models, and methods until sound decisionmaking becomes comfortable, and unsound becomes uncomfortable.

23

Special Methods
for Complex Decisions

For *very complex* decisions, advanced CBA training is sometimes required, and typically, a single-use CBA method must be designed for each individual decision. In contrast, the methods presented in this chapter are for *complex* decisions, they do not require special training, and each is suitable to be reused for many decisions. These methods include:

- The D/T-I Process

- The One-Text Process

- Choosing from a Large Number of Alternatives

- Choosing from an Infinite Number of Possibilities

- Setting Priorities among Nonexclusive Proposals

- Allocation Decisionmaking

- The Prior–Anchoring Process

THE D/T-I PROCESS

The process of designing, testing, and improving, or D/T-I (pronounced DTI) has been effectively used throughout human history. This CBA method, which is also called the Continuous Improvement Process, or Continuous Quality Improvement, is used for simple as well as for complex decisions. Following is a diagram of the D/T-I Process:

The D/T-I Process

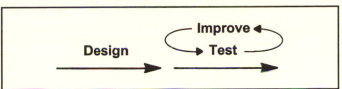

The D/T-I Process applies to virtually all types of improvements, ranging from very small changes to major breakthroughs. Major improvements sometimes require organized, managed, quality-improvement projects. Most, if not all, versions of the Total Quality Management (TQM) Process include the use of quality-improvement projects.

In organizations where TQM is being implemented, and in those where TQM has been accepted as a way of doing business, a good way to implement the CBA system is to designate its implementation as a continuous quality-improvement project, or as one of the organization's quality-improvement goals. This is how the Field Services Unit of the Animal and Plant Health Inspection Service (APHIS) in Minneapolis, Minnesota, implemented CBA.

The aircraft industry has thrived on the D/T-I Process. The Wright Brothers, who were pioneers in the aircraft industry, designed and constructed an airplane they thought would fly. Then, they tested it and improved it. Today, as a result of countless cycles of testing and improving, many types of modern airplanes are now in service. Each valid *improvement,* from one airplane design to the next, was either an individual *advantage* or a change in which, collectively, the advantages of changing outweighed the advantages of not changing. Therefore, when properly used, the D/T-I Method is a CBA method. It bases decisions on the importance of advantages.

As a result of countless cycles of testing and improving in virtually all areas of our social and economic systems, we have modern safety pins, shoes, computers, and an enormous number of the other conveniences that we now enjoy. Most of our modern conveniences have been produced by the D/T-I Process. This same process has also produced successful democracies. Like other CBA methods, the D/T-I method is a scientific method. It is a very effective method of Choosing By Advantages.

To improve a plan, process, product, or service, we should not search only for a major breakthrough. We should search, also, for many small improvements. Making improvements (creating advantages) should be a continuous, forever process. Of course, major breakthroughs are needed in many areas of our economic and social systems. Here are just two of many examples: We urgently need to find better ways to decrease our use of energy, especially from nonrenewable resources. At the same time, we need to find effective ways to produce more energy from renewable resources. These and countless other needs call for the D/T-I Process.

The evolution of decisionmaking methodology, which can be divided into five periods of time, or eras, is an example of the D/T-I Process. The product, in this case, is the CBA system. CBA is the result of many cycles of testing and improving, and it will need to be further improved in the future. While most of the improvements that have been incorporated into the CBA system are small, some are major breakthroughs. One breakthrough is the recognition that when we consider making changes, the advantages of making a particular change must outweigh the advantages of not making the change.

The first three eras in the evolution of decisionmaking methodology—the primitive–decisionmaking era, the frontier era, and the proposal–evaluation era—are in the past. However, the methods from these eras are still being used today. We are now in the impact–evaluation era, and the era of Choosing By Advantages could be emerging. I hope that in this era, sound decisionmaking will become the standard and that unsound methods will no longer be widely accepted. Examples of methods that came into use during each of the five eras are outlined on the next page and described in the following text.

Primitive Decisionmaking

While we were learning how to crawl, and walk, and talk, we were also learning how to make decisions. The first few methods we learned were primitive, natural methods—as natural as walking and talking. Some primitive methods are sound and effective, at least for some types of decisions. But others are unsound. Examples of primitive methods include:

- Basing decisions on power ("I see, I want, I take"). Modern forms of this method include basing decisions on political power or economic power. Fighting, striking, warring, and terrorizing—and in some cases, debating and voting—are additional examples.

- Unsound primitive methods include Choosing By Emotions—also, obtaining decisions from Stone-Age oracles, modern fortune tellers, or horoscopes. Sometimes, these methods produce sound decisions, but only by accident.

The Evolution of Decisionmaking Methodology

PRIMITIVE DECISIONMAKING
- Basing Decisions on Power or Authority
- The Instinctive Method: This is a method we all use, naturally. Here is what we do when we use this method: In response to beliefs, thoughts, feelings, observations, or displays of data—or whatever triggers the need for a decision—we:
  1. Make assumptions to fill in data gaps.
  2. Jump to a conclusion.
- Other Primitive Methods

THE FRONTIER ERA
- The Typical Frontier Decisionmaking Process: In response to the need for a decision, those who use this method:
  1. Collect data to fill in data gaps.
  2. Jump to a conclusion.
- Other Frontier Methods

THE PROPOSAL–EVALUATION ERA
- Reasons-Pro Versus Reasons-Con
- Advantages Versus Disadvantages
- Benefits Versus Costs (B/C)

THE IMPACT–EVALUATION ERA
- Pros and Cons Versus Pros and Cons
- Advantages and Disadvantages Vs. Advantages and Disadvantages
- Benefits/Costs Versus Benefits/Costs (and other B/C methods)
- Numerous Unsound Methods that are Mechanically Simple and Seemingly Sensible
- Many Variations of Weighting-Rating-and-Calculating (WRC)

CHOOSING BY ADVANTAGES
- Special Methods for Complex and Very Complex Decisions
  - Special Methods for Money Decisions
  - Other CBA Methods for Complex and Very Complex Decisions
- Simple Methods for Simple Decisions
  - The Tabular Method
  - The Two-List Method
  - The Simplified Tabular Method
  - The Simplified Two-List Method
  - Instant CBA
- Very Simple Methods for Very Simple Decisions

- The Instinctive Method: This is a method we all use, naturally. It is a very simple method: In response to whatever triggers the need for a decision, we:

  1. *Make assumptions* to fill in data gaps.

  2. Jump to a conclusion.

When decisionmakers base decisions on assumptions, where do the assumptions come from? Indirectly, they are derived from past experience, traditions, superstitions, success stories, testimonials, and so forth. Directly, however, they come from inside the decisionmaker's mind. Therefore, they seem, to the decisionmaker, to be relevant and true—even when they are untrue. As stated before, primitive methods are severely inadequate in a complex, rapidly changing, modern society. The emergence of science and the recognition of the pivotal cornerstone principle moved decisionmaking methodology from the primitive–decisionmaking era into the frontier era.

The Frontier Era

The purpose of moving to the frontier era was to bring about a change from basing decisions on assumptions to basing them on facts. Following are two commonly used frontier methods:

- The Typical Frontier Decisionmaking Process: In response to whatever triggers the need for a decision, those who use this method:

  1. *Collect data*, but not in writing, to fill in data gaps.

  2. Jump to a conclusion.

- The same as the Typical Frontier Decisionmaking Process, except that data are collected in writing.

The shift from basing decisions on assumptions to basing them on facts was a major improvement. However, the second step in the Frontier Process is the same as in the Instinctive Method: Both require decision-makers to jump to a conclusion. Neither of these methods constructs a solid, visible bridge from the data to the decision. For example, here is a five-step Frontier Method that is recommended in a high-school textbook— one that is in use today:

  1. State the situation that requires a decision.

2. List the possible choices available.

3. Consider the consequences of each possible choice.

4. Make a decision based on everything you know and act on it.

5. Evaluate your decision.

This process doesn't build a bridge from "everything you know" to the decision. Nevertheless, it is a large improvement, compared with the Instinctive Method, because it tells decisionmakers to base their decisions on facts, rather than assumptions.

Some decisionmakers haven't accepted the change from basing decisions on assumptions to basing them on facts. They have confidence in their own assumptions, because their assumptions come from inside their own minds. They don't have confidence in facts, especially those that come from outside. As has been demonstrated many times by the bridge design experiment (described in chapter 12), we naturally, automatically, make assumptions to fill in data gaps.

When members of the public saw that government officials were using primitive and frontier methods to make major public decisions, they said, "Wait. Before you spend our tax dollars, we want you to propose and evaluate all major projects and programs, to be sure they are worthwhile. And we want you to disclose the rationale for your decisions, so we can participate in the decisionmaking process." This moved decisionmaking methodology into the proposal–evaluation era.

The Proposal–Evaluation Era

The move from the frontier era to the proposal–evaluation era required decisionmakers to address new questions: What data should be collected? How can we build a bridge from the data to the decision? In response, the following and other proposal–evaluation methods were developed:

- The Ben Franklin Method: Reasons-Pro Versus Reasons-Con

- Advantages Versus Disadvantages

- Benefit/Cost Ratio Methods (B/C)

- Net Benefit Methods (B - C)

Patterns of thought and speech from the proposal–evaluation era are now very common. When those who use proposal–evaluation patterns go shopping, for example, they look at individual items, or proposals, and ask themselves, "Is this item worth its cost?" As is shown in chapter 24, this pattern of thought can produce financial disasters because it ignores two money–decisionmaking principles: Wellington's rule, which was initially presented in chapter 18, and the principle of interdependency, which is presented in chapter 24.

Many times, proposal–evaluation methods produce conflict instead of effective participation. Here is an example: Often, in public meetings to review project or program proposals, the proponents line up on one side and the opponents line up on the other. Then they shout at each other. To make matters worse, proposal–evaluation methods do not consider alternatives, and they often leave out significant effects that are not priced in the market. Therefore, concerned members of the public said, "Wait. We don't want to be faced with only the money-valued benefits and costs of a take-it-or-leave-it proposal. We want to see all the social, economic, and environmental impacts—positive and negative—of all the reasonable alternatives." This moved decisionmaking methodology into the impact–evaluation era.

The Impact–Evaluation Era

Some of the methods that came into use during the impact–evaluation era are simply modifications of proposal–evaluation methods. Following are examples:

- Pros and Cons Versus Pros and Cons

- Advantages and Disadvantages Versus Advantages and Disadvantages

- Benefits/Costs Versus Benefits/Costs, Net Benefits, and other Benefit/Cost Methods

Sometimes, some of the decisionmaking methods that are being used today are called *Cost-Benefit Analysis,* with the same initials as Choosing By Advantages (CBA). Therefore, when you see the label "CBA," it might not mean "Choosing By Advantages." In the CBA vocabulary, these methods are called Benefit/Cost Methods. Why? Because a Benefit/Cost ratio looks like this: B/C, not like this: C/B.

In addition to the methods listed above, the following methods, and many others, came into use during the impact–evaluation era:

- Numerous unsound methods that are mechanically simple and seemingly sensible

- Many variations of Weighting-Rating-and-Calculating (WRC)

As I have stated several times, the WRC methods are now widely viewed as the standard of how decisions should be made. As a result, they are being taught in all levels of the educational system, from elementary school classes for gifted and talented students to training seminars for business and government leaders.

Nevertheless, as you know, they are unsound methods. By violating the fundamental rule of sound decisionmaking, the principle of anchoring, the methods principle, Wellington's rule, and other sound-decisionmaking principles, they too often produce faulty decisions. To make matters worse, the impact–evaluation process has become horribly complex. In some cases, environmental impact statements have been hundreds of pages long and incomprehensible. The urgent need for methods that are sound, clear, and simple produced the CBA concepts and methods.

Choosing By Advantages

A key breakthrough in the development of the CBA system was the recognition of the methods principle: Different types of decisions call for different sound methods of decisionmaking. The methods that are now included in the CBA system came from three sources: Some are sound methods from the first four eras (these have simply been adopted into the CBA system), some are previously unsound methods that have been transformed from unsound to sound, and some are new.

The CBA system includes methods for the following and other types of decisions: responding to one-option situations, choosing from only two alternatives, choosing from several alternatives, choosing from a large number of alternatives, choosing from an infinite number of possibilities, and setting priorities among nonexclusive proposals. CBA also includes methods for work planning, workforce planning, budgeting, day-to-day scheduling, and so forth. As an outcome from many cycles of the D/T-I Process, the CBA system now includes a wide variety of concepts and methods, to meet the needs of:

- Individuals, Groups, Families, Organizations, and Communities

- Parents, Children, Teachers, and Students

- Business and Government Executives, Leaders, and Front Line Employees

- Engineers, Scientists, Technicians, Architects, Doctors, Teachers, Psychologists, Counselors, and Consultants

- *Everyone who participates in the decisionmaking process*

Why was the CBA system developed? The first reason, as stated previously, was the urgent need for methods that are sound, clear, simple, congruent, and effective. The second reason was skepticism. Without skepticism, the old standard methods wouldn't have been challenged and scrutinized, their mistakes wouldn't have been uncovered, and the CBA system wouldn't have been developed.

Skepticism will keep us moving forward. The development of CBA will be continued, using the D/T-I Process. However, CBA is already a very effective system. And I believe that the basic principles of sound decision-making, those that are presented in this book, have always been valid in the past, they are valid today, and they will always be valid in the future.

THE ONE-TEXT PROCESS

The One-Text Process is another sound method that existed before the CBA system was developed. This method is a variation of the D/T-I Process. The difference is that in the One-Text Process, we *study* and improve a written plan, instead of *testing* and improving a physical product. The One-Text Method is an excellent method to use during a planning process, an interactive decisionmaking process, or a difficult negotiation process. For example, this is the method President Carter used, in 1978, in achieving the Camp David accords (Fisher and Ury 1983: 121).

In many situations, you will first need to consider two or more plans. In those situations, use either the Two-List Method or the Tabular Method, as applicable, in concert with the One-Text Process. Or use the Scoring-Sheet Method, which is presented in the following section. First, compare the alternative plans—usually, not in detail—and choose the best one. Then, during the reconsideration phase, study the selected alternative and improve it. Complex, difficult decisions may require several cycles of studying and improving.

CHOOSING FROM A LARGE NUMBER OF ALTERNATIVES

The Scoring-Sheet Method

As demonstrated in chapter 22, the Tabular Method is designed for choosing from several alternatives—three or more, but not a large number. A method called the Scoring-Sheet Method is for choosing from a large number of alternatives. For example, this method is an ideal method for choosing from dozens of applicants for only one job opening. The Scoring-Sheet Method is the same as the Tabular Method, except that an individual scoring sheet is prepared for each alternative, instead of preparing one gigantic display of all the alternatives.

The Scoring-Sheet Format

There is no standard Scoring-Sheet Format. Instead, a special format has to be designed for each decision. Then, a copy is made for each alternative, and data are added. For simple decisions, 3" x 5" cards are often used as scoring sheets. Usually, for complex decisions, one or more 8-1/2" x 11" pages are used as scoring sheets, and they are attached to detailed displays of data. Different decisions call for different formats, but usually the Tabular Format is used as a guide. Typically, a scoring sheet includes brief summaries of some or all of the following data: attributes, advantages, importance, and total importance; also, revenue and cost data.

CHOOSING FROM AN INFINITE NUMBER
OF POSSIBILITIES

In the Forest Service, developing a forest plan is an example of choosing from an infinite number of possibilities. On each national forest, there is an infinite number of possible combinations of ways to manage and use timber, forage, recreational opportunities, wilderness, water, and other resources. Developing a strategic plan for a business is another example of choosing from an infinite number of possibilities. Designing a canoe is another example.

Use either the Tabular Method or the Scoring-Sheet Method, in combination with the One-Text Process, to choose from an infinite number of possibilities. First, formulate (design)—not in detail—a moderate number of alternatives, scattered throughout the range of possibilities. Depending on the number of alternatives, use either the Tabular Method or the Scoring-Sheet Method to evaluate (study) this first set of alternatives. Then, based on what you learn from evaluating this set of alternatives, narrow the range of possibilities and formulate a second set (improve).

Use either the Tabular Method or the Scoring-Sheet Method, again, to evaluate the second set. If necessary, use additional cycles of formulating and evaluating (studying and improving) to narrow the choice to the preferred alternative—the one text. Next, add details to the selected alternative. And then, using the One-Text Process, make additional improvements.

When choosing from an infinite number of possibilities, decisionmakers often face large numbers of stakeholders with differing (and sometimes conflicting) viewpoints. The CBA methods for dealing with this complexity are called *multiple–viewpoint decisionmaking methods,* or *Interactive CBA*.

All of the decisionmaking skills that are required in single–viewpoint decisionmaking—and more—are required in multiple–viewpoint decision-making. Therefore, the Interactive CBA Methods are presented in the effective–decisionmaking area of the CBA training process—after sound and congruent. Sound decisionmaking training is the foundation for effective decisionmaking training. Congruent decisionmaking training is the foundation and framework.

Using sound methods, so that decisions are anchored to the relevant facts, greatly reduces the need for using the special CBA methods for multiple–viewpoint decisionmaking. But using sound methods doesn't eliminate the need for these special methods.

SETTING PRIORITIES AMONG
NONEXCLUSIVE PROPOSALS

Counselors, consultants, psychologists, and other professionals who give advice about how to make decisions too often give unsound advice about selecting and scheduling work, leisure, and other activities. In "time management" workshops, for example, people are often advised to make a list of the things they need to do, with the list arranged according to importance—with their most important activity at the top of the list, and their least important at the bottom. Then they are advised to do the activities on their list, in order, starting with the one at the top. Unfortunately, this is a very unsound method. It often causes low-priority activities to be completed at the expense of high-priority activities.

We are continuously selecting, scheduling, and performing work, leisure, and other activities, and we need to be able to instantly make sound decisions pertaining to these activities. This requires clearly understanding why methods that set priorities only according to importance are unsound. There are two major reasons:

- First, methods that prioritize activities according to importance do not take into account the difference between choosing from mutually exclusive alternatives versus setting priorities among nonexclusive proposals. What needs to be emphasized is that the sound methods for choosing from mutually exclusive alternatives are unsound for setting priorities among nonexclusive proposals, and vice versa.

- Second, methods that tell us to do our most important activities first are confusing three very basic, very different decisionmaking concepts: most important, highest priority, and first-in-sequence. In contrast, CBA recognizes that a person's most important activity isn't necessarily a high priority activity. Furthermore, a person's highest priority activity isn't necessarily the one that should be performed first. The distinctions between these three concepts are vital—and simple.

To set the stage for presenting the methods for setting priorities among nonexclusive proposals, we will first examine the distinction between things that are mutually exclusive versus things that are nonexclusive. Next, we will examine the distinction between proposals versus alternatives. Then, we will distinguish between most important, highest priority, and first-in-sequence. Decisionmakers need to study and practice these distinctions until they automatically take them into account when selecting, scheduling, and performing activities.

Mutually Exclusive Versus Nonexclusive

To show the distinction between mutually exclusive and nonexclusive, let's use examples, rather than abstract definitions:

- Two things that are mutually exclusive: In a garage that is large enough to hold only one car, we can park a Ford Taurus or an Oldsmobile Ciera, but not both. In this case, the one excludes the other, and the other excludes the one. (It would be physically impossible to park both cars in this garage, at the same time.)

- Two things that are nonexclusive: In a garage that is large enough to hold two cars, we can park a Ford Taurus and an Oldsmobile Ciera, at the same time. The one does not exclude the other, and the other does not exclude the one.

As another example, here is a pair of mutually exclusive activities: At a particular point in time, a particular person—an auto mechanic—could be viewing Old Faithful Geyser in Yellowstone Park. Or, at that same point in time, the same person could be repairing an automobile in Phoenix, Arizona. The one activity excludes the other, and the other excludes the one. In contrast, the same mechanic could view Old Faithful on June 23, and repair an auto in Phoenix on July 10. In this case, the one activity does not exclude the other, and the other does not exclude the one.

Proposals Versus Alternatives

The methods of decisionmaking that have been presented in this book, so far, are for choosing from mutually exclusive alternatives. They are not for setting priorities among nonexclusive proposals. With this in mind, let's use the canoe purchase example to distinguish between proposals and alternatives.

Proposals can be either general or specific. Here is an example: At first, when the stakeholders proposed buying a new canoe, they were not proposing a particular canoe. Therefore, it was not a specific proposal. It was simply to buy a canoe. After looking at several alternatives, they narrowed their choice to Canoes C and K. Then, they decided that C is preferred to K. This process narrowed the canoe proposal to a single alternative, Canoe C. The selection of Canoe C changed the canoe proposal from general to specific.

- When they selected Canoe C, they excluded Canoe K. That was an example of choosing from mutually exclusive alternatives.

- The next section illustrates setting priorities among nonexclusive proposals. It also shows the difference between most important and highest priority.

Most Important Versus Highest Priority

To illustrate the distinction between most important and highest priority, a simple, hypothetical set of proposed work activities is shown in the chart on the following page. The names of the activities are represented by the letters A, B, C, and D, and they are arranged according to importance, not priority.

Let's suppose that we need to select from these four activities to create a plan of action, and that we have a total of only five hours available to do the set of selected activities. In this case, there are two mutually exclusive alternatives to choose from:

Alternative I: Select C, only, for a total importance of 15.

Alternative II: Select B plus D, for a total importance of 26.

In accordance with the fundamental rule, Alternative II is the preferred alternative. (Before adding the importance of D to the importance of B, we had to make sure that B and D were independent proposals. If they had been interdependent, it would have been a mistake to total their scores).

Proposed Activities, Listed According to Importance

Activity Name	Importance	Duration
A	20	10 Hours
B	18	3 Hours
C	15	5 Hours
D	8	2 Hours

Sometimes the importance scores for individual activities are the totals of the importance scores of two or more advantages. In this case—in which a zero-to-ten scale was used—this is why three of the totals of importance are greater than ten. For example, Activity A has three advantages (which aren't shown), compared with not doing the activity, and the total importance of the three is twenty.

Now, let's suppose that we are selecting from the same four activities to create a ten-hour plan of action. As in the five-hour example, there are two mutually exclusive alternatives to choose from, and the second is the preferred alternative:

Alternative III: Select A, only, for a total importance of 20.

Alternative IV: Select B, plus C, plus D, for a total importance of 41.

These examples demonstrate that if we have a small number of activities to choose from, we are able to create an action plan by formulating and choosing from mutually exclusive alternatives, where each alternative is a set of activities. But typically, we will have a large number of activities to choose from—sometimes, a very large number. In that case, it is much easier to achieve *exactly the same results* if we start by arranging the activities according to priority, rather than importance (a simple way to do this is to use 3" x 5" cards, as scoring sheets).

In the next chart, the activities are arranged according to their priorities—that is, according to importance per hour. For example, the priority of Activity B is 6.0 ($= 18 \div 3$), and the priority of Activity D is 4.0 ($= 8 \div 2$). (Notice that B is not only higher in priority than D, it is also more important.) In some cases, the number one activity in importance will be the number one in priority. But in this case, the number one in importance (Activity A) has the lowest priority.

Proposed Activities, Listed According to Priority

Activity Name	Importance	Duration	Priority	Total Duration
B	18	3 Hours	6.0	3 Hours
D	8	2 Hours	4.0	5 Hours
C	15	5 Hours	3.0	10 Hours
A	20	10 Hours	2.0	20 Hours

When the activities are listed according to priority, we don't need to formulate alternatives. We simply start at the top of the list and work our way downward until we run out of time. The priority list tells us that:

If we have a total of **3 hours**, we should select **B**.

If we have a total of **5 hours**, we should select **B**, plus **D**.

If we have a total of **10 hours**, we should select **B**, plus **D**, plus C.

There are three things we need to mention concerning this example. First, it is obvious that this method—arranging the activities according to their priorities—is much simpler than arranging them according to importance and then formulating mutually exclusive alternatives. Second, because the results from the two methods are exactly the same, we should use the simpler method. Therefore, we should arrange the activities according to priority, not importance. Third, in the ten-hour plan of action, it is probably safe to assume that by the time we complete Activities B, D, and C we will have a new set of high priority activities to choose from. Therefore, we might not be simply postponing Activity A. We might be eliminating it forever.

We often need to remind decisionmakers that their judgments about importance must be anchored to the relevant facts. Therefore, they must judge the importance of each advantage with care and precision. For example, a natural tendency that must be avoided is the tendency to treat both small and large as average. What this means is that decisionmakers tend to assign too much importance to small advantages when they are being compared with large advantages.

In one example, a decisionmaking team was setting priorities among a number of proposed activities, including installing guard rail on road L and installing guard rail on road Q. On a zero-to-ten scale, they assigned the guard rail for L an importance of 3.0. Then, with very little discussion, they assigned the guard rail for Q an importance of 1.5, because Q was considerably less important than L. When the CBA facilitator asked them to reconsider the importance score that had initially been assigned to Q, the team realized that the length of the protection provided by Q was only one-seventh the length provided by L—not one-half. Therefore, they changed the importance score for Q from 1.5 to 0.43 ($= 3.0 \div 7$).

One of the team members argued that, "On a scale of one-to-ten, the importance score can't be less than one." So the facilitator pointed out that the scale of importance is zero-to-ten, not one-to-ten. Then, he asked the team, once more, to reconsider the importance of Q. This time, someone pointed out that road Q has only one-seventh as much traffic as road L. So they changed the importance of Q from 0.43 to 0.06 ($= 0.43 \div 7$).

This example demonstrates why we have said, several times, that importance scores must be assigned carefully and accurately. In total, the two revisions (from 1.5 to 0.43, and from 0.43 to 0.06) produced a very large correction in the priority of installing guard rail on road Q.

Highest-Priority Versus First-In-Sequence

Now, let's return to the ten-hour plan of action. Which one of the three activities that are included in the plan—B, D, or C—should be first-in-sequence? The priority display doesn't answer this question. But the answer is simple: First, do the one that logically should be first. And remember: The highest priority activity isn't necessarily the one that logically should be first-in-sequence. (The CBA methods for deciding sequence are beyond the scope of this book; they are in the congruent decisionmaking area of the CBA system.)

ALLOCATION DECISIONMAKING

A motivational speaker reminded her listeners that it is impossible for anyone to do everything for everyone—including for themselves. Therefore, we all need to set priorities. Then she said that her most important life-roles, in order of priority, are as follows:

- Church and community service
- Self-improvement
- Family
- Work

It should be obvious to anyone who understands the principle of anchoring that the motivational speaker should not have selected her service role as her number one priority. I hope that, by now, you understand this principle.   Therefore, you should be able to respond immediately, correctly, to the following question: In your view, which one of her roles should she have selected as her number one priority?

I hope you recognized, instantly, that this question is an unanchored question, and that any judgments about the priorities of the four roles would be unanchored judgments.   As you know, we must never set priorities among factors, goals, roles, categories, or other high-order abstractions. To demonstrate why we must never set priorities among roles, imagine that you have made a list of all the prospective service activities, large and small, in your community.   Could you, personally, do all of them?   Of course not.

The motivational speaker faces the same situation. If she truly selected her service role as her highest priority, the only activities she would do would be service activities, and she would be neglecting her other roles.

People often say, "Your family, not your work, should be your first priority."   What they probably mean—and should say—is that we must establish a proper balance between work and family activities. How can we establish a proper balance among all our roles? It is true that we need to set priorities—but not among roles, or categories of activities.   Instead, we must set priorities among specific activities, in all the roles. At the same time, by applying the standard rule of allocation, we need to allocate the proper amount of time, according to our values and preferences, to each of the roles. Following is the concept of this allocation process, considering only two roles—service and work:

SERVICE ACTIVITIES	WORK ACTIVITIES
S1	W1
S2	W2
S3	W3
S4	W4
S5	W5
S6	W6 — Margin
S7	W7
S8	W8

In both lists, the activities are arranged according to their priorities, not according to their importance. That is, they are arranged according to importance per hour. None of the activities are low in priority. In the service role, for example, all the activities (S1 through S8) are very high in priority, and S1 has the highest priority. Similarly, W1 has the highest priority in the work role. Although all sixteen of these activities are vital, "must-do" activities, we don't have time to do all of them.

In *concept* (not in reality, except for major decisions), we draw a line across the lists of activities to allocate the proper amount of time to each role. This line is called the *margin.* According to our best estimates of activity durations, we are capable of doing, in total, only those activities that are above the margin. And here is the standard rule of allocation: The priorities of all the activities that are at the margin must be equal, or nearly equal. For example, Activities S4 and W6 have the same priority—the same importance per hour.

In *actuality*, it would take too much time to physically arrange our daily activities in priority order and to draw the margin. But we do need to mentally apply the concept, as accurately as we can.

THE PRIOR ANCHORING PROCESS

When business organizations and government agencies select contractors to build products or provide services, they must avoid favoritism. Therefore, what contracting officers often do, prior to requesting proposals from prospective contractors, is to assign numerical weights to the factors that the decision will be based on, and that is a mistake. As shown in earlier chapters, all methods that assign weights to factors—including both prior weighting and post weighting—are unsound. They do not anchor judgments about importance to relevant, real-world facts. Therefore, they need to be replaced as soon as possible.

In order for contracting decisions to be sound, they must be based on anchored judgments. At the same time, favoritism must be avoided. Therefore, *prior anchoring*—prior weighting of advantages—must replace prior weighting of factors ("weighting" is the same as "weighing").

The Four Central Activities

After defining the purpose and circumstances of the decision, the needs and preferences of the stakeholders, and the applicable criteria, complete the four central activities of the Prior Anchoring Method. The key words for remembering these activities are the same as for the Tabular Method: attributes, advantages, importance, and total importance.

1. Estimate the expected range of ***attributes*** in each factor.

   a. Prepare a list of factors—containers for the criteria, attributes, and advantages—for the decision. Include all factors in which there are applicable criteria, plus others in which there might be differences among the alternatives. If you need to collect data in a particular factor, just to be sure there are no differences, that factor should be included. For complex decisions, both factors and sub-factors might be required.

   b. If allowed by your organization's regulations, include a factor called "other" so that unforeseeable advantages can be taken into account. Of course, cost will nearly always be a factor. However, as is shown in chapter 24, cost must be included as a special factor, not as a regular factor.

2. Decide the expected range of ***advantages*** in each factor.

   a. In each factor:

      • Based on the must-criteria, identify the worst acceptable attribute (WA).

      • Estimate the worst expected attribute (WE).

      • Estimate the best expected attribute (BE).

   b. In each factor, select either the worst acceptable attribute or the worst expected attribute as the base for identifying advantages. If the two are the same or nearly the same, select the worst acceptable attribute. If not, select the worst expected attribute (see 3c, on the following page). The selected attribute is labeled as ***the least-preferred attribute.***

   c. In each factor, describe—or state—the difference between the least-preferred attribute and the best expected attribute. This difference is labeled as the most important advantage, or the ***anchor-statement advantage,*** in this factor. Statements describing these advantages are called anchor statements, because they anchor the decision to the relevant facts.

3. Decide the ***importance*** of the expected advantages.

   a. Select the paramount advantage—the most important of the anchor-statement advantages. Then, to establish a scale of importance for the decision, assign the paramount advantage an importance of 1, 10, or 100—or any convenient number. (Usually, a 0-to-100 scale is selected.)

b. Weigh the importance of each anchor-statement advantage, compared with the paramount advantage.

c. In each factor, construct either a preference chart or a preference curve, extending from the least-preferred attribute to the best expected attribute.

The following example of an attribute scale of a preference curve illustrates selecting the worst expected attribute (WE), instead of the worst acceptable (WA), as the least preferred. In this case, the curve from WE to best expected (BE) would be significantly easier to construct than the curve from WA to BE. (It would not be a mistake to select the worst acceptable as the least preferred. It would simply be more work.)

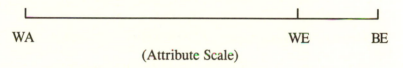

WA   WE   BE

(Attribute Scale)

4. Choose the preferred alternative, based on the *costs* of the alternatives, and the ***total importance*** of their advantages. In this activity, as detailed in the following sections, collect data (request and receive proposals), measure the importance of each actual advantage, incorporate new or unexpected information, and objectively choose the preferred alternative.

Request and Receive Proposals

After completing the set of preference charts and preference curves, you are ready to prepare a Request for Proposals (RFP) and to send a copy to each prospective contractor (this is actually a request for alternatives).

In the RFP, list the factors and sub-factors for the decision. Also, in each factor describe the must-criteria. Prospective contractors need to know whether or not they would be able to meet the minimum requirements, and if so, exactly what information they would need to provide in each factor. Although the factors must be identified, factor weights must never be established, and factors must never be listed "in order of priority."

If weighing factors is a requirement in your organization—as it is in many organizations—you can meet the intent of the requirement by using the weights assigned to the anchor-statement advantages. However, by using the anchor-statement weights you will definitely not be weighing the factors. Therefore, do not label the weights as factor weights. What is important to remember is that prior weighting of *factors* does not achieve its own purpose, which is to avoid favoritism. In many situations, weighing factors actually opens the door to favoritism. As soon as possible, the requirement to weight or rank factors needs to be eliminated.

Because methods that weigh factors create distortions and faulty decisions, they are unfair both to contractors and to contracting organizations. Nevertheless, those who have used such methods in the past should not be criticized. Although they were basing decisions on unanchored judgments, they were using the methods that were viewed, at that time, as the standard of how decisions should be made. But now that the CBA methods have been developed and validated, it's time to change—from Weighting-Rating-and-Calculating to Choosing By Advantages.

Measure the Importance of Each Actual Advantage

The proposals from prospective contractors are actually descriptions of mutually exclusive alternatives. Therefore, the methods for choosing from mutually exclusive alternatives must be used—not the methods for setting priorities among proposals.

After receiving the proposals, score their advantages—objectively—as follows: Locate the attributes of each proposal on the applicable preference charts and preference curves. Then, simply read the importance of each associated advantage.

Incorporate New or Unexpected Information

In some situations, the CBA methods for incorporating new or unexpected information must be applied during the scoring process. Incorporating such information sometimes requires extending one or more of the preference charts and preference curves in one direction or the other. The following is a brief discussion of how to incorporate unexpected information when evaluating contract proposals.

Suppose that we assigned the paramount advantage an importance score of 100. Now, in the factor with the paramount advantage, suppose that a proposal from one of the prospective contractors has an attribute that is even better than the best expected. In this case, we would assign the corresponding advantage an importance score greater than 100, based on extending the preference curve or chart. In any factor, if there is an attribute that is better than the best expected, the advantage corresponding with that attribute should be assigned an importance that is greater than the importance of that factor's anchor-statement advantage.

If one of the attributes is less desirable than the one that was originally selected as the least preferred, but at least as desirable as the worst acceptable, one option is to move the vertical scale of the curve or chart downward to establish a new zero point, as shown in chapter 10. The other option is to extend it downward and to use negative importance scores.

Choose the Preferred Alternative

If the costs are equal—which will seldom be the case—choose the alternative that has the greatest total importance of advantages. If the costs are unequal, apply the CBA concepts and methods for money decision-making, as outlined in chapter 24.

Prior Anchoring can be used in situations other than contracting—for example, in hiring personnel or in judging a talent contest. Furthermore, CBA can be used in the contracting process without using prior anchoring. Simply state in the RFP that Choosing By Advantages will be used in the selection process. Then, to minimize the chance of favoritism, make sure the contractors are not identified with their proposals until after the proposals have been evaluated. This is much simpler than the Prior Anchoring Process; however, if you need to avoid both favoritism and the suspicion of favoritism, you need to use prior anchoring.

According to several contracting specialists who have attended CBA workshops, existing laws and regulations do not allow the use of prior anchoring. They say that, although Weighting-Rating-and-Calculating is unsound and opens the door to favoritism, they are required to continue weighing factors and rating attributes due to legal precedence. I hope they are wrong. In my view, legal precedence should not require anyone to knowingly use unsound, unfair methods.

It is likely that legal precedence will be established, in the future, discouraging, or even prohibiting the use of factor-weighting methods in the contracting process. It would not be difficult to prove, in court, that factor weights and attribute ratings are unanchored judgments, and that decisions should not be based on unanchored judgments. Such proof could establish that selecting a contractor based on unanchored judgments is legally unacceptable. Of course, it's already ethically unacceptable.

Obviously, the Prior Anchoring Method can be misused. But when it is used correctly, it is exceptionally objective. It isn't totally objective, of course. However, it is far more objective (when used correctly) than the methods in common use today—especially those that weigh factors and rate attributes. But don't try to make it unreasonably objective or unreasonably precise. Keep it simple. If it is becoming too complex, or if it is taking too long, you are not doing it correctly.

Usually, decisions that call for prior anchoring are money decisions. And many other decisions, as well—including many personal and family decisions—are money decisions. Therefore, we all face the need to properly take money into account, in many of our decisions. Key differences between sound methods for money decisionmaking and sound methods for nonmoney decisionmaking are presented in chapter 24.

24

Special Methods
for Money Decisions

Due to the vital role of money in a modern economy, and due to the complexities of money decisionmaking, money decisions require special methods. This chapter introduces a few of the unique complexities of money decisionmaking and outlines how to deal with them.

The CBA concepts and methods for *nonmoney decisions,* such as the campsite decision, apply to *equal-money decisions* (which we label as nonmoney decisions), such as the canoe decision. These same concepts and methods apply to *unequal-money decisions* (which we label as money decisions). However, money decisions require additional definitions, principles, models, and methods. Furthermore, the methods for nonmoney decisions must be adjusted before being used for money decisions.

Money decisionmaking is a whole field of study. Therefore, most of the details pertaining to money decisionmaking are beyond the scope of this book. For example, this book ignores life-cycle costs, but the CBA system as a whole doesn't ignore life-cycle costs. It's the same with compound interest calculations, *business income and profit calculations,* and so on.

In the CBA training process, many of the money-related decisionmaking concepts and methods are presented in the congruent-decisionmaking area. Only those that are the most basic are presented in the sound-decision-making area. This chapter presents only part of what is typically presented in this area. To introduce a few basic sound-decisionmaking concepts and methods for money decisionmaking, the first four sections of this chapter outline the evolution of money decisionmaking methodology, from the primitive decisionmaking era to Choosing By Advantages.

The diagram on the following page brings together the histories of the cornerstone principles—histories that were presented in the introduction to part I and in chapters 13, 18, and 23. This diagram shows, first, that the fundamental rule, the principle of anchoring, and the methods principle each has its own history, and that each evolved in response to the initial version of the pivotal cornerstone principle. Second, it shows that the CBA system emerged when the cornerstone principles converged. Third, it shows that the future of CBA will depend on how well the CBA definitions, principles, models, and methods are accepted—especially, the revised pivotal cornerstone principle. Now, within this historical framework, let's outline the evolution of money decisionmaking methodology.

PRIMITIVE DECISIONMAKING

As you know, in the Instinctive Method (which came into use during the primitive decisionmaking era), decisionmakers observe the situation, make assumptions to fill in data gaps, and jump to a conclusion. The purpose of the following example is to show that people can easily be misled by this method.

As recently as late in the nineteenth century, there were Americans infected with tuberculosis who concluded that one of their relatives was a vampire. The vampire died of tuberculosis. What the vampire's infected relatives *observed* was that they became ill after the vampire had been buried. Because the relatives didn't understand how diseases are transmitted, and because they didn't understand incubation times, they *assumed* that the illness had been transmitted after the vampire had been buried. And they *concluded* that they should treat their own illness by exhuming and performing rituals with the remains of the vampire. Their assumption was based on experience and observations. Nevertheless, it was a false assumption, and it produced a wrong conclusion.

Basing decisions on assumptions not only happens in the Instinctive Process, it is also what happens in methods that weigh factors and rate attributes—including money decisionmaking methods. Unfortunately, the assumptions are often false, producing wrong conclusions.

During the primitive–decisionmaking era, people made key assumptions about money—especially, what money is, and what it does. Like the assumptions made by those who believed in vampires, these money assumptions didn't come out of thin air; they were based on experience and observations. Nevertheless, some of them were false and they produced wrong conclusions about how to include money in the decisionmaking process.

Histories of the Cornerstone Principles

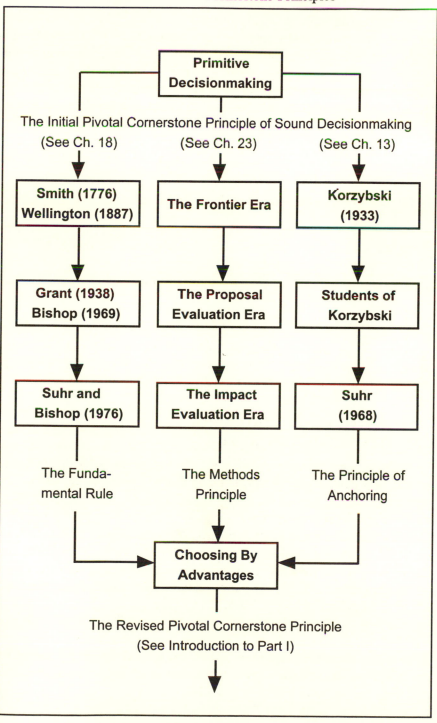

FRONTIER DECISIONMAKING

When decisionmaking methodology moved into the first scientific era—the frontier era—many assumptions pertaining to money didn't change. These same assumptions continued into the proposal–evaluation era and the impact–evaluation era. As a result, many of the money decisionmaking methods that are commonly used today are unsound.

A hypothetical example will be used to illustrate a few of the unsound methods that came into use during the proposal–evaluation era and impact–evaluation era: Our vacuum cleaner stopped working yesterday afternoon; this morning we went shopping for a replacement. We will use the vacuum cleaner example to illustrate the following methods:

Proposal–Evaluation Method *(this method is unsound)*

- Benefits Versus Costs (B/C)

Impact–Evaluation Methods *(these methods, also, are unsound)*

- Benefits/Costs Versus Benefits/Costs

- Incremental Benefits/Costs

- Other Impact–Evaluation Methods

Although the above methods are unsound, they played a major role in paving the way for CBA. Becoming familiar with them will help you understand the CBA methods that are presented later in this chapter.

A PROPOSAL–EVALUATION METHOD:
BENEFITS VERSUS COSTS (B/C)

In the vacuum cleaner example, soon after we began shopping we found an excellent new cleaner (Proposal E) on sale for a special low price. To help us decide whether or not to buy this proposed new cleaner, we listed its benefits. Then, we assigned a money value to each of the benefits, calculated the total value of the benefits ($220), calculated the Benefit/Cost ratio (B/C) of the proposal, and constructed the following graphical display. In this display, the benefits of the proposal are stacked against the costs, and the proposal's B/C ratio is compared with a B/C ratio of one (the slope of the line represents the B/C ratio).

The display shows that the B/C ratio of E is 1.7 (= $220 ÷ $130), which is much greater than one. Therefore, supposedly, selecting Proposal E would be the correct decision. However, as will be clearly shown by principles and methods that came into use during the impact–evaluation era, selecting this proposal would be a mistake.

Benefits Versus Costs (B/C)

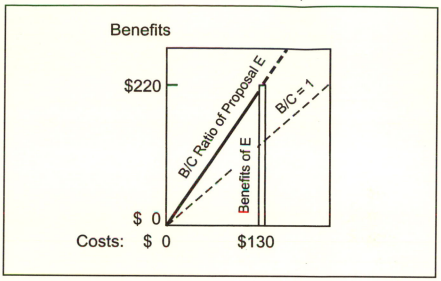

One of the mistakes in this method is that decisionmakers often include only those benefits that are priced in the market, as if they were the only benefits that matter. This mistake is one of the reasons members of the public objected when government officials used proposal–evaluation methods for major decisions. Another mistake is that market prices are used as a proxy for importance, as if the market price of a benefit represents its importance. What might be more significant is that the benefits of *without-the-proposal* are often ignored. Also, benefits and costs to future generations are often either ignored or severely discounted.

Therefore, many said, "Wait. We don't want to be faced with only the money-valued benefits and costs of a take-it-or-leave-it proposal. We want to see all of the social, economic, and environmental impacts—positive and negative, short-term and long-term—of all the reasonable alternatives. And the do-nothing alternative must be included." These demands moved decisionmaking methodology into the impact–evaluation era.

IMPACT–EVALUATION METHODS

In contrast with proposal–evaluation methods, impact–evaluation methods require considering a full range of reasonable alternatives, instead of a take-it-or-leave-it proposal. Therefore, we changed the name of "Proposal E" to "Alternative E," and we searched for other alternatives.

Benefits/Costs Versus Benefits/Costs

In the vacuum cleaner example, we considered two additional alternatives: Repair the old cleaner (Alternative R) and a superior-quality cleaner (Alternative S). As shown in the following display, Alternative S has a lower cost than E, and its benefits are greater than those of E. Therefore, E is obviously not the preferred alternative.

In this display, the slopes of the dashed lines represent the B/C ratios of the alternatives. As you can see, Alternative R has a much higher B/C ratio than either of the other alternatives. Therefore, according this method—in which the decision is based on comparisons of B/C ratios—we should select Alternative R. However, as the following sections demonstrate, this is not a sound method. The rule is: Never use Benefit/Cost ratios to choose from mutually exclusive alternatives with unequal costs.

Benefits/Costs Versus Benefits/Costs

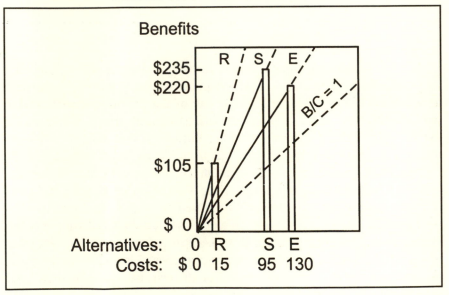

Incremental Benefits/Costs

Chapter 18 introduced a seemingly complex principle of sound decision-making, called Wellington's rule. This rule is actually surprisingly simple when applied to what we now call *increments*. Before CBA, an increment was defined as: An increase in cost, coupled with an increase, a decrease, or no change in total benefits (the CBA definition will be given later).

Wellington's Rule, Revisited

> No increase of expenditure over the unavoidable minimum is expedient or justifiable, however great the probable profits and value of the enterprise as a whole, unless the INCREASE can with reasonable certainty be counted on to be, in itself, a profitable investment.

The next display shows that in the vacuum cleaner decision there are three increases, or increments: (R minus 0), (S minus R), and (E minus S). To illustrate Wellington's rule, let's start with the third increment (E - S). In this increment, Alternative S is what Wellington would have called *the unavoidable minimum.* Alternative E is what he would have called *the enterprise as a whole.* It is obvious that Increment (E - S) (the increase from S to E) *is not* a profitable investment. Therefore, Alternative E is not the preferred alternative.

Incremental Benefits/Costs

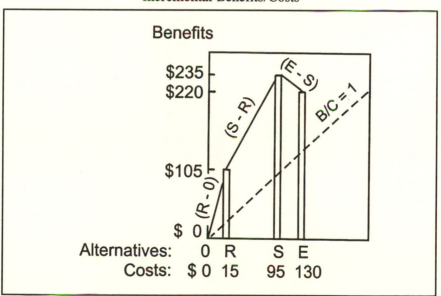

In contrast, the first increment (R - 0) *is* a profitable investment. This increment has a very small increase in cost, coupled with a large increase in benefits. (In this first increment, Alternative 0 is the unavoidable minimum, and Alternative R is the enterprise as a whole.)

According to the philosophy of the impact–evaluation era, the second increment (S - R) is also a profitable investment. Why? Because the B/C ratio of Increment (S - R) is 1.6 [= (235 - 105) ÷ (95 - 15)], which is much greater than one. This is shown by the slope of the line representing Increment (S - R). Therefore, according the Incremental Benefits/Costs Method, Alternative S is the preferred alternative. In many families, however, as the CBA process will demonstrate, Alternative S would not be the preferred alternative. Therefore, this is an unsound method.

Other Impact–Evaluation Methods

One of the unsound Impact–Evaluation methods that is sometimes used today is the Net-Benefits Method. This method compares the benefits minus the costs (B - C), or net benefits, of the alternatives—as measured in the following diagram by the lengths of the filled-in lines:

Benefits Minus Costs Versus Benefits Minus Costs

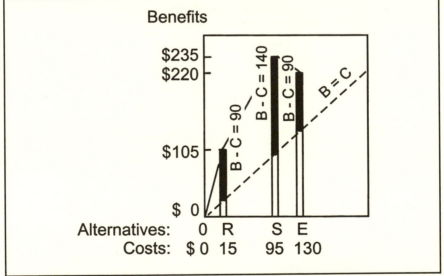

According to this method, Alternatives R and E are equally preferred, because their nets of benefits minus costs (B - C) are equal. And, according to this method, Alternative S is the preferred alternative, because it has the greatest net of benefits minus costs. However, as will be shown by the CBA process, Alternatives R and E are not equally preferred. And in many families, Alternative S would not be the preferred alternative.

The Net-Benefits Method is just one of several unsound methods that are called Cost-Benefit Analysis or Benefit/Cost Analysis. Although they do not qualify as sound methods, they do recognize that *cost must be included as a special factor.* In this regard, the WRC Process, which was presented in chapter 18, took a giant step backwards (the WRC methods typically include cost as a regular factor, and that is a critical mistake). Now, let's move from unsound methods of money decisionmaking to sound methods.

THE PROBLEM: MONEY DECISIONMAKING COMPLEXITIES

Like the impact–evaluation methods, the CBA methods for money decisions simultaneously consider a full set of reasonable alternatives, as required by Wellington's rule. A major improvement, compared with the impact–evaluation methods, is that the CBA methods also consider a full set of reasonable proposals, as required by the principle of interdependency. The principle of interdependency—as it relates to money decisions—is just one of several additional complexities that we must deal with, as we move from nonmoney to money decisionmaking.

The Principle of Interdependency

In itself, the principle of interdependency is very simple: If we spend $80 for one purchase, such as Increment (S - R), that same $80 is no longer available for a different purchase. Therefore, the decision about the one purchase and the decision about the different purchase are interdependent decisions. Although this principle is very simple, it is one of the most significant of all the money decisionmaking principles. Taking various types of interdependencies into account is essential in both nonmoney and money decisionmaking. For both, interdependencies can add a significant amount of complexity to the sound-decisionmaking process.

A Law That Cannot Be Repealed

The fact that money decisions are often financially interdependent is not the only complexity that we must take into account. It is impossible to avoid the following reality: Money decisions are more complex than corresponding nonmoney decisions. This reality is like a law of nature; it cannot be repealed. Many of the complexities of money decisionmaking are unavoidable. Remember: Computers are more complex than calculators, battleships are more complex than canoes, and money decisions are more complex than nonmoney decisions.

To simplify learning the CBA money-decisionmaking concepts and methods, divide learning these concepts and methods into two parts. First, learn what the complexities are. Then, learn how to correctly deal with them. Mechanically, the CBA methods for money decisions are almost as simple as those for nonmoney decisions. Therefore, the key to simplifying money decisionmaking is to clearly understand the complexities and to know, instantly, how to deal with them. First, carefully review what money is and what it does.

What Money Is and What Money Does

For many, something that is not tangible is harder to understand than something that is; and money, surprisingly, is not tangible. Money is an abstraction, a special type of abstraction. It is a message. And using money is a communication process, a powerful communication process. Decisionmakers have often made critical mistakes because they have not recognized this principle. To prevent these mistakes, CBA sharpens the definition of what money is and what it does. Here is the CBA definition: *Money is an official message that serves as a medium of exchange.*

Take a few minutes to memorize this definition, and share it with others. To make better decisions, people need to stop viewing money as a tangible commodity. Because it is not a tangible commodity, it must be included in the decisionmaking process as a special factor, not as a regular factor.

Money, the message, can be stamped on a metal coin. It can be stamped on a precious metal, such as silver. Or, it can be stamped on an abundant metal, such as copper. And a dollar that is stamped on an abundant metal is exactly the same as a dollar that is stamped on a precious metal. To clarify what money is and is not, think about what happens to the money when you melt a coin: When you melt the coin, the money is destroyed. What remains is not money. It is just a piece of metal.

Money, the message, can be printed on paper. And a dollar that is printed on paper is exactly the same as a dollar that is stamped on a coin. It is real money. Money can be written on a check, or it can be stored in a computer system. In fact, most of the money that exists in today's modern economy is in the form of electronic signals (messages) in computer systems.

For transferring large amounts of money, it is enormously more practical to use computers, rather than coins. By using electronic systems of communication, money can be sent from one country to another in almost no time at all. If a computer breaks down the money isn't lost, because banks keep back-up files.

A Close Connection Between Money and Debt

For some decisions, the relationship between money and debt increases the complexity of decisionmaking, and for those decisions this relationship needs to be clearly understood.

The American banking system is a fractional-reserve system. In this type of system, money is created when someone borrows from a bank. That transaction doesn't just create money, it creates both money and debt. And, as everyone knows, the debt begins to grow, immediately, according to the laws of compound interest—not according to the laws of physics. But the money from the same transaction stays the same; it doesn't grow, at all.

To illustrate this connection between money and debt, let's return to the canoe decision. Let's assume that we have decided to buy Canoe C, and the price is $400. Although we don't have $400, and our paycheck won't come until Friday (and this is Monday) we have decided to buy the canoe today. So, how will we obtain the $400? The answer is simple: We will create it. We will create a $400 increase in the world's supply of money. Then, we will use the $400 that we have created to buy the canoe.

We are able to add $400 to the world's supply of money because we have an excellent credit rating and our bank has more than $400 of lending authority. (Lending authority is not the same as money.) First, we write a $400 promissory note to the bank. (The note *is not* money.) In return, the bank writes a $400 deposit to our checking account, and this transaction reduces the bank's lending authority by a small fraction of the $400. (The deposit *is* money—money that didn't exist before).

Whenever we use this method to create $400 of new money, we also create $400 of new debt. And, as stated above, the debt begins to grow immediately. This explains why the debt that is associated with the creation of the money supply is continuously growing in both the public and private sectors of the economy. And obviously, debts grow faster during times when interest rates are higher.

"A Dollar" Is Not "A Dollar"

Because money is a message, not a commodity, "a dollar" is not "a dollar." To see what this means, let's examine the income and expenses of a hypothetical, very wealthy individual. The following sketch pertains to only those dollars she or he receives and spends for personal consumption. It does not include such expenses as taxes, investments, donations to charities, and so forth. The sketch shows that each additional item purchased for consumption is less important (per dollar) than the one before—if the decisionmaker properly sets priorities.

Dollars Received and Spent for Personal Consumption

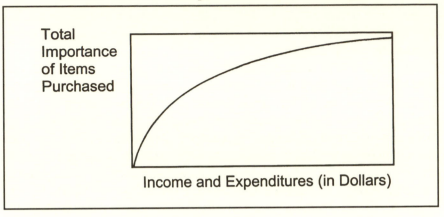

Income and Expenditures (in Dollars)

Starting at the left-hand side of the diagram, the first dollar would be used for essential purchases, such as items of food. Therefore, the first purchase would be very important (per dollar). At the right-hand side, the last dollar would be spent for something that has almost no importance at all. The owner of a very successful oil exploration company said, "Additional income has no personal value to me, whatsoever. I have an accountant who records my income, but just to keep score."

Now, let's look at the same concept from the opposite direction. That is, let's start at the right-hand side of the curve and move toward the left—toward lower levels of income. The first decrease in income would take away something that isn't very high in priority, such as an extra luxury automobile that is seldom used. But at the far left, a decrease would take away basic essentials, things that are necessary for survival. Therefore, near the left-hand end of the curve, each item taken away would be extremely important (per dollar).

Now, let's imagine a family that is shopping for a new car. The members of this particular family do an excellent job of managing their finances. Therefore, they know exactly what they can and cannot afford. Specifically, they know that their maximum expenditure for a car is $21,000. With this limit in mind, they identified several alternatives. The four that are at their price extremes are shown in the following display of cars and prices.

Notice that the increase in cost from A to B is $500. Also, the increase from K to L is $500. But each is a different $500. Neither of these $500 increases has any importance, in itself, but each does have importance in terms of what the family can purchase with $500.

Some of the Cars Being Considered

Car A: $10,000

B - A = $500

Car B: $10,500

•

•

•

Car K: $20,000

L - K = $500

Car L: $20,500

The principle of interdependency tells the family that if they spend $500 more in the purchase of a car, that particular $500 will not be available for something else. Therefore, before choosing a car, they need to ask themselves: What would be the something else? And how important is that particular something else, compared with the advantages that would be gained from spending the additional $500 for a car?

Although money, in itself, has no value, it is sometimes useful—pertaining to certain types of decisions—to talk about money as if it does have value. This simplifies discussions about money. And this is what we are going to do in the following discussion which demonstrates, again, that "a dollar" is not "a dollar."

Q. Which of the two $500 increases [(B - A = $500) or (L - K = $500)] is the most important one?

A. The $500 increase from K to L is far more important than the $500 increase from A to B.

Many people argue, at first, that the increase from K to L is less important than the increase from A to B, "because," they say, "the $500 increase from $20,000 to $20,500 is a much lower percentage of the total cost" (salespersons love this argument). What everyone needs to clearly see, however, is that the $500 increase from $20,000 to $20,500 is a much higher percentage of the funds that would remain for something else, after buying the car. This is demonstrated by the following comparison between the two $500 increases:

- After buying the $10,000 car, the family would have $11,000 left over for other purchases. A $500 increase from $10,000 to $10,500 would take away only 4.5 percent of the $11,000.

- After buying the $20,000 car, the family would have only $1,000 left over for other purchases. A $500 increase from $20,000 to $20,500 would take away 50 percent of the $1,000.

With the above in mind, let's look at the tradeoffs that would result from each of the $500 increases. In response to an increase from $10,000 to $10,500, the family would trade off things that, to them, are not extremely important (per dollar). But in response to an increase from $20,000 to $20,500, they would be forced to trade off things that are very important (per dollar), things that are high in their list of priorities. Furthermore, in response to an increase above $21,000 (their upper limit), they would be forced to trade off basic essentials, such as food and clothing.

These examples show that a dollar does have value, in terms of what it can be exchanged for in a particular situation. Nevertheless, it has no value in itself. Any judgments about the importance of so-called money-advantages would be unanchored judgments, which must be avoided. This means that we must use methods that do not require deciding the importance of dollars or differences in dollars—except approximately, in terms of tradeoffs, in Stage I decisionmaking (described later in this chapter). Remember: Sound methods do not require judging the importance of money-differences.

The Methods Principle for Money Decisions

Another unavoidable complexity is that there are many types of money decisions, and *different types of money decisions call for different methods of money decisionmaking.* Also, many money decisions are money-and-debt decisions, requiring compound interest calculations. In one of the ways that money-and-debt decisions have been classified, they are labeled as financial, commercial, economy, or economic decisions.

Financial decisions are borrowing and lending decisions. A financial institution, such as a bank, acquires lending authority for the purpose of creating money and debt (and collecting interest). *Commercial decisions* are decisions by commercial enterprises, those that create products and services. These decisions pertain to business revenues and costs. *Economy decisions,* as in *Principles of Engineering Economy* (Grant 1938), pertain to nonmoney effects, in addition to revenues and costs.

Economic decisions pertain to the allocation and use of resources (economists say scarce resources). Therefore, virtually all of our decisions, including most of our nonmoney decisions, are economic decisions. For example, many of our decisions pertain to the allocation and use of ourselves or other people. Because we are scarce resources, and because decisions that pertain to the allocation and use of scarce resources are economic decisions, our decisions pertaining to selecting and scheduling the things we do can be viewed as economic decisions.

Most decisionmakers don't need to be concerned with these four distinctions. But they do need to clearly understand the distinctions, described next, between *choosing from mutually exclusive alternatives* versus *setting priorities among nonexclusive proposals*.

The Distinction Between Mutually Exclusive Alternatives Versus Nonexclusive Proposals

As stated earlier, the CBA system was born in 1981, when the cornerstone principles converged. Of course, in its early stages of development the system required a lot of nurturing, and parts that were missing had to be invented. One of the parts that was missing was a set of sound methods for money decisionmaking.

Some of the money decisionmaking methods that came into use during recent eras are obviously inadequate. Others are in conflict with basic sound-decisionmaking principles. They do not qualify as CBA methods. Therefore, starting in 1981, I intensified my search for sound, clear, simple methods for money decisionmaking. In this search, I talked to economists, engineers, scientists, educators, and others, in addition to studying papers and books on subjects related to money decisionmaking. One of the questions that needed to be resolved was the question of whether or not the various Benefit/Cost methods that are in use today are sound methods.

Some experts said that Benefit/Cost methods are unsound and must not be used. Others said that they are sound and must be used. This disagreement might have been caused, in part, by conflicting definitions of *benefits* and *costs*. But the major cause, I believe, was that they were talking about different types of decisions.

Apparently, those who argued that Benefit/Cost methods are unsound were talking about choosing from *mutually exclusive alternatives*. If so, they were correct; Benefit/Cost ratios must not be used to choose from mutually exclusive alternatives. At the same time, those who argued that Benefit/Cost methods are sound were apparently talking about setting priorities among *nonexclusive proposals*. If so, they were almost correct.

Perhaps both sides recognized why they were in disagreement, but didn't recognize its significance. To review the distinction between mutually exclusive and nonexclusive, let's repeat the examples from chapter 23:

- Two Things That are Mutually Exclusive: In a garage that is only large enough to hold one car, we can park a Ford Taurus <u>or</u> an Oldsmobile Ciera, but not both. In this case, the one excludes the other, and the other excludes the one.

- Two Things That are Nonexclusive: In a garage that is large enough to hold two cars, we can park a Ford Taurus <u>and</u> an Oldsmobile Ciera. In this case, the one does not exclude the other, and the other does not exclude the one.

Now, let's use the vacuum cleaner example, presented earlier in this chapter, to review the distinction between alternatives and proposals. During the proposal–evaluation era, Cleaner E was viewed as "The Vacuum Cleaner Proposal." (There was just a proposal with no alternatives, except doing nothing.) When decisionmaking methodology evolved from the proposal–evaluation era into the impact–evaluation era, the decisionmaker's field of vision was expanded to bring Wellington's rule into view, and the term *proposal* took on a new meaning. During the impact–evaluation era, Cleaner E was viewed as only one of several alternatives, within "The Vacuum Cleaner Proposal."

Now, as decisionmaking methodology is evolving from the impact–evaluation era into the era of Choosing By Advantages, the decisionmaker's field of vision is being further expanded to bring the principle of interdependency into view. Besides asking, what additional *alternatives* should be considered? CBA decisionmakers ask, "What additional *proposals* should be considered?" This, necessarily, adds complexity to the process. Therefore, it is essential to simplify as much as possible. So, let's move from the topic of identifying the complexities of money decisionmaking to the topic of dealing with these complexities.

THE SOLUTION: CHOOSING BY ADVANTAGES

Of course, we could simplify money decisionmaking by just going back to using unsound methods, including those that ignore many of the complexities. But, to me, that would be unacceptable. Unsound methods produce too many unsound decisions. A much better way is to simplify by correctly dealing with the complexities. For both nonmoney and money decisionmaking:

- CBA simplifies complex decisions by taking smaller steps.

- CBA simplifies simple decisions by taking fewer steps.

- CBA simplifies all decisions by using correct data, and by using data correctly.

- The more you practice the CBA methods, including the methods for money decisions, the simpler they will become.

CBA simplifies considering a full range of proposals, and a full range of alternatives within each proposal, by taking smaller steps. To take smaller steps in the money decisionmaking process, CBA divides the decisionmaking phase (Phase III) into three stages, as follows:

Stage I: In each proposal, exclude the easy-to-exclude alternatives.

Stage II: Set priorities among the proposals.

Stage III: Allocate funds and resources.

Stage I: Exclude the Easy-to-Exclude Alternatives

In the original version of the canoe decision, the costs of the two canoes were the same. Now, to illustrate Stage I, let's suppose that the costs of Canoes C and K are $400 and $450, so that the cost of Canoe C is $50 less than the cost of K. This $50 difference must *not* be displayed as shown in the following chart (as an advantage). Displaying it as an advantage would encourage the decisionmakers to assign it an importance score, and that would be a mistake.

This Is Not a Sound Method

Advantages of Canoe C		Advantages of Canoe K	
• 10 Pounds Lighter		• Moderately Smoother Finish	
• Slightly Greater Stability		• Much Nicer Color	
• $50 Less Cost		• Slightly Better Keel Depth	
Total Importance:		Total Importance:	

Using the canoe example, this section demonstrates three things: First, methods that require judging the importance of money differences are unsound (money differences are not advantages, they represent advantages). Second, methods that use money scales to express importance are unsound (a money scale is not a valid importance scale). Third, sound methods use Importance/Cost reference lines, instead of Benefit/Cost reference lines.

We must use methods of decisionmaking that do not require or encourage assigning importance scores to money attributes or money differences. Therefore, the CBA formats for including money are designed to discourage this mistake. Following is an example of how to include money in the Two-List Format:

This Is a Sound Method

Advantages of Canoe C		Advantages of Canoe K	
• 10 Pounds Lighter	70	• Moderately Smoother Finish	5
• Slightly Greater Stability	75	• Much Nicer Color	100
		• Slightly Better Keel Depth	10
Total Importance:	145	Total Importance:	115
Total Cost:	$400	Total Cost:	$450

Notice that when there is a difference in cost the greatest total importance isn't underlined, because when there is a difference in cost the alternative with the greatest total importance isn't necessarily the preferred alternative. It is often impossible to make an informed judgment about which one of the alternatives is preferred until after Stage II and Stage III. In this case, however, we can easily exclude Canoe K, and the only remaining alternative is C. Obviously, Canoe C is the preferred alternative. It has both the greatest total importance and the least total cost.

If we had assigned an importance score to the $50 difference in cost, we would have been violating the fundamental rule of sound decisionmaking. As previously stated, differences in cost are not advantages, they represent advantages. In contrast with an advantage, which is an objective reality, a difference in cost is an abstraction. A similar example of the distinction between an abstraction and an objective reality is the distinction between a map and the territory represented by the map. As stated by Alfred Korzybski and his students:

- The map *is not* the territory.

- The map *represents* the territory.

"The map is not the territory" is a key sound-decisionmaking metaphor. It reminds us of the difference between symbols and actuality. While I was a scoutmaster, whenever I led a scout troop on a backpack trip in a wilderness area I helped the scouts increase their awareness of this difference. I would lay out a map of the area. Then, I would say to one of the scouts, "It's your turn. Where is," for example, "Hidden Lake?"

At first, most of the scouts pointed toward the symbolized location of Hidden Lake (or wherever we were going) on the map. Very few pointed toward the actual location of Hidden Lake, on the ground. Then, we talked about the relationship between the symbolized location and the actual location. Sometimes I pointed to the symbol of Hidden Lake on the map, and said, "This is the location of Hidden Lake, *on your map*. This is not Hidden Lake." Then, while pointing in the right direction, I would say, "Hidden Lake is on the other side of that ridge." Next, we talked about how to keep from getting lost. We reviewed, many times, the following rules (violations of these rules have caused a significant number of fatalities):

- The First Rule of Hiking: When hiking in a group, stay with the person behind you.

- The Second Rule of Hiking: Keep yourself oriented, and know your location, *on your map,* at all times.

I am happy to report that none of our scouts were ever lost—and there were no close calls. Furthermore, by understanding and skillfully using map symbols, they were able to reach their hiking goals. And they enjoyed doing it. Similarly, by understanding and skillfully using financial symbols, people can achieve their financial goals.

The $50 difference between the $400 cost of Canoe C and the $450 cost of Canoe K is similar to a map symbol. During Stage I, however, this $50 difference is not as specific as a map symbol. It is at a higher level on the ladder of abstraction. During Stage I, the $50 difference *represents* at least one advantage of at least one proposal. But at this time, we have not yet identified the particular advantage, or advantages, represented. Obviously, since it is an unknown advantage, we don't know its magnitude or the magnitudes of its associated attributes. Therefore, it is impossible for us to make an accurate judgment about its importance.

In some cases, we are able to deal with this complexity by transforming the unequal-money decision into an equal-money decision. That is, we are able to decide what item, or items, would be purchased with the difference in cost and include them in the evaluation. For example, the stakeholders could have included a $50 pair of wicker canoe seats, as follows:

This Is a Sound Method

Advantages of Canoe C		Advantages of Canoe K	
• 10 Pounds Lighter	70	• Moderately Smoother Finish	5
• Slightly Greater Stability	75	• Much Nicer Color	100
• Wicker Seats	35	• Slightly Better Keel Depth	10
Total Importance:	180	Total Importance:	115
Both alternatives have the same cost ($450).			

In the CBA training process, when we point out that money attributes and money differences are abstractions, we need to also point out that we are talking about real money. Real money is like a real map. It is very useful—it makes our economic system work—but it is not the territory. The next time you are using a map, point to a map symbol (representing Chicago, for example) and to say to yourself, "This is not Chicago." And the next time you write a check to pay for a purchase, such as a new chair, point to the message on the check and say to yourself, "This is not a new chair." Nevertheless, the money you wrote on the check is real money.

The next principle is that sound methods do not use money scales as importance scales, because the money that is used in importance scales is not real money. To introduce this principle, let's return to the vacuum cleaner decision. During previous eras, the vertical scale in a graphical display of benefits versus costs was viewed as a money scale, and that was a mistake. A so-called dollar in the vertical scale is entirely different from an actual dollar in the horizontal scale. The vertical scale is not a money scale; it is an importance scale, and it is subjective. Therefore, as in the next display, CBA labels the vertical scale as an importance scale. Notice, also, that the alternatives have been renamed—as V0, V1, V2, and V3.

Establishing a Reference Line

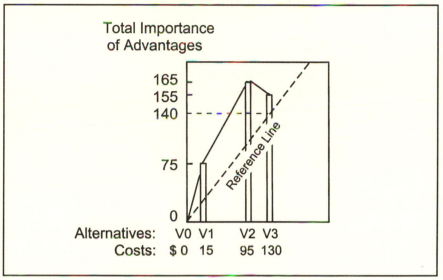

Because the vertical scale is an importance-scale, not a money-scale, the reference line represents an Importance/Cost ratio, not a Benefit/Cost ratio. To locate the reference line in this example, we estimated the following: In the proposals that are competing with the vacuum cleaner proposal for the same funds, a typical high priority advantage that costs $130 has an importance of 140.

Remember, it is not *$130* that has an importance of 140. Instead, it is something tangible, such as *a $130 chair,* that has an importance of 140. Or, it could be a $130 computer program, or some other high priority item (with a cost of $130) that has an importance of 140. Remember, we can make an anchored judgment about the importance of a tangible reality, such as a chair. But a judgment about the importance of an amount of money would be an unanchored judgment.

When using the reference line, remember that money has a special role in the decisionmaking process; it is an official message that serves as a medium of exchange. Therefore, money, in itself, has no importance. Also, the reference line is, at best, a rough estimate. Nevertheless, as the following demonstrates, it is a very useful estimate in Stage I.

In the Incremental Benefits/Costs Method, an increment is defined as an increase in cost, coupled with an increase, a decrease, or no change in benefits. In CBA, it is defined as follows:

- An *increment* is an increase in cost, coupled with an increase, a decrease, or no change in total importance of advantages.

Stage I of the CBA Process

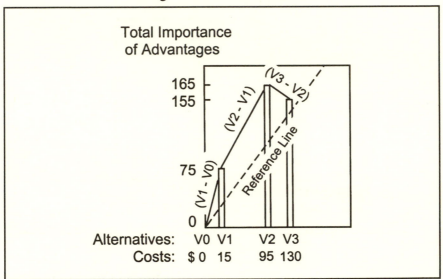

In this display, the increments are (V1 - V0), (V2 - V1), and (V3 - V2). During Stage I, we examine each increment, and we exclude the easy-to-exclude alternatives. As in the Incremental Benefits/Costs Method, if the slope of the reference line is approximately 45 degrees, and if the slope of the line representing the increment is nearly vertical, the alternative on the left is easily excluded. And that is how V0 was excluded. If the slope of the line representing the increment is negative, horizontal, or nearly horizontal, the alternative on the right is easily excluded. And that is how V3 was excluded.

In many cases, when all the easy-to-exclude alternatives have been eliminated there will be only one remaining—the preferred alternative. In other cases, such as in the vacuum cleaner example, two or more alternatives will remain. To identify the preferred alternative in those cases, Stage II and Stage III of the CBA process are required. (In the Incremental Benefits/Costs Method, there is no Stage II or Stage III.)

This is where CBA is very different from the Incremental Benefits/Costs Method: CBA takes the principle of interdependency into account. CBA recognizes that *if the slope of the increment is between nearly vertical and nearly horizontal, neither of the two alternatives in the increment should be excluded during Stage I.* In the example, we didn't exclude V1 or V2 during Stage I. The reason we didn't is that—in addition to (V2 - V1)—there are other proposals that are competing for the same funds. And at this time we don't know if the other proposals are higher or lower in priority than (V2 - V1). Therefore, in this case, Stages II and III are required.

When the Prior Anchoring Method is used in selecting a contractor, it sometimes isn't feasible to do Stages II and III, even when they are needed. In that case, greater care must be exercised when establishing the reference line, and it is precisely used in choosing the preferred alternative. In the vacuum cleaner example, based on comparing the slope of (V2 - V1) with the slope of the reference line, V2 would be selected.

To illustrate the need for stages II and III, think about going shopping in a large department store. As we push a shopping cart down the first aisle, we will soon come to an item that we would really like to buy. In the Incremental Benefits/Costs Method, we would ask ourselves, "Is this item, or this increment, worth more than its cost?" That is a dangerous question. If we perceived that the benefits of the item are worth even slightly more than the cost, we would load it into the cart.

Those who are exceptionally frugal would arrive at the check-out counter with almost nothing in the cart. As a result, they would have money left over. But they would be leaving behind several high-priority items that they should have purchased. On the other hand, many of us would quickly fill the cart with "worthwhile" items. It would be filled so quickly that we would run out of money before we would come to the aisle with our highest-priority items. Therefore, our money would be gone, and we would be leaving behind a number of high-priority items that we should have purchased. Of course, some would simply add the high-priority items to the cart, and they would pay for them by borrowing and over-spending.

How can we avoid the mistakes of under-spending, low-priority spending, and over-spending? The key is to use the three-stage money decisionmaking process, *but include Stages II and III only when necessary.* To demonstrate why Stages II and III are not always necessary, let's convert the campsite decision that was presented in chapter 22 to a money decision. Let's suppose that the three sites are in a commercial campground. Let's suppose, also, that Site No. 19 has utility connections (that we are not equipped to use), and the costs are as follows:

Site No. 8: $ 3.00   Site No. 19: $ 20.00   Site No. 23: $ 4.50

This might not be a realistic example, but that doesn't matter; selecting a campsite is not its purpose. It's purpose is to demonstrate Stage I of the money-decisionmaking process. Study the discussion and displays that follow to learn the *process;* don't worry about the *content* of the decision. After you have studied the campsite example, practice with simple, hypothetical examples of your own invention. Then, practice with simple, real-world decisions.

In Stage I, the alternatives are arranged—in a Two-List Display, a Tabular Display, a graphical display, or a set of scoring sheets (or simply in mind)—according to their costs. Also, they are named, or renamed, according to their costs (in the example, S1 is first, then S2, and then S3). The greatest total importance isn't underlined, because the alternative with the greatest total isn't necessarily the preferred alternative.

As demonstrated by the vacuum cleaner example, an Incremental-Importance/Incremental-Cost reference line is used in Stage I to exclude the easy-to-exclude alternatives. In this case, S2 (Site No. 23) is the only alternative that was not excluded. Therefore, S2 is the preferred alternative. And, as in many cases in real-world decisionmaking, Stages II and III are not required.

If funds had been unlimited, a reference line would not have been needed, and S3 (Site No. 19) would have been selected. But, as we all know, funds are seldom, if ever, unlimited. For the stakeholders in this example, special items of food they planned to buy on the way home from the camping trip had a much higher priority than the advantages that they traded off by not spending the extra $15.50 for Increment (S3 - S2).

Some argue that this method is unsound, because they think (incorrectly) that constructing the reference line requires assigning money values to nonmarket advantages. They say that it is impossible to assign correct money values to nonmarket advantages. Their argument is true, but it doesn't go far enough. It is not only impossible to assign correct money values to nonmarket advantages; it is also impossible to assign correct money values to advantages that are priced in the market. There is no such thing as "correct" money values.

Some try to find "correct" market prices to use—rather than using importance scores—so they won't need to take personal responsibility for their judgments about importance. But due to interdependencies among money decisions, finding a "correct" price is somewhat like finding a "correct" ritual for the remains of a vampire. On the other hand, as shown by the campsite example, we can estimate (approximately, in Stage I) the importance of other advantages that a particular amount of money ($15.50, in this case, as shown by the dot in the graphical display) would buy.

Tabular Display of the Campsite Decison

FACTORS	ALTERNATIVES		
	S1 (SITE NO. 8)	S2 (SITE NO. 23)	S3 (SITE NO. 19)
1. WATER Attributes:	60 Ft. Away	150 Ft. Away	260 Ft. Away
Advantages:	200 Feet Closer 40	110 Feet Closer 30	
2. TENT SPOT Attributes:	Moderately Level	Quite Sloping	Almost Level
Advantages:	Mod. More Level 30		Much More Level 70
3. TABLE Attributes:	Without	With	Without
Advantages:		With Versus Without 65	
4. PRIVACY Attributes:	Not Very Private	Moderately Private	Very Private
Advantages:		Mod. More Privacy 45	Much More Privacy 100
TOTAL IMPORTANCE:	70	140	170
TOTAL COST:	$3.00	$4.50	$20.00

Graphical Display of the Campsite Decision

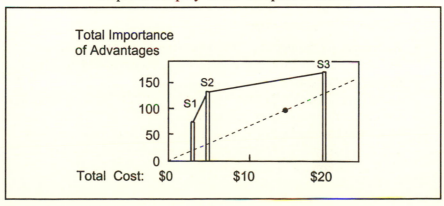

When used for a simple decision, both a tabular display and a graphical display (such as those for the campsite decision) can be constructed in only a few minutes. To be able to quickly and easily construct them for decisions where they are needed, practice constructing them for decisions where they are not needed. When they are needed, their precision should be no more than what is required for the decision; and usually, even for complex decisions, they can be hand constructed and hand lettered.

Stage II: Set Priorities Among the Proposals

As demonstrated by the campsite example, the Stage I CBA methods respond to Wellington's rule. Then, building on the results from Stage I, the Stage II methods respond to the principle of interdependency. This section will be only a brief introduction to Stage II.

There is a very important distinction between Stage I and Stage II. In Stage I, we choose from mutually exclusive alternatives. Specifically, we exclude the easy-to-exclude alternatives. In Stage II, we set priorities among nonexclusive proposals. This distinction is simple: When choosing from a pair of mutually exclusive alternatives, we are able to choose one, or the other, *but not both.* In contrast, after setting priorities between a pair of nonexclusive proposals, we are able to choose one, or the other, *or both*—except as limited by funding constraints. This distinction is vital, because the sound methods for choosing from mutually exclusive alternatives are unsound for setting priorities among nonexclusive proposals; and vice versa.

Before we begin the discussion of Stage II, let's review the distinctions between proposals, alternatives, increments, and proposed increments.

- In Stage II, we will be considering several *proposals*, including the proposal to buy a new vacuum cleaner. These proposals are all competing for the same funds.

- In the vacuum cleaner proposal, we considered four *alternatives:* V0, V1, V2, and V3. Therefore, this proposal has three *increments,* as shown in the next graph.

- By comparing the slopes of the increment lines with the slope of the reference line, we excluded V0 and V3. This narrowed the proposal to only one *proposed increment,* with a cost of $80 (the cost of the cleaner will be either $15 for V1, or $95 for V2). By excluding V0, we included the $15 cost of Increment (V1 - V0). Therefore, we didn't need to display, or even to know, its incremental importance and its priority (this is why they are shown in parentheses in the chart at the bottom of the following page).

A proposed increment is a specific proposal (therefore, we sometimes label proposed increments simply as *proposals*). Stage II sets priorities among proposed increments within a particular category of funding. For example, the vacuum cleaner proposal is in the furniture and appliance category. Specifically, it is increment (V2 - V1) that has been proposed. By including or not including Increment (V2 -V1) in our final budget, we will be choosing between Alternatives V2 and V1.

The Vacuum Cleaner Proposal, Revisited

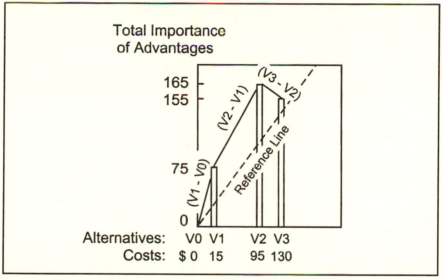

In addition to the vacuum cleaner proposal, other proposals in the furniture and appliance category include a proposal to repair a refrigerator (Proposal R) and a proposal to buy a new dishwasher (Proposal D). Following are the increments in this category, listed in order of their priorities (V0, R0, and D0 are the do-nothing alternatives):

Increment Identification	Incremental Importance	Incremental Cost	Priority (Imp./Cost)	Total Cost
(V1 - V0)	(75)	$ 15	(5.0)	$ 15
(R1 - R0)	360	120	3.0	135
(V2 - V1)	90	80	1.1	215
(D1 - D0)	360	510	0.7	725

Along with setting priorities within the furniture and appliance category, priorities must also be established in other categories; such as food, clothing, education, and recreation. When constructing a display of priorities, the proposed increments are arranged, in each category, according to incremental importance per incremental dollar.

This has been one of the most controversial of all the steps in the CBA process. For some, apparently, it is very counter-intuitive. Most of those who disagree with this step argue that the increments should be arranged according to importance. For example, they say that (D1 - D0) should be higher in priority than (V2 - V1)—instead of as shown below—even though (D1 - D0) has a much higher cost than (V2 - V1).

Increment Identification	Incremental Importance	Incremental Cost	Priority (Imp./Cost)
(V2 - V1)	90	$ 80	1.1
(D1 - D0)	360	510	0.7

They say, also, that because (D1 - D0) and (R1 - R0) have the same importance they should have the same priority—even though (D1 - D0) has a cost of *$510,* while (R1 - R0) has a cost of only *$120.* They argue that cost should not be a consideration.

A few who disagree with this step argue that the increments should be arranged according to their costs. They argue that (V2 - V1), with a cost of $80, should be higher in priority than (R1 - R0), with a cost of $120—even though (V2 - V1) is a lot less important than (R1 - R0).

Most observers strongly disagree with both of these arguments. On the one hand, arranging the proposals according to importance, with the greatest total importance at the top of the list, would create an irrational bias in favor of large, high-cost proposals. On the other hand, arranging them according to cost, with the least cost at the top of the list, would create an irrational bias in favor of small, unimportant proposals.

To prevent both types of bias—to make sound decisions—the increments must be arranged, within each category, according to their *incremental-importance/incremental-cost* ratios. This method doesn't favor small, medium, or large proposals. Instead, it maximizes individual and organizational performance. Nevertheless, some say that they agree with everything about CBA, except that they disagree with using incremental-importance/incremental-cost ratios. To see this from their perspective, let's look, again, at increments (V2 - V1) and (D1 - D0).

Why do some people argue that Increment (D1 - D0) should have a higher priority than (V2 - V1)? Here, I believe, is the answer: From their perspective—particularly in government agency work units—it is very logical to prefer the higher cost. Priority decisions affect their budget allocations, and members of work units would prefer *receiving* $510 for Increment (D1 - D0), rather than receiving $80 for Increment (V2 - V1). In their view, a $430 increase, from $80 to $510, would be an advantage. (Salespersons also prefer higher costs.)

Deciding Advantages. When deciding advantages, especially in the money decisionmaking process, keep in mind what an advantage is and is not. It is a difference between two alternatives, within a proposal; it is not a difference between two proposals. In Stage II, each proposal (each proposed increment) has two alternatives: with-the-proposed-increment and without.

Remember that in a priority list, each importance is the net importance—the incremental importance—of the proposed increment. That is, it is the importance of the advantages of with-the-proposed-increment minus the importance of the advantages of without-the-proposed-increment. The cost is the net cost—the incremental cost. Most of all, remember that the ratio of incremental importance per incremental dollar is what establishes the priority of the increment. An example of this ratio is shown in the following display.

Using the Correct Ratio

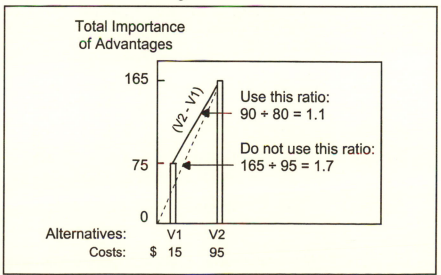

Deciding Importance. In stage II, scoring sheets can be used (one for each increment) each with a Two-List Display. On the left, list the advantages of without-the-proposed-increment. (When working with decisionmakers who are unfamiliar with CBA, we sometimes label the advantages of without-the-proposed-increment as the *disadvantages* of the increment.) On the right, list the advantages of with-the-proposed-increment. Then, weigh both sets of advantages on the same scale. When deciding importance, *all the advantages,* of *all the alternatives,* in *all the proposals* must be weighed on the same scale of importance. Also, as shown in chapter 23, to avoid a bias in favor of small proposals we must studiously avoid assigning average importance scores to smaller-than-average advantages.

Constructing a Priority List. After deciding the importance of each advantage and calculating the incremental importance and incremental cost of each proposed increment, arrange the increments according to importance per dollar. When using the scoring-sheet method, arrange the scoring sheets in order (according to importance per dollar). For most proposals, there will be only one increment. But for the vacuum cleaner proposal, there will be two.

When we are dealing with a set of major proposals (such as a set of highway construction proposals), we actually construct a priority list. But in the furniture and appliance example, we would simply apply the concept mentally, without constructing a list. The following list, which was presented earlier, shows what we would have in mind. It includes the two increments of the vacuum cleaner proposal (V), the one increment of the refrigerator repair proposal (R), and the one increment of the dishwasher proposal (D)—arranged according to their priorities.

Increment Identification	Incremental Importance	Incremental Cost	Priority (Imp./Cost)	Total Cost
(V1 - V0)	(75)	$ 15	(5.0)	$ 15
(R1 - R0)	360	120	3.0	135
(V2 - V1)	90	80	1.1	215
(D1 - D0)	360	510	0.7	725

Choosing the Preferred Alternative. In Stage III, based on this list of priorities, we will choose between Alternatives V1 and V2.

Stage III: Allocate Funds and Resources

In Stage III, the final stage of Phase III, we allocate funds and resources, and construct a budget. This requires setting priorities across categories, using a process that was introduced in chapter 23. In this process, a line *(the margin)* is drawn so that at the margin the priorities are approximately equal. Also, the amount of funds needed for those proposals that are above the margin is equal to the amount of funds available. Therefore, those that are above the margin are selected, and those below are excluded. In the furniture and appliance example:

If the margin is at **$15**, select **V1.**

If the margin is at **$135,** select **V1,** plus **R1.**

If the margin is at **$215,** select **V2,** plus **R1.**

If the margin is at **$725,** select **V2,** plus **R1,** plus **D1.**

It is in Stage III where, for example, the canoe proposal competes with the vacuum cleaner proposal (this is where we decide whether or not to purchase a canoe). As just demonstrated, it is in this same stage where we choose between Alternatives V1 and V2. The priorities of other competing proposals (other competing increments) and the availability of funds determines the location of the margin. In the vacuum cleaner example, if the family's margin is at $135 or less, they should select V1. If their margin is at $215 or more, they should select V2 (instead of V1).

(Due to the simplicity of this decision, the family—guided by a written budget—would probably use the Instant CBA process for money decisions, described in the following chapter, for this decision.)

Phase IV: The Reconsideration Phase

The next example is similar to the campsite example. In this example, a business organization or a government agency has selected Alternative M2—one of the alternatives in a major project proposal. The next phase of the CBA process is the reconsideration phase (Phase IV).

One of the ways to effectively reconsider a major decision is by using a process that is called Value Engineering, or VE. (It is also called Value Analysis, or VA.) In the VE process, a specially trained VE team finds ways to improve the decision. In many cases, large improvements have been made by using the VE process. Of course, the ideal improvement is a decrease in cost, coupled with an increase in total importance, as shown in the next diagram.

Using the VE Process in the CBA Process

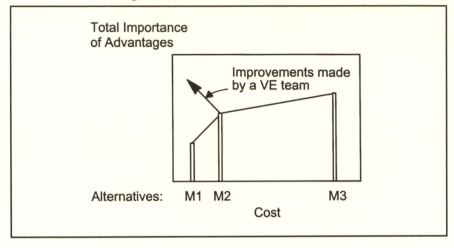

In the CBA system, there is a two-way relationship between VE and CBA. First, CBA decisionmakers who have VE skills use VE, when it is applicable, during the reconsideration phase of the CBA process. Second, they use CBA during the evaluation phase—and, where applicable, during other phases—of the VE process. VE facilitators, consultants, and others who participate in the VE process must avoid using unsound methods of decisionmaking—such as Weighting-Rating-and-Calculating or Choosing By Advantages and Disadvantages. Therefore, they need to thoroughly learn and skillfully use the CBA methods.

Value engineers who understand and use CBA have suggested including CBA skills as a requirement for certification in the value engineering field. Others have suggested including CBA skills as a requirement in the licensing of all professional engineers. Obviously, engineers need to learn and skillfully use sound methods of decisionmaking, even if sound decisionmaking skills do not become a requirement for professional licensing. Engineers must not only use correct data, they must also use data correctly.

If engineers should be required to learn and use sound methods, what about members of other professions, especially those who make significant decisions that affect other people? For example, shouldn't economists, educators, psychologists, counselors, consultants, lawyers, doctors, employees in governments, and—most of all—leaders in organizations be expected to use sound methods? Shouldn't we all be expected to use sound methods? Some have said, "Yes, but not necessarily CBA methods."

In theory, I agree. In practice, however, when additional sound methods are discovered, or invented, they will probably weigh advantages, either explicitly or implicitly. Remember that we selected the name, Choosing By Advantages, in response to the following question: What do sound methods have in common? The answer: They base decisions on the importance of advantages.

So far, we haven't been able to find any exceptions. But that is just one of the reasons we gave the name Choosing By Advantages to sound methods. We decided not to just call them sound methods, because many of the unsound methods they will replace—including Weighting-Rating-and-Calculating, Choosing By Pros and Cons, Choosing By Advantages and Disadvantages, Choosing By Benefit/Cost Ratios, and others—are commonly viewed as "sound" methods. Usually, therefore, in response to requests for sound methods, unsound methods would be provided. Another reason for not calling them sound methods is that the total Choosing By Advantages system includes congruent decisionmaking methods and effective decisionmaking methods, not only sound decisionmaking methods.

Complex and difficult decisions are not the only decisions that call for CBA methods. Simple, day-to-day and minute-to-minute decisions call for them, as well. The CBA methods for simple decisions and those for very simple decisions—presented in the following chapters—are for both nonmoney decisions and money decisions.

25

Simple Methods
for Simple Decisions

The following display reminds us that, compared with decisions that call for the Two-List Method, CBA simplifies simple decisions by taking fewer steps. For example, the Simplified Two-List Method requires only two central activities, instead of three.

Sound Methods

SPECIAL METHODS FOR	SIMPLE METHODS FOR SIMPLE DECISIONS					VERY SIMPLE METHODS FOR
	The Tabular Method	**The Two-List Method**	Simplified Tabular Method	Simplified Two-List Method	Instant CBA	
COMPLEX	Attributes	—	Attributes	—	—	VERY
AND VERY	Advantages	**Advantages**	(Advantages)	Advantages	(Advantages)	
COMPLEX	Importance	**Importance**	—	—	—	SIMPLE
DECISIONS	Total Importance	**Total Importance**	(Total Importance)	(Total Importance)	(Total Importance)	DECISIONS
SPECIAL METHODS FOR MONEY DECISIONS						

Fewer Steps

This chapter presents the Simplified Tabular Method, and it reviews the Simplified Two-List Method and the Instant CBA Process. Chapter 26 reviews the Recognition–Response Process, and it presents additional very simple methods for very simple decisions.

THE SIMPLIFIED TABULAR METHOD

The Simplified Tabular Method is used in situations where it quickly becomes obvious, after just summarizing the costs and attributes of the alternatives, that one of them is preferred. Therefore, only the first of the four central activities—summarize the costs and attributes—is performed in writing. The second activity is required, but not in writing. Therefore, in the display of sound methods, the second activity of this method is shown in parentheses. The third activity isn't required, at all. The fourth is required, but not in writing.

In the Simplified Tabular Method, the Tabular Format is used, right from the start—in case it turns out that additional activities of the Tabular Method must be performed in writing. Following is an outline of the Simplified Tabular Method for money decisions:

The Simplified Tabular Method

1. In the Tabular Format, summarize the *costs* and the ***attributes*** of the alternatives.

2. Mentally perceive the ***advantages*** of each alternative.

3. Without deciding the importance of each individual advantage, choose the preferred alternative, based on the *costs* and the ***total importance*** of advantages.

If the decision isn't obvious—after summarizing the costs and the attributes—write the advantages in the spaces provided in the Tabular Format. Then, if the decision still isn't obvious, complete the Tabular Method, as follows: After displaying the advantages, decide and display the importance of each individual advantage. Then, calculate totals.

THE SIMPLIFIED TWO-LIST METHOD, REVISITED

As in the Simplified Two-List Method for nonmoney decisionmaking, presented in chapter 5, the Simplified Two-List Method for money decisionmaking requires only one of its activities to be displayed in writing. The difference is that for money decisionmaking the costs of the alternatives must be included.

The Simplified Two-List Method

---

1. In the Two-List Format, summarize the *costs* and the ***advantages*** of the alternatives.

2. Without deciding the importance of each individual advantage, choose the preferred alternative, based on the *costs* and the ***total importance*** of advantages.

To demonstrate the Two-List Format, chapter 5 presented an outline of the Simplified Two-List Method, for nonmoney decisions, and introduced the choice between Canoes C and K. But in that case, the Simplified Two-List Method was inadequate. After listing the advantages of the alternatives, the stakeholders were unable to choose the preferred alternative. Therefore, they completed the Two-List Method (as shown in chapter 9) to make the decision. By using the Two-List Method, they easily selected Canoe C. Following, again, is the choice between Canoes C and K:

In This Decision, the Two-List Method Was Used

Advantages of Canoe C		Advantages of Canoe K	
• 10 Pounds Lighter	70	• Moderately Smoother Finish	5
• Slightly Greater Stability	75	• Much Nicer Color	100
		• Slightly Better Keel Depth	10
Total Importance:	145	Total Importance:	115
Both Alternatives Have the Same Total Cost.			

In contrast with the canoe example, following is an example of where the stakeholders were able to use the Simplified Two-List Method to choose the

the preferred alternative. They were choosing between two backpacking tents, J and Q. After just listing the costs and the advantages of the two alternatives, the choice was obvious. Without deciding the importance of each individual advantage, they easily decided that the four advantages of Tent J far outweighed the two advantages of Tent Q. In addition, the cost of J was less than the cost of Q. Therefore, they quickly selected Tent J, and they were confident that they had made the right decision.

Notice that they used the Two-List Format, right from the start, in case it became necessary for them to complete the Two-List Method, by deciding the importance of each individual advantage and calculating totals.

In This Decision, the Simplified Two-List Method Was Used

Advantages of Tent J	Advantages of Tent Q
• Slightly Better Ventilation	• With Versus without A Small Vestibule
• Much Easier to Set Up	• Slightly More Floor Space
• 12 Ounces Lighter (5 lb. 7 oz. Versus 6 lb. 3 oz.)	
• Better Stuff-Bag	
Total Importance:	Total Importance:
Total Cost: $268	Total Cost: $310

The Simplified Two-List Method is an ideal method to use during decision meetings. It keeps the participants focused on advantages, with a minimum of writing. But it isn't just for unimportant decisions; it's for important decisions, as well—if they are simple. And remember: By practicing the Simplified Two-List Method, you will soon be able to use the Instant CBA Process, whenever it is applicable, instead of the Instinctive Method. Also, you will soon be able to use the very simple CBA methods for very simple decisions, and you will be making excellent decisions more often than ever before.

INSTANT CBA, REVISITED

As shown in chapter 6, Instant CBA requires one activity with two simultaneous tasks. In the first task, we mentally perceive the costs and advantages, instead of listing them on paper. The second task is the same as the second activity in the Simplified Two-List Method: Without deciding the importance of each individual advantage, simply choose the preferred alternative, based on the *costs* of the alternatives and the *total importance* of their advantages.

In response to thoughts, feelings, observations, displays of data, or whatever triggers the need for a decision, Instant CBA requires the same number of mental tasks as the Instinctive Method—where decisionmakers make assumptions to fill in data gaps and jump to a conclusion. But the two methods are not at all the same. For many decisions, Instant CBA is faster, because it quickly clarifies the situation; and it also produces better decisions, because it is a sound method.

To learn the Instant CBA Process, start by practicing the CBA vocabulary. To learn the vocabulary, study the Tabular Format, as suggested in chapters 5 and 8. Keep on practicing the CBA vocabulary until it becomes a well-established habit.

Obviously, when designing a new building it would cause a lot of confusion if the architect used such words as *windows, foundations, walls,* and *shingles* interchangeably. And, obviously, when teaching someone how to drive a car it would cause confusion to use such words as *clutch, brake, accelerator,* and *light switch* interchangeably. It should be just as obvious that decisionmakers cause confusion when they use such words as *factors, criteria, attributes,* and *advantages* interchangeably.

In addition to practicing the CBA vocabulary, practice the Two-List Method until you can use it almost instinctively. Then, practice the Tabular Method, the Simplified Tabular Method, and the Simplified Two-List Method. Once you are skilled in using the Simplified Two-List method, you can easily add the Instant CBA Process to your repertoire of sound-decisionmaking skills.

As shown by the sound-decisionmaking model in chapter 20, and as shown by the diagram that follows, the decisionmaking phase of the sound-decisionmaking process can be viewed as a five-step process. (The five steps include the four central activities, plus the first task in the second activity.) As shown, sound methods move back and forth between the objective and subjective sides of the decisionmaking process.

OBJECTIVE STEPS   **SUBJECTIVE STEPS**

ATTRIBUTES

Least-Preferred Attributes

ADVANTAGES

IMPORTANCE

TOTAL IMPORTANCE

Instant CBA requires only one activity with two tasks. It combines the first three steps into the first task. At the same time, it combines the last two steps into the second. Following are the two tasks: Perceive, in your mind, the costs and advantages of each alternative. At the same time, and without deciding the importance of each individual advantage, simply choose the preferred alternative—based on the costs and the total importance of the advantages.

In the simple CBA methods, decisions are based explicitly on the importance of advantages. In the very simple CBA methods, decisions are based implicitly on the importance of advantages. The very simple methods combine all five steps into one: Choose the preferred alternative—instantly, intuitively—based on the costs and the total importance of advantages.

26

Very Simple Methods
for Very Simple Decisions

The sound-decisionmaking model, presented in chapter 20, highlighted two types of decisions: Decisions that guide further decisionmaking are *criteria;* those that steer the course of events are *action decisions.*

From one moment to the next, the course of events is being guided by a complex network of decisions. The hierarchy shown below is contained, many times for many decisions, in this network. In the hierarchy, the first four levels are criteria. That is, they are decisions that guide further decisionmaking. One general criterion is likely to be guiding further decisionmaking for many specific decisions.

Long-Range Decisions

Mid-Range Decisions

Short-Range Decisions

Very Short-Range Decisions

Action Decisions

ACTIONS

The methods presented in this chapter are for very short-range decisions and action decisions. The decisions produced by these methods have an effect that is similar to the photographs that are shown on a television screen, or a movie screen, to produce a motion picture. Guided by previous decisions and present circumstances, very short-range decisions and action decisions are created continuously, producing a flowing stream of actions and outcomes. The following methods for very simple decisions are presented in this chapter:

- One Factor Decisionmaking

- Responding to One Option Situations

- Choosing in Advance

- The Recognition–Response Process

- Using Good Intuition and Good Judgment

These methods are for decisions where the other CBA methods, including the Instant CBA process, would be too slow. While the other CBA methods base decisions *explicitly* on the importance of advantages, these methods simplify very simple decisions by basing them *implicitly* on the importance of advantages.

ONE FACTOR DECISIONMAKING

In many situations, there will be advantages—differences among alternatives—in only one factor. Choosing between flavors of ice cream for an ice cream cone is an example. Some people spend more time then they wish to spend when they make this type of decision. They say to themselves, "Worry, worry, woe is me. I really don't need so many calories. I don't know which flavor to choose."

This not-so-uncommon thinking confuses the decisionmaking process. To avoid confusion and to simplify one factor decisionmaking, use the CBA process. As shown in the outline in chapter 22, clarify the purpose of the decision. Are you deciding whether to have an ice cream cone, or are you choosing a flavor? At the same time, clearly perceive the attributes of the alternatives. That is, form a clear, accurate, sensory-rich perception of each alternative—how it looks, tastes, sounds, or feels. In the ice cream example, perceive the flavors. In almost the same instant, decide. (By choosing the alternative with the preferred flavor, you will be choosing the one with the greatest advantage in flavor.)

While clarifying the purpose of the decision and forming a sensory-rich perception of each alternative, instantly exclude the easy-to-exclude alternatives. Now, what if you have narrowed the list to only two alternatives, and it's hard to decide between the two? What should you do? The difficulty in deciding could mean that the two are almost equally preferred. If so, you can't go very far wrong with either option. So, mentally flip a coin, and do whatever the coin tells you to do. Flip an imaginary coin, because it takes too long to flip a real one.

All the differences among the alternatives must be taken into account. For some decisions, however, due to interdependencies among their prospective factors, it is better to treat those decisions as one factor decisions—even when it seems they could be divided into several factors. As an illustration of interdependencies, suppose we were choosing between two ice cream sundaes. The desirability of the flavor of a sundae, as a whole, is not the same as the total of the desirabilities of the flavors of its components. Therefore, we would not divide the flavor decision into factors, such as the flavor of the ice cream, the flavors of the toppings, the nuts, and so forth. An economist gave a similar example of interdependencies: He said, "I like ice cream, and I like sauerkraut. But I don't like ice cream mixed with sauerkraut."

Usually, when making a very short-range decision or an action decision, dividing the decision into factors isn't a possibility. In most of these decisions, identifying the factors and explicitly thinking of individual advantages would take far too much time. Therefore, the Instant CBA Process—where we do think of individual advantages—would be too slow. Instead, *we must perceive each alternative as a whole.*

Very short-range decisions and action decisions must truly be made instantly. That is why they must be based implicitly, not explicitly, on the importance of advantages. And that is why they require an exceptionally high level of skill.

Do not use one factor decisionmaking when there are significant differences in two or more independent factors. For example, a popular method called The-Reason Reasoning looks a lot like one factor decisionmaking. However, while one factor decisionmaking is a sound method, The-Reason Reasoning is unsound. To illustrate The-Reason Reasoning, let's go back to the canoe decision. As you recall, the stakeholders selected Canoe C, because—in total—the two advantages of Canoe C are more important, to them, than the three advantages of K.

By using The-Reason Reasoning, they probably would have selected Canoe K, by mistake, as follows: "The reason for selecting Canoe K was its kelly-blue color."

RESPONDING TO ONE OPTION SITUATIONS

Technically, there is probably no such thing as a one option situation. However, in many real-world situations we face only one alternative that is realistic and reasonable. For example, think about driving along a freeway and coming to a bridge. The freeway crosses the bridge, but should you cross it? Of course. Unless the situation is an unusual one, simply recognize it, and respond. As they say in the television commercial, "Just do it."

The decision to cross the bridge is a very short-range decision. The continuous flow of decisions that steer you across the bridge are action decisions. Very short-range decisions guide action decisionmaking, and action decisions produce the things we say and do. Therefore, action decisions—perhaps more than any other decisions—call for Choosing By Advantages.

Many times it isn't easy for us to do what we have decided to do—even in one option situations. An example is the decision to stop smoking. Deciding is the easy part. After deciding, it is difficult to implement the decision. CBA can help. First, we must use a sound method to decide. Using a sound method to decide makes it easier to implement the decision. Therefore, we must get rid of the old advice, which is to weigh the advantages and disadvantages of smoking against the advantages and disadvantages of not smoking.

CHOOSING IN ADVANCE

After mentally choosing, the next step is emotionally choosing (becoming motivated); for example, to emotionally choose to stop smoking, form clear, accurate, sensory-rich perceptions of the advantages of not smoking. A person can form positive, motivational pictures of himself or herself as a nonsmoker—with more energy, other things purchased with the money that would be saved, and so forth. There is power in positive thinking—if it is realistically positive. Of course, avoiding smoking in the first place is much easier than quitting. The key is to make positive, effective mental and emotional choices—in advance.

If you are a parent, teach your children how to correctly choose in advance. To help them avoid becoming addicted to drugs, for example, teach them how to choose by advantages. This is essential. It puts thinking (instead of feeling) in control of their behaviors. If no one teaches them how to choose by advantages, they will automatically use the Instinctive Method, which far too often produces unsound decisions.

After teaching your children how to choose by advantages, help them form strong, sensory-rich, motivational perceptions of the marvelous advantages of addiction-free living. Also, teach them how to avoid addictions. Of course, avoiding addictions is easier to decide than to do. This is why it is important not only to mentally decide in advance, but also to form strong, emotional, motivational pictures of the advantages of the selected alternative in advance. Most of all, correct responses must be practiced in advance. Mentally, emotionally, and physically choosing in advance is much more effective than waiting for difficult decisionmaking situations to arise.

In my view, another example of a one option situation, coupled with the need for choosing in advance, is the choice of whether or not to learn how to read and write. To me, learning to read and write is the only reasonable alternative, but too many just don't do it. Parents can help their children learn to read and write by helping them form clear, accurate, emotional, motivational pictures of the marvelous advantages of reading and writing.

In my view, the choice of whether or not to learn and use CBA is another one option situation. Do you agree? If you do, then decide, today, to rule out all unsound methods—those that cause or encourage critical mistakes. (Again, you don't need to throw them away. Just transform them, from unsound to sound.) Next, form vivid, motivational perceptions of the advantages of Choosing By Advantages. Then, continue the five-step skill-learning process. And don't leave out Step Five. To strengthen your own CBA skills, teach the CBA definitions, principles, models, and methods to at least one other person. And certainly, use CBA, continuously, for your own decisions.

THE RECOGNITION–RESPONSE PROCESS, REVISITED

As outlined in chapter 6, researchers estimate that expert decision-makers—those who most often make excellent decisions—use the Recognition–Response Process for 85 to 90 percent of their decisions. And I think the researchers' estimate might be low.

Here is what expert decisionmakers do when they are using the Recognition–Response Process: They *observe* the situation, *recognize* that they have either considered or experienced similar situations before, and *respond*. An expert draws from a mental reservoir containing countless numbers of excellent previous decisions. And she or he simply reuses a previous decision, adjusted according to the present situation.

Those who most often make excellent decisions are not the only decisionmakers who use the Recognition–Response Process. Those who least often make excellent decisions also use this process—for at least 85 to 90 percent of their decisions. They too draw from large reservoirs of previous decisions. But their reservoirs contain too many faulty decisions; and because they don't make adequate adjustments, they keep repeating their mistakes.

To bring this pattern to the attention of participants in CBA workshops, they are asked to describe things that expert decisionmakers do and others fail to do when both are using the Recognition–Response Process. The participants nearly always list the following behaviors of experts: First, they are better observers; second, they are more responsive to feedback.

Different decisionmakers are not necessarily using the same method when they appear to be using the Recognition–Response Process. When the decisionmaking process is not displayed in writing, the following methods— and the Instinctive Method—appear to be the same.

The Decision–Response Process (Instant CBA, for example):

Observe ——▶ Formulate Alternatives ——▶ Decide ——▶ Respond

The Recognition–Response Process:

Observe ——▶ Recognize ——▶ Respond

The Stimulus–Response Process:

Perceive ——▶ Respond

I believe that those decisionmakers who most often make poor decisions most often use the Stimulus–Response Process, and those who most often make excellent decisions most often use the Decision–Response Process. (They use the Decision–Response Process when the old decisions in their mental reservoirs don't apply.) Furthermore, I believe that in the future, by skillfully and consistently using CBA—in writing when necessary— expert decisionmakers will make excellent decisions more often than ever before. By using CBA, they will be continuously adding excellent new decisions to their reservoirs, and they will be able to make more of their decisions in advance.

There are countless situations where the key to instantly making sound decisions is to skillfully decide what to do in advance, and then to use the Recognition–Response Process. Firefighters, for example, need to select and practice, in advance, the best possible responses to a wide variety of dangerous situations.

Of course, this process doesn't apply only to firefighters. Everyone needs to select and practice correct responses to a wide variety of situations. Therefore, everyone needs to become adequately skilled in both explicitly and implicitly Choosing By Advantages.

It is much easier to base a decision explicitly on the importance of advantages if it is made in advance. For motivation—to be sure the response to the situation will be in accordance with the decision—the decisionmaker needs to form vivid perceptions of the advantages of the selected alternative. In some situations, decisionmakers need to prepare written lists of advantages. A written list helps in both selecting the best alternative and successfully implementing the decision.

A written display of advantages—using the Two-List Format, the Tabular Format, or scoring sheets—can be used in combination with the Recognition–Response Process. To demonstrate this, let's look at the canoe decision once more. Following is a revised comparison between Canoes C and K (in this version of the Two-List Format, the attributes are displayed).

The Choice Between Canoe C and Canoe K

Advantages of Canoe C		Advantages of Canoe K	
• 10 Pounds Lighter (65 Lbs. vs. 75 Lbs.)	70	• Moderately Smoother Finish (Very Smooth vs. Mod. Smooth)	5
• Slightly Greater Stability (Excellent vs. Very Good.)	75	• Much Nicer Color (Kelly-Blue vs. Starry-Brown)	100
		• Slightly Better Keel Depth (5/8 Inch vs. 7/8 Inch)	10
Total Importance:	145	Total Importance:	115
Both Alternatives Have the Same Total Cost.			

As before, this display tells us that we should try to find another alternative, one with the weight and stability of Canoe C, and with the color of K. If we find a canoe with these characteristics, it won't be necessary to update the Two-List display. By using the Two-List Method, we have already clarified our preferences. So, if we find a canoe that has the weight of C, the stability of C, the color of K, and the other attributes that we prefer, we will simply recognize it and respond—by selecting it.

Skillfully voting in the political process calls for using the Recognition–Response Process, sometimes in combination with a written display of advantages. Before going to the voting booth, use the CBA process to decide how to vote. Once in a while—only for difficult choices—we need to prepare either a Tabular Display or a Two-List Display to help us clearly see the advantages of each candidate. In the voting booth, we simply recognize the candidates we have decided to vote for and respond.

Again, as stated previously, practicing is another way to improve the success of a decision. For example, an excellent quarterback on a football team drops back to pass. He observes that the pocket is collapsing. At the same time, he recognizes a seam through the defense, and he responds by running for a first down. The play-by-play announcer comments that the quarterback made the right "decision." What the announcer said is true. The quarterback did make the right decision. However, he formed most of the decision before the game. During the game, he repeated what he had decided earlier and had practiced—many times—both in his mind and in actuality. While implementing the decision, he made adjustments, according to the circumstances. In harmony with the sound-decisionmaking model and based on experience, he used correct data, he used data correctly, and he responded to feedback.

By the choices we are making, day-to-day and minute-to-minute, we are shaping the future. Of course, it is important to remember that many things in the world around us are chaotic and that, to a great extent, the future is unpredictable and uncontrollable. Therefore, steering the course of events is a turbulent, muddy, searching–discovering, negotiating–bargaining, decisionmaking process. Furthermore, when we are basing our decisions on the importance of advantages, we are basing them on prospective, uncertain, future advantages. Therefore, we must remain open and flexible; we must be fully responsive to feedback.

USING GOOD INTUITION AND GOOD JUDGMENT

As this chapter has shown, we all carry in our minds large reservoirs of data for decisionmaking—including memories of previous decisions. We also carry in our minds various models and methods of decisionmaking. At any particular moment, most of what we have stored in our minds is at the subconscious level.

In CBA, using stored items of data, without becoming aware that we are using them, is called intuition. (Some call this intuition with precedence, to distinguish it from intuition without precedence—without drawing from stored data.) Using stored models and methods is judgment. Of course, as everyone knows, not all intuition is good intuition, and not all judgment is good judgment. In CBA, intuitively using correct data is good intuition; intuitively using data correctly is good judgment.

CBA doesn't replace intuition and judgment, that would be both impossible and undesirable. Instead, CBA enhances good intuition and good judgment. The key is to store, in our minds, *valid data,* including excellent previous decisions, and *sound methods.* Therefore, to improve your intuition and judgment, study and practice the CBA definitions, principles, models, and methods. Restudy and practice as many times as necessary, until CBA becomes your natural, effective, intuitive system of decisionmaking.

Conclusion

Making sound decisions doesn't guarantee that all your decisions will be accepted and implemented. Sound decisions are sometimes accepted, and sometimes not. Furthermore, using sound methods doesn't guarantee that you or others will always make sound decisions. Remember; sound decisionmaking requires sound methods, integrity, and skill—not only sound methods. Sound decisionmaking also requires experience, knowledge of the situation, vision, determination, patience, and many other essentials.

SOUND METHODS

Remember that the question of whether a particular method is or is not a sound method is a scientific question, not a matter of opinion or preference. If a method causes or encourages multiple-counting or omissions, it is, scientifically, an unsound method. If it causes or encourages distortions, unanchored judgments, or other critical mistakes, it is, scientifically, an unsound method. The attractiveness of a method is not a measure of its soundness. Instead, *sound methods are those that use correct data, use data correctly, and respond to feedback.*

Participants in CBA workshops have asked: "Compared with unsound methods, do sound methods actually produce better decisions?" Some have suggested using different methods in the same decisionmaking situation to find out which method produces the best decision. This experiment has been performed several times. Those who compared the results nearly always preferred the decisions that were produced by sound methods. However, their preferences were subjective and, therefore, the experiment was subjective and not necessarily valid.

We are on shaky ground when we try to judge the quality of a method by examining a decision that it produced. But we are on solid ground when we judge the quality of a decision (at least in part) by examining the method that produced it, by asking process questions, such as:

- Did the method use correct data? (Was the decision based on the applicable criteria, the relevant facts, and the appropriate viewpoints?)

- Did the method use data correctly? (Did it anchor the decisionmaker's viewpoint to the relevant facts, by basing the decision on the importance of advantages?)

- Was the method responsive to feedback? (Was Phase IV as thorough as Phase III?)

- Was the correct sound method used? (Remember that different types of decisions call for different sound methods.)

It would be dangerous to judge the validity of a decisionmaking method by examining the decisions it produces. To judge a method, we must examine the method, itself.

INTEGRITY

Participants in CBA workshops sometimes ask, "If people are dishonest when they are using the CBA process, isn't it possible for them to make the decision that they wanted to make in the first place—even if it is an unsound decision? Wouldn't it be easy for them to cheat, by assigning incorrect importance scores to the advantages?"

The answer is yes. Obviously, CBA doesn't prevent cheating or lying (or stealing). But in many cases, it discloses cheating and lying. What's more important, however, is that it discloses innocent mistakes so they can be corrected. I believe that unsound decisions are more often methods-caused than people-caused, and that blaming the decisionmaker for a methods-caused faulty decision is like blaming the pilot for a mechanically caused airliner crash. Nevertheless, sound decisionmaking does require high integrity.

For the same reasons that people with high integrity would never cheat, or lie, or steal, they would never knowingly use, require, accept, or teach unsound methods. So, I hope that, from now on, everyone who teaches decisionmaking skills, or related skills, will teach sound methods—and only sound methods. In particular, I hope that those who have been teaching unsound methods in seminars for business and government organizations will change to sound methods, as soon as possible.

In organizations, should using CBA be mandatory or optional? It depends on the organization. In some organizational cultures, not mandating CBA will create less emotional resistance to it, and this would be a major advantage of not mandating it. In one case, a person who seemed to feel threatened by CBA was able to veto its use in an entire organization. This case is exceptional. Most people accept and enjoy CBA once they understand it. Nevertheless, as this case demonstrates, veto power can be much stronger than performance power.

In some situations, mandating the use of CBA tools and methods could inadvertently cause some CBA tools and methods to not be used. Why? Because there are some CBA tools and methods that, at first glance, do not look like they would belong to CBA. Here is just one example: When a method called Linear Programming is used properly, it is an excellent component of the CBA process. It is not used in Phase III to select a course of action. (That is a common misuse of Linear Programming.) Instead, it is used in Phase II, for certain types of decisions, as an aid in formulating a full range of alternatives.

As stated, leaders with high integrity would never knowingly use or accept the use of unsound methods. Nevertheless, I believe that teaching CBA, encouraging its use, and rejecting the use of unsound methods will be much more effective than simply mandating the use of CBA.

SKILL

As stated in the beginning of this book, one of the greatest of all human abilities is the ability to make choices. And because human performance, including organizational performance, is a decisionmaking process, people can significantly improve the quality of their lives and the lives of others by skillfully using sound methods of decisionmaking. Therefore, your decisions about how to make decisions are among the most important of all the decisions you will ever make. Fortunately, now that you know what CBA is, what it does, and what some of its advantages are, deciding how to make decisions could be one of the easiest of all the decisions you will ever make.

Of course, deciding to use sound methods is not the part that is difficult. As anyone can see, the advantages of methods that are sound, clear, and simple far outweigh the advantages of those that are unsound, unclear, and too complex. But deciding and doing are two different things. So take a few minutes to list the advantages of continuously improving your decisionmaking skills. Next, form sensory-rich motivational perceptions of these advantages. Then, assess where you are in the five-step skill-learning process; and continue the process.

The Five-Step Skill-Learning Process, Revisited

---

1. Learn the basic sound-decisionmaking concepts and methods—those that have been presented in this book. Especially, learn the cornerstone principles:

   - Decisionmakers must learn and skillfully use sound methods.

   - Decisions must be based on the importance of advantages.

   - Decisions must be anchored to the relevant facts.

   - Different types of decisions call for different sound methods.

2. Unlearn the unsound methods that are in common use today. Examples of commonly used unsound methods include Choosing By Advantages and Disadvantages, Choosing By Pros and Cons, Weighting-Rating-and-Calculating, and numerous unsound methods that are mechanically simple and seemingly sensible.

3. Relearn the sound-decisionmaking concepts and methods. Relearn as many times as necessary. Very soon, reread and restudy this book.

4. Practice the CBA methods. If you haven't done so already, start using CBA, today. And remember: Practicing is good, but practicing with feedback—especially from a CBA facilitator or a CBA instructor—is much better.

5. Teach the CBA definitions, principles, models, and methods to others. This step will strengthen your understanding of the CBA methods and your ability to use them successfully. You can begin teaching CBA, immediately, mostly by example. And in the future, you might want to teach by formal instruction.

Education is key to the successful implementation of the CBA system. To see why it is key, think about the question that has so often been asked about human behavior: "Why is it that modern society has made so many improvements in technology, but so few in human behavior?" (Of course, not all changes in technology have been improvements.) Two answers to this important question show why education is the key to improving human behavior.

First, in the area of technology members of each new generation start from where the previous generation ended; then, they make improvements (they create advantages). For example, today's medical technologies and today's factories are much improved, compared with those that were used by previous generations. In contrast, each new human born today is practically the same as one born many generations ago. Therefore, as in previous generations, new infants, if not taught otherwise, will acquire and use, throughout their lives, the same primitive methods of decisionmaking that Stone Age children acquired and used. As demonstrated by the bridge design experiment, one of the methods they certainly will acquire and use is the Instinctive Method. Learning the Instinctive Method is as natural as learning to walk and talk.

Second, people can buy new technologies, but they must learn new behaviors, and some new behaviors must be taught. For example, people can buy new telephones, but they must learn better ways to communicate with one another, and they must be taught how to read and write. Similarly, they must be taught how to choose by advantages. Using sound methods of decisionmaking is not a natural skill.

This book has emphasized that human performance is a decisionmaking process. Of course, it is, in part, the product of heredity (nature). But, it is also the product of nurture and choice. Therefore, education (nurture) and using sound methods of decisionmaking (choice) are the keys to improving human performance, and they must go hand-in-hand. Successful education requires sound decisionmaking, and sound decisionmaking requires successful education. Both call for CBA. So, how can we incorporate CBA into the education and performance of individuals, families, organizations, and communities?

I believe that success will depend, to a great extent, on CBA champions. They help people learn what CBA is, what it does, and why it is essential in a modern society. They help people discover that we all are continuously making mental, emotional, and physical choices; that by our choices, we are steering the course of events and shaping our future; and that CBA does produce better choices. Therefore, CBA will help us create a better future.

CBA champions help people discover that virtually all types of choices, from the simplest to the most complex, call for Choosing By Advantages. In organizations, CBA champions help to establish using sound methods as one of the organization's basic values.

Leaders, trainers, and other professional decisionmakers have a special role in bringing about improvements in organizational culture and values. Therefore, they need to become the leading CBA champions. First, they need to learn and skillfully use CBA themselves. Second, they need to provide CBA training to the other members of their organizations. And third, they need to discourage the use of unsound methods.

In some organizations, unfortunately, unsound methods are mandated. That is, members are required by custom or by written direction to use methods that we now know are unsound. Certainly, unsound methods must not be mandated. Therefore, leaders in those organizations that require the use of unsound methods need to get rid of that requirement, as soon as possible.

Obviously, those in the highest levels of leadership need the highest levels of CBA skill, and they need to be the strongest advocates of using sound methods. However, the responsibility for learning, using, and teaching CBA needs to be a shared responsibility. So, whether or not you are a leader in an organization, I challenge you to become an active CBA champion, starting today.

A mid-level manager came into my office and said, "I need to use CBA for an important decision. I've looked and looked, and I can't find any other acceptable methods. But it's been two years since I attended your training session, so I can't remember how to do it. Would you please give me a refresher?" By the time he asked for a refresher, it was too late; what he really needed, before using CBA for a major decision, was experience. He could have gained plenty of experience by using CBA for two years, but he didn't. He could have received many benefits from using it, but he didn't. If he had been using it for two years, he would not have needed a refresher.

Apparently, he thought that learning CBA is an event. But successfully learning and using CBA is a journey, not an event. The initial event (attending a CBA training session or reading this book) is essential, but it is just the beginning. As I stated in the introduction, I hope you will thoroughly enjoy your journey.

References

Bishop, A. Bruce. 1969. *Socio-economic and community factors in planning urban freeways*. Project on Engineering-Economic Planning. Report EEP-33. Palo Alto, CA: Stanford University.

Brown, Ginger. 1993. *A series of lessons for CBA decision-making skills*. Master's project. Ogden, UT: Weber State University.

Bois, Samuel J. 1966. *The art of awareness: A textbook on general semantics*. Dubuque, IA: Wm. C. Brown Co., Inc.

Fisher, Roger and William Ury. [1981] 1983. *Getting to yes: Negotiating agreement without giving in*. Reprint. New York: Penguin Books.

Grant, Eugene L. [1930] 1938. *Principles of engineering economy*. Rev. ed. New York: The Ronald Press Company.

Grant, Eugene L. and W. Grant Ireson. 1970. *Principles of engineering economy*. 5th ed. New York: The Ronald Press Company.

Hayakawa, S. I. 1939. *Language in action*. New York: Harcourt, Brace and Company.

Herrmann, Ned. 1988. *The creative brain*. Lake Lure, NC: Brain Books.

Korzybski, Alfred. [1933] 1958. *Science and sanity: An introduction to non-Aristotelian systems and general semantics*. 4th ed. New York: The International Non-Aristotelian Library Publishing Company.

Smith, Adam. [1776] 1986. *An inquiry into the nature and causes of the wealth of nations*. New York: Penguin Books.

Wellington, Arthur Mellen. 1887. *The economic theory of the location of railways*. 2d ed. New York: John Wiley and Sons.

Index

About the Author

JIM SUHR is co-founder and president of the Institute for Decision Innovations, Inc. Throughout his career as a farmer, teacher, civil engineer, and consultant he has continuously searched for practical ways to improve human performance.